WARN  Y

S

WAS WAR NECESSARY?

Volume 105, Sage Library of Social Research

SAGE LIBRARY OF SOCIAL RESEARCH

WAS WAR NECESSARY?
NATIONAL SECURITY AND U.S. ENTRY INTO WAR

MELVIN SMALL

Volume 105
SAGE LIBRARY OF
SOCIAL RESEARCH

 SAGE PUBLICATIONS   Beverly Hills   London

Copyright © 1980 by Sage Publications, Inc.

2 - 9 - 83

All rights reserved. No part of this book may be reproduced or utilized in any form or by any means, electronic or mechanical, including photocopying, recording, or by any information storage and retrieval system, without permission in writing from the publisher.

E 181 .S54
Small, Melvin.
Was war necessary? :

For information address:

SAGE Publications, Inc.
275 South Beverly Drive
Beverly Hills, California 90212

SAGE Publications Ltd
28 Banner Street
London EC1Y 8QE, England

Printed in the United States of America

Library of Congress Cataloging in Publication Data

Small, Melvin.
    Was war necessary?

    (Sage library of social research ; 105)
    Includes bibliographies.
    1. United States--History, Military. 2. United
States--National security. I. Title.
E181.S54   973   80-13536
ISBN 0-8039-1486-5
ISBN 0-8039-1487-3 (pbk.)

FIRST PRINTING

CONTENTS

For Mark and Mike—May They
Never Have To Ask My Question

PREFACE

For most of my academic career, I have studied the causes of war in hopes of contributing to the creation of a more peaceful world. I still hope that my writings and lectures in peace research and diplomatic history might have some impact on our understanding of international conflict. Nevertheless, I have grown impatient directing my intellectual energies almost exclusively to the academy.

In this volume, I write for college students and lay people about the irrationality of most wars. As we shall see, even the United States' entries into international war from 1812 to 1950 were not justified in terms of the defense of national security. Some of my arguments will be overdrawn, others provocative. I want to make the reader think about the justifications for war and to determine under what circumstances she or he would support a call to arms. An exploration of these questions and their relationship to the United States' experience may also reveal something about our history, our political system, and how we may look to observers in other countries.

I began working on this project in a seminar at Wayne State University in the spring of 1972 and continued that fall at Aarhus University in Denmark. I am indebted to the American and Danish students who participated in both seminars, and especially to my three Danish colleagues who sat in on the class: Niels Amstrup, Ib Faurby, and Nikolaj Petersen. Over the succeeding years, many friends have read all or part of one of the versions of the manuscript. Gilbert Gall, Douglas Haller, Chris Johnson, Marc Kruman, Thomas Maddox, Glenn Paige, Lynn Parsons, Alan Raucher, Sam Scott, Michael Small, and Athan Theoharis were especially generous with their time and comments.

Most helpful, as they have been ever since graduate school, were Bradford Perkins and J. David Singer of the University of Michigan. Although they chide one another about the unbridgeable gap between the historian humanist and the social scientific quantifier, Perkins and Singer share a singular commitment to good scholarship and the development of a saner international system.

All of the members of the support staff of the History Department at Wayne State University contributed to my project. Under the able direction of Donna Monacelli, Tricia Abbott, Linda Blakely, Linda Brownstein, and Ginny Corbin efficiently and cheerfully assisted in the production of a final manuscript.

As is the case with most projects of this kind, spouses and children are crucial in helping to see it through to completion. Sarajane, Mark, and Mike Small have all left their imprint on this book.

—M.S.

INTRODUCTION

The appalling wars in Southeast Asia made many Americans deeply ashamed of their country's foreign and military policy. The spectacle of the world's leading democratic state conducting what appeared to many to be a savage imperialist war unleashed a storm of protest which, in its intensity and longevity, surpassed any comparable protest in American history. It was understandable that the neocolonialist Fourth Republic of France could fight such a war in Indochina from 1945 to 1954 and even more understandable that the authoritarian Portuguese regime could engage in such activities in Angola and Mozambique. But the United States?

After Bunker Hill, Gettysburg, and Iwo Jima, we apparently strayed from the pathway of righteousness. In his quixotic Children's Crusade of 1968, even Senator Eugene McCarthy adopted this theme when he asked his listeners to "sort out the music and the sounds, and again respond to the trumpet and the steady drums." A few critics contended that it was unreasonable to expect Americans to respond again to the trumpet and steady drums since they had rarely done so before. For those to the left of the poet-candidate, the intervention in Vietnam was the most recent in a series of oppressive actions of a nation that exterminated Indians, enslaved blacks, and intervened in a host of little wars from the Philippines at the turn of the century, to Haiti during World War I, to Nicaragua in the late 1920s, and to the Dominican Republic in 1965.

Even taking into account these ugly interludes, many citizens still maintain that the United States has compiled a relatively wholesome record in the seedy business of international politics. According to them, we have been less aggressive than other major powers and have injected a much-needed measure of morality into the diplomatic process.

To muster evidence to support such a conclusion is easy. Our collective memories overflow with snatches of glorious history from school lessons, Independence Day addresses, and innumerable songs, films, and teleplays. When most of us think about our diplomatic and military encounters, we remember Commodore Perry in the War of 1812 defending the fledgling republic against British piracy, Teddy Roosevelt charging up San Juan Hill to free the Cubans from their hateful Spanish masters in a splendid little war, or our titanic struggle against the ruthless Axis powers who threatened to destroy civilization. All of these popular images involve a peaceful, defensive United States provoked into war by the attacks of others. According to our school texts, we chose war only after General Taylor's brave young lads were ambushed by Mexicans in Texas, after the Kaiser's U-boats sent American seamen to the bottom of the Atlantic, or after Joseph Stalin's puppets in North Korea stormed across the 38th parallel to attack our Free World ally.

Other nations fight wars of aggression, other nations strike the first blow, but the democratic United States has, until recently at least, fought only defensive wars. To admit that we entered a war for less than selfless motives or even that we were wrong to take up arms would challenge the American way. Our mythology suggests that we are different from other states. They produced their Napoleons and Bismarcks, we our Lincolns and Wilsons. Our primary, high school, and even college courses in history often resemble civics classes in which deviations from the patriots' catechism are rare. Consequently, there is a good deal of misunderstanding in this country about our diplomatic history and our relations with other nations. This misunderstanding contributed to world outlooks that either supported intervention in Southeast Asia or considered it just one terrible mistake, an aberration in an otherwise impressive record in international affairs.

Much of the misunderstanding revolves around a simplistic view of how the United States came to enter her celebrated wars. We remember episodes from our military history, thrilling exploits on Normandy beach or Pork Chop Hill. How we came to fight in France or Korea is another matter. Such a memory lapse is not surprising. Citizens of all nations tend to remember stories of combat and heroism before they remember the often sordid, and always complicated, tales of diplomatic intrigue that precede military hostilities.

Were we to ask the proverbial average Americans why their country fought in World War II, they would respond, undoubtedly, "because the Japs attacked Pearl Harbor." As we move back in time, their memories would become a bit more foggy. They might remember that we entered the Spanish-American War because the Spanish blew up the *Maine* ("Remember the *Maine,* to Hell with Spain!"). Were we to press them further and ask why the Japanese attacked Pearl Harbor and the Spanish the *Maine,* they would probably scratch their heads and mumble something about the Japanese and Spanish being aggressive sorts who wanted to conquer us.

We should not single out the much-maligned persons in the street for their lack of historical knowledge. When I ask students the same questions, most respond in terms comparable to those of citizens outside the university. If anything, today's students are less knowledgeable about the United States' past than the rest of the population. Ahistorical and bored, they fail to see the relevance of such esoteric subjects as the entry of the United States into World War II, let alone the War of 1812. Why, they ask, must we study these questions? Is it not sufficient to know that we fought in World War II because of the sneak attack on our fleet in Pearl Harbor? Obviously, since the Japanese were imperialists bent on taking over the Pacific basin, a detailed account of what precipitated their unparalleled treachery merits little attention.

The story of Pearl Harbor is not that simple. Americans might be surprised to discover that experts the world over believe that the United States was responsible, in part, for the outbreak of war with Japan in 1941. Japan's brief against us is not that outlandish. It must be examined. By studying the background of World War II and other U.S. wars, we will be able to learn more about our *real* diplomatic tradition, the relationship between democracy and foreign policy, and, perhaps, the nature of American society in general. Armed with the knowledge of where we have been, we might be better able to understand where we are today and where we might be in the future. Above all, as we study our past with patriotic blinders removed, we may develop an appreciation of how we look to others.

The United States fought in six major international wars from 1783 to Vietnam—the War of 1812, the Mexican-American War of 1846, the Spanish-American War of 1898, World War I, World War II, and the Korean conflict. Our entry into these wars was unnecessary. In all cases, our national security was not threatened sufficiently to justify the call to arms.

Almost all wars are products of miscalculation. Except in a few flagrant cases of unprovoked aggression such as Hitler's attack on Poland in 1939, they are not entered into eagerly by national leaders, even by those who strike the first blow. World War I may be the best example of a war that everyone wanted to avoid. In more recent years, the Arab-Israeli War of 1967, although precipitated by provocative Egyptian moves, was one war which Cairo did not want to fight. Similarly, the India-Pakistan War of 1971, brought on by the Pakistani Army's brutal suppression of East Bengali rebels, was not desired by the government in Islamabad that knew it could not defeat the Indian Army.

If almost all wars were launched by mistake, is it fair to single out the United States for censure? I feel that it is, because although Americans would accept the proposition that most of history's wars were irrational, they feel that theirs made sense.

Admittedly, the U.S. record is good. Even if our wars were unnecessary, we fought in "only" six major international wars. We were, however, involved in over a hundred small skirmishes against peoples who were not members of the nation-state system. In addition to these colonial and imperial wars, we did endure a long and bloody civil war. Yet, aside from our Civil War, most major powers had comparable experiences and so, when it comes to *international* wars alone, we look relatively pacific. From the end of the Revolutionary War to Vietnam (1783-1961) or a period of 178 years, we fought in 6 international wars or an average of 1 every 30 years. Over the same time span, the British fought in 8 major international wars or 1 every 22 years, the Russians in 13 or 1 every 14 years, and the French in 14 or 1 every 13 years.

The United States appears even more pacific when one considers the numerous international crises that we peacefully resolved. We did not go to war with England in the early 1790s when she violated our neutrality or did we escalate the undeclared naval war with France of 1798-1800. Both of these difficulties could have easily erupted into full-scale war. During the next decade, the *Chesapeake* crisis did not lead to war with Britain. After the War of 1812, the Florida affair was handled with finesse by James Monroe and John Quincy Adams who pried today's sandy playground from the Spanish without employing too much force. And only a few years after this success, we were able to operate a rhetorically aggressive Latin American policy without provoking a military response from the conservative powers in Europe. During the next two decades, we stopped short of the brink in disputes over the Canadian border as well as the Oregon question, despite, or maybe because of, James Polk's legendary "54° 40' or Fight." Secretary of State William Seward was masterful in handling severe crises with England and France during the Civil War, while conflict with Chile in 1891-1892 and with England over Venezuela in 1895 did not lead to war.

In the twentieth century, war was averted with Colombia during the Panama affair of 1902, England during the Canadian-Alaskan boundary flareup of the same period, and Mexico in 1916, although Black Jack Pershing and more than 5,000 men spent a good deal of time as unwelcome guests on Mexican soil. Later on, we did not take up arms against Japan in 1937 after her attack on the *Panay*. In our era, we did not fight Stalin in

Greece, Turkey, and Iran, or his heirs in Hungary in 1956, Cuba in 1962, and Czechoslovakia in 1968. And we did not attack North Korea after she seized the *Pueblo*. And these are only highlights of a lively diplomatic history.

Beginning from the premise that most of these incidents, if not all of them, could have led to war and arguing that most, if not all, wars should be avoided, then the United States—with its six international wars to 1961, only three of which are of any magnitude in terms of battle deaths—has maintained a remarkably pacific record. This record is all the more remarkable when we consider our feeble condition, small population, and monarchical enemies who surrounded us when we began to make our way alone in the world in 1783.

There is another way to interpret our record. The Atlantic Ocean was a formidable barrier that protected Americans against any invading force. Even the British, with their mighty navy, should not have been able to hold Canada in 1812. The odds that the Spanish, French, or British would have started a war with us were long indeed, even if bumptious Young Jonathan gave them just cause for complaint. Despite our domestic schisms and logistic difficulties inherent in the defense of thousands of miles of land and sea borders, at bottom, we held almost all of the trumps. In particular, Canada was a hostage for British good behavior. Although our standing armies and navies were pathetically weak through most of the nineteenth century, as long as we struck a defensive posture, our strength was augmented by the Atlantic Ocean, while the strength of our potential adversaries was diminished to a similar degree.

Our oceanic defense was formidable right through to the 1950s and the ICBM age. In World War II, the United States and England prepared for almost three years to launch an amphibious invasion of France, even though they had to cross only 30 to 50 miles of English Channel. Moreover, in 1944 they were moving into a friendly country occupied by a German garrison of old men and untrained schoolboys who lacked air and sea support. Yet, the Allies ran into immense problems on D day and the months thereafter. Imagine the problems facing a potential enemy force trying to cross the Atlantic or Pacific or even invading by way of Canada or Mexico. Throughout most of our history, Europeans thought more than twice before they tangled with the United States in this hemisphere. Thus, although we fought in only six international wars, six may have been more than our quota. Perhaps we should have become involved in far fewer wars than the Europeans who were crowded together on a small continent, each surrounded by rivals only a mountain range or a river's width away. That we did stumble into six wars, especially the three in the nineteenth century, may demonstrate a proclivity for war.

Whether we consider the United States unusually martial or pacific, she did participate in several unnecessary wars. Before going any farther, I must explain what I mean by unnecessary war. First of all, I do not think there is such a thing as a splendid little war. At the same time, I do not consider myself a pacifist. In the system in which we have been operating since our earliest days, a system without an international police force, a nation must take up arms when it is attacked or is in imminent danger of being attacked. War may also be justified when a nation's bases, vessels, or formal allies are attacked. From my perspective, all other wars should be avoided whether they are fought to defend the balance of power, to secure markets, or to uphold international morality.

Is this, as some contend, a naive neoisolationist position? Cannot all threats to the balance of power, markets in Asia, and international morality ultimately become imminent threats to national security? Obviously, the definition of "imminent" needs clarification. Would not an attack have been imminent had hitler defeated Russia and England in 1941, or Germany won World War I and established economic supremacy throughout the developing world, or the British been able to continue to trample on our flag with impunity during the Napoleonic Wars?

Of course, if we accept these arguments, then we should seriously consider taking out Libyan nuclear installations before those alleged fanatics develop the capability to bury us. Or perhaps we should contrive a way to destroy the Organization of Petroleum Exporting Countries before our economic system falls apart, or declare war on South Africa for her affronts to human dignity.

Few would seriously consider such policy recommendations today although they are the logical corollaries of perceiving threats to our national security as more than just *direct* military threats. All of which brings us back to that sticky problem of national security. If we are going to argue that the only wars that are justified are those fought to protect national security, then we must define that elusive concept. When is national security threatened? What is national security?

It might help if we considered threats to national security to be of three general kinds—direct military threats, economic threats, and threats to national honor. All, except pacifists, would take up arms when an enemy invaded our shores, and even pacifists might resist nonviolently. Almost everybody would take up arms when the enemy was aboard vessels on the way to the attack. But in the latter case, how do we know that they are not on a training mission? To take the most extreme example, suppose that on December 6, 1941, we had intercepted the Japanese fleet 500 miles from Pearl Harbor. A good number of Americans would have opposed an aggressive move on our part until we knew for sure that those aircraft carriers were not on a goodwill visit to Mexico or Chile. How could we have established for certain what their intentions were? Did we have to wait until the bombs started to fall?

Still on the military threat, most of us agree that we should go to war when someone makes a military incursion across our frontier. Where is our frontier? On the Rhine? The 38th Parallel? Havana? Had Hitler beaten England and then decided to take over Canada, could we have allowed him time to gain a foothold along our vast northern border? Or to change the perspective somewhat, could the Russians have afforded to sit idly by in 1956 while their fraternal neighbor, Hungary, was invaded by agents of the CIA? Did not Russia's strategic frontier begin at the Hungarian border? Although the definition of

frontier is ambiguous, I define national security in terms limited
to a direct military attack on our own soil or on the soil of a
near neighbor whose conquest would leave us in a dangerously
weakened position. Such a definition would exclude the
domino theory that said we must stop "them" in Vietnam
because Vietnam is only four jumps away from the United
States, as in Vietnam-Malaya-Philippines-Hawaii.

Many argue that national security can be threatened by
enemy activities that fall well short of military attack. If a
nation threatens to upset the balance of power—as did Napoleon, Hitler, and perhaps Stalin or Truman—it may capture so
much of the world's wealth and resources that other nations
will suffer a serious decline in their living standards. With that
decline could come mass unemployment, depression, and
domestic political instability. Therefore, as in the case of
America's relationship to Germany in World War I, even though
the Kaiser posed no immediate military threat, had he won the
war, his economic leverage would have been so great and his
intentions so hostile that our economic and political stability
would have been placed in jeopardy. Ultimately, Germany
would have been able to convert economic dominance into
military or political dominance.

To make the economic threat even more direct and relevant,
one might argue that if forces opposed to our survival gained
control of all of the oil-producing areas of the world, our
national security would be threatened and we would have to go
to war. For myself, I do not think economic arguments justify
the loss of one citizen in war. I would prefer to do without oil
and lower my standard of living than go to war for markets and
raw materials. Of course, as the quality (or is it quantity?) of
life declines, many lives might be lost in civil war—but I would
take my chances on that happening.

Naturally, an American can more easily hold to such principles than citizens of countries such as Japan, who are dependent on free international trade. At various times in history,
sustained economic blockades and boycotts directed against
them could have led to mass starvation.

Attacks on a nation's honor or prestige represent a third sort of national security threat, and perhaps the most complicated one of all. If another nation invades disputed border areas, attacks our citizens and their property, makes illegal seizures of our vessels, or otherwise assaults our sovereignty, national security is said to be threatened. For one thing, if we accept such offenses without a fight, third parties may consider us a weakling nation, easily bullied and dominated. The international system is full of countries looking for easy prey. That nation which does not stand up for its honor will ultimately face a direct military threat to its security. In addition, a nation that allows its honor to be sullied will suffer a loss of general respect among its own people that could lead to political dislocation and civil turbulence.

In 1898, Spain faced a difficult choice. Either give the Cubans their freedom and lose the last vestige of imperial glory or fight a war against the United States she knew she could not win. To give in to U.S. demands for Cuban independence would have been humiliating and so, with only the slightest chance of finding European allies, Spain chose the path of war. As expected, she lost not only the war but also Cuba, the Philippines, Puerto Rico, and Guam. At the cost of all this real estate, in addition to 5,000 battle deaths, Spanish honor was maintained.

In 1939, Finland refused to give the Russians a huge chunk of territory near Leningrad in exchange for barren arctic wastes. Russia proceeded to invade its tiny neighbor, a nation whose friends were already involved in their own war. After a bloody struggle, Finland surrendered. She suffered 50,000 battle deaths, thousands more were injured, made homeless, and orphaned, and much of the country lay in ruins. She also was compelled to relinquish more territory than the Russians had originally demanded. Undoubtedly, Finnish honor was preserved. Observers thrilled to the courageous struggle waged by the little Davids in the infamous Winter War. Today, Finns walk proudly in the world; their national integrity and self-respect have been enhanced because of their celebrated resistance to aggression. They may also have escaped satellization in 1948 because of the toughness displayed in 1939-1940. But were other options available in 1939 and was not the price they paid for protecting national honor too high?

In a comparable situation, Czechoslovakia, a strong and progressive small power, did not take up arms against Germany when the Sudetenland was wrenched from her in 1938 and she did not fight the following year when the entire country was absorbed into the Third Reich. Most likely, though the Czechs could have mounted a stiffer resistance than did the Poles later in the same year, in the end the Germans would have crushed them. Deciding that in this case discretion may have been the better part of valor, the realistic Czechs chose to sully their reputation and accept aggression without a fight. In exchange, the country emerged from World War II relatively unscathed. Although forced to live as Nazi vassals, and although some citizens and minorities were shipped off to the camps or suffered Lidices, many Czechs were able to protect their lives and property.

Denmark's experience with the question of national honor in World War II may be the most interesting of all. To this day, many Danes profess to be disturbed by their countrymen's attitudes in the spring of 1940. Unlike the Norwegians, Dutch, Belgians, and Poles, the Danes did not resist a German takeover. More important, they even accepted, albeit without enthusiasm, membership in the Anti-Comintern Pact which made them tacit allies of the Nazis. From 1940 to 1943, Denmark enjoyed self-government, there was little underground activity, and scant personal and physical damage to the country. An effective underground did develop after 1943, especially after the Nazis took away what was left of Danish political freedom. In the fall of that same year, the Danes were able to foil Hitler's secret plans to round up Danish Jews. Almost the entire nation worked together to smuggle 7,500 Jews to Sweden before the Gestapo could ship them off to the crematoria. Despite this well-publicized gesture, Denmark's position during the war is still an important issue in the country. Why, they ask themselves, did they not fight like other small European states? Of course, what did the Poles, Belgians, Dutch, and Norwegians gain from their futile struggles—a clearer conscience, greater national peace of mind? In exchange for those unmeasurable rewards, they were visited with devastation, death, quislings, and concentration camps. Was Denmark's honor soiled in 1940? If so, what has been the effect on her national character and her respect among her own citizens and the rest of the nations of the world?

Given logistic considerations, the Danes made the wisest choice in 1940. Had they resisted for a while, the Nazi effort elsewhere (especially in Norway) conceivably might have faltered, but this was unlikely. Above all, the Danes can always talk about their assistance to the Jews, unique assistance that salvaged national honor with a realistic and effective gesture. The Danish people were too sensible to waste their lives by throwing themselves at Nazi tanks. What would have happened to their national consciences had they not the glorious Jewish incident to recall? Very little, I think, for a history of resistance and heroism would have been written anyway.

Some cynical Danes even claim that their resistance was not effective. To those who have grown up on Hollywood portrayals of European resistance movements, this comes as a shock. We expect that every Frenchman, Dane, Belgian, and Norwegian helped the Allies by blowing up rail lines, protecting downed fliers, and sending secret coded messages from short-wave transmitters hidden in the basements of local cafes. As the powerful documentary film *The Sorrow and the Pity* demonstrates, most Frenchmen, like most citizens in similar plights, sat out World War II, neither overtly collaborating nor covertly resisting. In a few years, after memories of the war faded, national honor was assuaged by inflating scattered acts of resistance into a widespread national patriotic movement. Is this merely self-delusion? If it is, can a nation survive it? I think so, and consequently am suspicious of arguments claiming that a failure to stand up to the stronger bully must lead to a decline in self-esteem that can be translated into a threat to national security.

If a nation sees that war is the only outcome of a diplomatic duel unless it accepts less than half a loaf, and if it does not stand much of a chance of winning that war, then it is best to take less than half the loaf. It is said that aggressors can never be sated—give them the Sudentenland and they will eventually come back for more. Perhaps, but not every diplomatic rival is Hitler. One should put off the day of final reckoning until national survival is at stake. Then "better dead than Red," and maybe not even then. This is not a pacifist's approach to international conflict. It represents a course of rationality and prudence.

Undoubtedly, justifications for war based upon unemotional analyses of the military, economic, and prestige components of national security are not entirely satisfactory. What is missing from these calculations is the righteous war, the war to save suffering peoples. To some degree, this moral criterion dovetails with the prestige criterion. Our national security is said to be dependent upon the maintenance of our prestige and our prestige is, in turn, partially dependent upon the fulfillment of our implicit national commitment to rescue nations from oppressors. Those who justify war according to some form of moral imperative do not like to talk about anything as base as national security. To them, any war fought to defend the freedom of others is a rational war.

Such an approach, though noble, makes little sense. In the first place, people who run nations do not make war for those exalted purposes, even though they may convince themselves and their citizens that they are entering the battle to save humanity. No doubt in many wars, one side's strategic interests coincided with what appeared to be the interests of humanity. Nevertheless, I cannot identify a single war in modern history that was launched *primarily* for reasons of morality. This is not to say that we cannot or should not support the morally preferable side in a war. Such a determination is easiest in wars in which one group is fighting for liberation from oppression. Nevertheless, the selection of the morally superior side should not be confused with the notion that governments go to war because of moral considerations.

All statesmen in recent times have claimed that they were fighting their wars for only the most moral purposes. The Nazis fought to save the world from Jewish domination, the United States to defend the democrats of Seoul against the butchers of Pyongyang, the Russians to liberate Hungary from counter-revolutionaries, the Chinese to destroy Tibetan feudalism, and the Indians to assist their persecuted brothers in Bangladesh. All of these cases, and countless more, represent ex post facto justifications for decisions based upon considerations of *Realpolitik*. Even the war the United States fought against the Axis had little to do with morality at the start. If we did enter for higher spiritual purposes, then why were we not in the ranks in 1939 and 1940 when Hitler was overrunning country after country? Once in the war, Americans were told they were fighting to rid the world of the fascist scourge. In the 1950s and 1960s, if our interventions were based upon a desire to free peoples from oppression in Korea, Vietnam, Cuba, and the Dominican Republic, where were we in Spain or Greece?

Our morality, as well as the morality of other nations, is highly selective and inconsistent. One leader's morality is another's immorality, one leader's freedom is another's oppression. Even philosophers and theologians are unable to agree on universally acceptable definitions of moral and immoral international behavior. In any event, moral justifications have never been directly related to the decision makers' definitions of national security. To oppose war on humanistic grounds and then to eliminate moral arguments from our analyses may seem paradoxical. Yet given the impossibility of defining morality, it would be futile to devote much attention to the issue of just wars. If anything, the case against war becomes all the stronger when we use the realpoliticians' own cost-benefit analysis against them.

In the pages to follow, I will examine the background of each of the United States' international wars. First, I will discuss the major events that led to war as well as the personalities involved on both sides of the tables and the trenches. The emphasis will be on the American scene, although there is some distortion inherent in the writing of diplomatic history primarily from the vantage point of only one of the capitals. As we travel this depressing path toward the outbreak of hostilities, I will occasionally pause to analyze the meaning of certain issues, and even raise general questions about the nature of the U.S. system. When we finally enter war, the historical narrative will terminate and I will consider the whys and why nots and finally the question of national security and America's decision to take up arms. In the concluding sections, I will bring together common strands from the six accounts that inform us about our diplomatic tradition and the relationships, if any, between our war entries and our strategic interests.

Since the book is directed to an audience beyond that of my academic colleagues, I have broken several canons of scholarship in an attempt to keep the stories clear and readable. Above all, I have attempted to prune my accounts of unnecessary details. Many names, dates, articles of treaties, and minor incidents have been eliminated. For example, when I mention a message from a U.S. minister in London, I will usually omit his name, the precise date it was sent and received (unless such facts are relevant), and its exact wording. It may well be that my definition of unnecessary details and those of my colleagues will differ. I only hope that any distortions produced in this drive for simplicity will not detract from the overall validity of my analysis. There is, of course, such a thing as being too simple. Some events in diplomatic interactions are impervious to lean and uncluttered narrations. To strike the correct balance between the prodigious monograph that frightens off lay readers and the popular essay that horrifies the experts because of its simplemindedness is difficult. I hope that I have come close to this balance.

In a further attempt to maintain clarity, I have kept direct quotations to a minimum. Although they enhance the aesthetic quality of a dry account and offer superficially supportive documentation for an author's judgments, they tend to distract the reader from the main flow of the narrative.

Finally, the footnote, a most useful scholarly appurtenance, has been eliminated entirely. This bit of streamlining is difficult to justify. Yet, I will not be reporting any new bits of evidence or archival discoveries. My material comes from monographs and articles discussed in the bibliographic essay accompanying each chapter.

BIBLIOGRAPHY

In the essays that follow each chapter, I will present those books and articles that I found most useful in my analyses. By no means are they meant to be complete bibliographies.

As far as I can tell, no one has attempted to do what I have done in this volume. The closest to my approach may be the obscure pamphlet by C.H. Hamlin, *The War Myth in United States History* (New York: Fellowship Publications, 1946), an antiwar tract that attempts to demonstrate that we did not belong in any of our wars. At first glance, other, more well-known works seem to deal with the subject at hand—a comparative analysis of the way the United States entered her international wars. Merlo J. Pusey's *The Way We Go To War* (Boston: Houghton Mifflin, 1969) does not do what the title suggests. Writing during the Vietnam war, Pusey presents an argument for renewed congressional assertiveness in U.S. foreign relations. Although, he traces the history of the growth of Presidential power in several chapters, he concentrates primarily on the era since the end of World War II.

Similarly, Ralph K. White's *Nobody Wanted War: Misperception in Vietnam and Other Wars* (Garden City, NY: Doubleday, 1968) is not very useful for our analysis. White looks only at two wars in which the United States did not fight before devoting the bulk of his work to the perceptions of the several antagonists in the Vietnam war. White's book is excellent for the general problem of misperception in international relations and for his use of current social scientific literature to highlight his material.

More attention has been paid to comparative military than comparative diplomatic history. Robert Leckie's long and readable *The Wars of Amer-*

ica (New York: Harper's, 1968) offers a concise introduction to the political background of our entries, but concentrates on the details of the action after the war had begun. A volume in the U.S. Army's Historical Series, *American Military History,* edited by Maurice Matloff (Washington, DC: Government Printing Office, 1969), is skimpy on the diplomacy preceding war entry.

Less concerned with day-to-day accounts of battles and formations is Russell F. Weigley's *The American Way of War: A History of the United States Military Policy and Strategy* (New York: Macmillan, 1973). Weigley carefully examines the strategic thinking that had much to do with the way the diplomats approached their confrontations. Disappointing for this study, but another example of important comparative history, is Ernest R. May (ed.), *The Ultimate Decision: The President as Commander in Chief* (New York: George Braziller, 1960). May and his colleagues emphasize the action after the wars began.

One of the most influential essays on the roots of American foreign policy is William A. Williams's *The Tragedy of American Diplomacy* (New York: Dell, 1962), which is concerned more with the hows and whys of intervention than with the shoulds. I suspect that Williams and his many followers would consider it irrelevant to examine the justification for wars in terms of national security since, they contend, the needs of U.S. capitalism and the Open Door policy made such interventions inevitable. A challenging analysis of the general neo-Marxist model is Robert B. Zevin's "An Interpretation of American Imperialism," *Journal of Economic History* 32(March 1972), 316-360. A useful survey of U.S. martial activities is Doris A. Graber's *Crisis Diplomacy: A History of the United States Intervention Policies and Practices* (Washington, DC: Public Affairs Press, 1959).

A good place to begin for an examination of national security is Gerald E. Wheeler's essay, "National Security" in Alexander DeConde (ed.), *Encyclopedia of American Foreign Policy,* II (New York: Scribner's, 1978), 523-634. Wheeler describes how U.S. strategists altered their definitions of national security over time as the world became more complex. For the tension between realism and idealism, Charles E. Osgood's *Ideals and Self-Interest in America's Foreign Relations* (Chicago: University of Chicago Press, 1953), though overdrawn and outdated, is still indispensable. Two other venerable classics are Hans Morgenthau's *In Defense of the National Interest* (New York: Knopf, 1951) and his widely read *Politics Among Nations* (New York: Knopf, 1951). The fuzzy nature of the concept of national security is explained in Arnold Wolfers's

" 'National Security' as an Ambiguous Symbol," *Political Science Quarterly,* 67(December 1952), 481-502. On the other side of the spectrum, no student of the rationality of and the rationales for war can ignore Michael Walzer's *Just and Unjust Wars: A Moral Argument with Historical Illustrations* (New York: Basic Books, 1977).

Several specialized works were helpful in the preparation of this study. Barry B. Hughes's *The Domestic Context of American Foreign Policy* (San Francisco: W. H. Freeman, 1978) is the best summary of the state of research on the role of public opinion in U.S. foreign policy. Most of his examples and discussions center around events since 1940. For statistical data on how the United States compares to other countries, J. David Singer and Melvin Small's *The Wages of War, 1816-1965: A Statistical Handbook* (New York: John Wiley, 1972) and Small and Singer's "The War Proneness of Democratic Regimes, 1816-1965," *The Jerusaleum Journal of International Relations,* I(Summer 1976), 50-69 are among the most important.

Chapter 1

THE WAR OF 1812

Whether the United States shall continue passive under these progressive usurpations and these accumulating wrongs, or, opposing force in defense of their national rights ... is a solemn question which the Constitution wisely confides to the legislative department of the Government.

—James Madison, June 1, 1812—

The story of the origins of the War of 1812 is confusing. None of our other wars has been explained in so many different ways by so many different people over such a long period of time. Depending upon the source, the war was fought for maritime rights, independence from Britain, national honor, the defense of the Republican Party, the defense of republican institutions, expansion into Canada and Florida, relief from economic depression, and combinations of these and other causes. In part, the ambiguity surrounding the origins of the war relates to the absence of an incident that precipitated hostilities. There was no Pearl Harbor in 1812, not even a sinking of a *Maine*. Why we went to war in June and not May or April is still something of a mystery.

Complicating matters further, the War of 1812 was one of those few wars without a victor. Had official referees been around to keep score of the telling military blows and knockdowns, they would have declared the contest a draw. To support this judgment, they could have pointed to the treaty of peace that provided for *status quo ante bellum.*

There are those, however, who maintain that the little War of 1812 was the only war the United States ever lost until Vietnam. According to proud Canadians, since American expansionists set out to capture Canada, and since they were repulsed after a series of bumbling campaigns, Canada won the war. Others who feel that the United States received the worst of it rest their case upon the insurmountable lead a belligerent builds when he burns his opponent's capital. Thus, the United States suffered a crushing blow when the Redcoats burned Washington and sent James Madison and his Cabinet fleeing, with Dolley bringing up the rear along with the portrait of George Washington rescued from British torches.

For most citizens, until the fall of Saigon in 1975, the United States had never lost a war. Indeed, many consider the War of 1812 our second successful war for independence. Despite the military and diplomatic outcome, the United States allegedly won the war because it stood up to the British and demonstrated that it could no longer be pushed around like some fifth-rate nation. In addition, by successfully resisting British attacks at Plattsburgh and especially New Orleans (albeit after the war was over), Americans gained new self-respect. They had been able to carry on a war against the greatest of world powers. And they achieved this so-called victory at the cost of only 2,200 battle deaths.

Such an analysis treats the loss of 2,200 lives callously. It also ignores the demographic repercussions of those losses and the physical and psychological wounds left in the bodies and minds of thousands of other soldiers and civilians who participated in the conflict. Is the alleged salvaging of national honor worth the life of even one human being? In considering our response to this question, we must remember that after the last round was fired, the grievances that compelled James Madison to ask for war remained unresolved.

THE ROOTS OF WAR

The story of the War of 1812 began in France in 1789 when Louis XVI called his Estates General into session and unknowingly set in motion a chain of events that terminated only in 1815 when Napoleon was banished to St. Helena. At first, Americans rejoiced at the tidings of the French Revolution. France was going to be the next domino to fall in the worldwide revolution against tyrannical monarchs, a revolution inspired by the earlier success of the American republicans. Hopes for France faded after the guillotining of Louis and the institution of the Terror that was too bloodthirsty for the tastes of most Americans. All of this was entertaining for transatlantic spectators who viewed the startling events on the continent as one might view a baseball game sitting in the last row of the center field bleachers on a foggy day.

After the onset of world war in 1792 between the French Republic and a group of English-led counterrevolutionary powers, the United States, initially an interested observer, became an unwilling participant. Previously, the old British North American colonies had been swept into four major European wars in the seventeenth and eighteenth centuries. The new United States would soon discover, much to its misfortune, that independence and the Atlantic Ocean could not completely isolate it from the Old World.

The emerging political factions within the new republic quickly chose sides, with Thomas Jefferson and his friends supporting France and Alexander Hamilton and his friends supporting England, or so it seemed. According to the political rhetoric of the day, the Jeffersonians were champions of the bloody *sans-culottes* and the Hamiltonians, champions of autocratic royalists. Jefferson was accused of wanting to institute an American Reign of Terror, Hamilton of wanting to crown someone, perhaps himself, King of the United States. Such charges would have been harmless had they only involved the exaggerated taunts of political rivals, but much more was at stake. The factions chose up sides as a byproduct of their need to develop a foreign policy to meet European threats to U.S. national security.

During the first round of Anglo-French War (1793-1800), problems arose that eventually led to the American War of 1812. In 1793 and 1794, the British enacted a series of Orders in Council severely restricting the ability of neutral nations to trade with France and her allies. To make matters worse, they also outraged Americans with their impressment practices, forcibly seizing presumed British sailors and citizens from American merchant vessels and "returning" them to British service.

A possible Anglo-American clash was delayed by the negotiation of the Jay Treaty in 1794, a *modus vivendi* ushering in the so-called First Rapprochement (1795-1804). During this 10-year period, the United States was almost continually on the brink of war with France. First, we fought an undeclared naval war from 1798 to 1800. Only the courage and wisdom of our second President, John Adams, saved us from a full-fledged war we could ill afford. Then, our third President, Thomas Jefferson, jockeyed for position with Napoleon over New Orleans. After implicitly threatening the new French ruler with an Anglo-American alliance, Jefferson secured not only New Orleans but also the windfall of the Louisiana Purchase. Once Louisiana was obtained in 1803, and after the Peace of Amiens (1802-1803) had broken down, the spotlight again shifted to our old enemy, Great Britain, and the problems papered over in 1795. Guiding us through the early years of trials and tribulations in the Napoleonic wars was Thomas Jefferson, one of the founders of our nation.

THOMAS JEFFERSON AND REPUBLICAN FOREIGN POLICY

Although many the world over still admire Thomas Jefferson's contributions to democratic political theory, architecture, and science, few turn to the sage of Monticello for guidance on foreign affairs. At first glance, this appears surprising. Jefferson was a cosmopolitan and urbane American, an experienced diplomat who served as minister to France and then, quite successfully, as the nation's first Secretary of State. But when, as President, he finally became the chief architect of American foreign policy, he seemed to forget many of the lessons learned during his lengthy apprenticeship.

In other endeavors, Jefferson appeared to be a practical man. In foreign affairs, he all too often rigidly adhered to lofty principles he claimed were universal and immutable. That was all well and good in the abstract. But what if other nations did not accept those principles? After all, from their point of view, Jeffersonian principles of international conduct blended quite neatly with what seemed to be American self-interest. In his disputes with the British, Jefferson insisted on a sweeping settlement that would have had his enemies in London renounce their illegal behavior on the high seas. All along, he could have achieved a workable arrangement that would have smoothed over relations for a while by removing questions of international law, and even morality, from the bargaining table.

His rivals, the Adams-Hamilton-Federalist faction, argued that the security of the United States depended upon the maintenance of proper, if not cordial, Anglo-American relations. According to them, when the British assaulted Americans on the high seas, a protest was in order, but we could never adopt a policy that might lead to a severance of the Anglo-American linkage. After all, England bought half of our exports including 80% of our cotton crop. Once before, in the heady afterglow of the Revolutionary War, we thought we could do without them. Rather quickly we found ourselves drawn back to England because of common tastes and methods of doing business, as well as complementary economies. Admittedly, we were also important to them, since we bought one-third of their exports. But given their vast empire and control of the seas, they would have an easier time compensating for the loss of American trade than we would have compensating for the loss of their trade. Thus, the Federalists asked, what purpose was served if, in defending principles, your country was destroyed? To this, Jefferson and his friends replied, if you do not defend your principles, your country will be destroyed in the long run.

Jefferson's idealism also affected his day-to-day handling of diplomatic affairs. For example, he was shocked by what he interpreted to be the cynical behavior of his international rivals, who were only playing the game according to the accepted code of Machiavelli. Jefferson's attitude here is again surprising for he understood well the skullduggery commonplace in American domestic politics. On one occasion, he even refused to purchase stolen documents because Americans, who had to set an example for the rest of the benighted world, did not traffic in such sleazy materials.

With his constant defense of international justice and his unwillingness to accept realistic compromises based upon considerations of national power, Jefferson became the first of that long line of American statesmen who led his people toward war for the sake of universal principles accepted only by the United States. Woodrow Wilson, Franklin Roosevelt, and John Foster Dulles are only the most prominent examples of American leaders who have drunk deeply at the well of Jeffersonian idealism. This approach has been practiced by many of our Presidents and accepted by most of our citizens. We continually fail to understand the other fellow's predicament and refuse to accept the notion that in diplomacy, in most cases, both parties are right. Of all of our diplomatic traditions, this is the one most enraging to other nations. They simply will not accept the idea that the United States represents truth and justice while her adversaries are always international sinners and prevaricators. To be sure, there is nothing wrong with American statesmen upholding international morality in proclamations to their own citizens and to world public opinion. But when those proclamations are also used in private diplomatic intercourse, war becomes likely. One of the best ways to create a stalemate is to come to the bargaining table armed with principles you refuse to surrender.

In the case of Jefferson and Madison from 1801 to 1812, they were only armed with principles. The two Republican leaders presided over a party suspicious of the military and wary of large federal expenditures. Unyielding on principles of international law with the British after 1806, they did not build the sort of defense force to compel their adversaries to accept those principles. We can credit Jefferson with another first. He set a precedent for those who followed him in Washington who bluffed and blustered, inflaming American jingoism, yet who resisted taking measures to prepare for war, war made more likely because of that bluff and bluster. "Speak loudly and carry no stick" might be the motto of such unrealistic statesmen who operated a vigorous rhetorical diplomacy on behalf of a nation capable of hurling only paper broadsides across the Atlantic. Even though his Secretary of the Treasury pointed out how easily the capital itself could be taken by England in case of war, Jefferson and, to a lesser degree, Madison refused to maintain the pitifully weak gunboat navy which, by 1812, had rotted and fallen into a state of disrepair.

Lurking behind this defense policy was the conviction that we did not need much of an army or navy because American yeomen could defeat any professional army in the world. One Kentuckian, fighting for freedom with his trusty longrifle, was the match for any 10 mercenaries. Such had been the case in the Revolution and so would it be in any future wars against Old World monarchies. This conviction was a long time dying. How was it, we asked only recently, that communist Vietnamese could fight so well for 30 years? At first, such dedication was explained in terms of drugs or soldiers chained to their guns. Today, most Americans are finally prepared to lay to rest the notion that the more democratic the cause, the better the soldier.

The Jeffersonian nondefense policy also involved a democratic aversion to standing military establishments. Armies, and especially navies, were playthings of monarchies that had no place in the New World. But an adequate military force was a necessary evil if one hoped to contend with aggression from Europe. In the years before the War of 1812, the British knew they would have had a difficult time holding Canada against a mobilized United States. Although such a prospect might have made them more conciliatory, so long as Jefferson and his Republicans did little about preparedness, the British had few reasons to meet Americans even halfway.

Aside from failing to develop the necessary muscle to back up their demands, the Republicans also failed to understand the nature of the international economic system. Few experts, even today, understand international economics. All the same, Jefferson and Madison misread the situation and above all overemphasized the importance of American trade for the British. From 1806 to 1812, the two Virginians waged economic warfare against England with a variety of measures. They believed that the severance of trade with America, or even the threat of such a severance, would frighten the British into coming to terms. Not self-sufficient, England needed the raw materials, foodstuffs, and naval stores we provided.

Though we could hurt England by cutting our exports, we could not hurt her severely enough to bring her to her knees, or even to one knee. In part, our economic offensive was blunted by the opening of the Spanish Empire in South America to British traders in 1808, something the Republicans could not have been expected to foresee. More important, England was weakened more when her *exports,* and not her imports, were prohibited from various markets. Indeed, the underlying principle of Napoleon's Continental System was to deny markets—not supplies—to the British, and this might have worked had he been able to enforce it effectively throughout his empire. Napoleon considered exports to be the key to the British economy. Close their markets and gold would stop flowing into London coffers. Neither the American nor the French policy worked, but it now appears that Napoleon had the better of the argument.

In the last analysis then, the Republicans approached their adversaries across the ocean laboring under a series of misconceptions about the nature of the diplomatic and economic system. Their nonexistent army and navy compounded their difficulties. Fortunately, the powerful British were too preoccupied with other matters to take Young Jonathan very seriously.

THE VIEW FROM LONDON

Although we are interested primarily in how and why the United States went to war, our story would be incomplete were we not to consider the British perspective. Above all, we must remember that affairs in the United States were trivial matters for England during the first 12 years of the nineteenth century and, for that matter, for much of the next 100 years. Indices of European history texts dealing with the period from the French Revolution to Waterloo offer few citations to American difficulties with the belligerents or even the War of 1812. Politically and militarily impotent, far off the beaten track, a republican pariah, the United States counted for little in European politics until the eve of World War I.

Today, American policies are crucial to the development and stability of Liberia. Liberian policies, on the other hand, are matters of marginal interest to all except those behind the African desk at the State Department. To draw the parallel with the British-American connection at the turn of the nineteenth century might be stretching a point, but not beyond credibility. To put it another way, the most important post for an American diplomat during the period was London; among the least important posts for a British diplomat was Washington. The latter would have preferred to serve in Naples, Dresden, or even Istanbul before remote and malarial Washington. This factor was significant in the prewar diplomacy since the British were ill-served by several amateurish diplomats here. Who else could they have found to make the voyage across the Atlantic to the rugged frontier of the civilized world?

The length of the voyage partially explains how we came to declare war in 1812 after the British had eliminated one of our most serious grievances. An average trip across the Atlantic took almost two months. Six weeks was a swift passage. In diplomatic time, this meant that instructions sent from London to Washington by fast packet boat on January 1 would reach the British envoy in Washington around the end of February. Reporting that the situation in the states had changed and that the instructions of January 1 were irrelevant, his dispatch would reach London somewhere in the middle of April. Who knows what might have happened in London and on the continent since that first despatch was sent on January 1? Until the Atlantic cable was laid in 1866, American relations with Europe were frustrated by this awesome communication problem. Our most glorious victory in the war, Andrew Jackson's Battle of New Orleans, was fought after peace had been signed in Belgium on Christmas eve in 1814.

Even considering these difficulties, the British were unnecessarily arrogant toward the Americans. Most ministers, antirepublican to begin with, thought they could get away with anything against those second-hand Englishmen. Some of this lack of concern for America's pretentious defense of neutral rights was understandable. England was fighting for her life and also, she argued, for the rights of free men everywhere against Napoleonic dictatorship. She had become a major international actor because of her naval power, a power she exercised ruthlessly and effectively with little concern for the rules of fair play. Any retreat from the amoral prerogatives of the ruler of the seas would have seriously weakened her ability to combat Napoleon.

Still, in the period prior to the War of 1812, Britain *appears* to have had the weaker case, especially since she was virtually alone on the seas while the rest of the world, enemies and neutrals, protested her policies. But international law, a fuzzy business, is interpreted by each nation according to its own precedents and best interests. With a straight face, the British could claim that even their most restrictive policies were within the bounds of proper international law. And with just as straight a face, those neutrals that wanted to be able to sell anything, any time, at any place, to any belligerent, claimed that their complaints against the British were supported by international law. Who was right? Such a question cannot be answered.

One can sympathize with the British. They felt they were shouldering the burdens of the world, maintaining the balance of power against the tyrant Napoleon, and losing lives and ships. Meanwhile, neutrals, making money hand over fist, were complaining about the niceties of international law. In considering our disputes with them, we must bear in mind how we looked to our enemies in London. Unfortunately, few contemporary Americans were able to maintain such an empathetic perspective.

THE SLINGS AND ARROWS OF OUTRAGEOUS BELLIGERENTS

In May of 1803, after the brief Peace of Amiens, the European conflagration, smouldering for two years, ignited once again and we soon found ourselves back where we had been in 1793. What to do about violations of our neutral rights? As in the earlier period, those with the most to lose, the merchants and ship owners, were willing to grin and bear it. They were prepared to live with the inconvenience and humiliation of illegal searches and seizures as long as they could maintain their lucrative war trade. They seemed to say that we might as well make as much out of this as we can and accept the insults to our honor and occasional thrusts into our pocket books since the belligerents were not going to improve their manners just for the United States. Jefferson and Madison did not agree with their position. They contended that their country could not withstand insults to her honor. At the start, Jefferson was willing to tolerate some British violations, especially since he felt it in our interest to see Napoleon restrained. After 1804, however, he decided that the British had gone too far. Although the British and the French were seizing ships and violating rights, British violations were more numerous, took place closer to home, and involved more than just traditional illegal practices.

From 1804 to 1812, the United States was in almost constant conflict with England over two issues—neutral rights and impressment. In terms of national honor, the impressment issue was the most important and also the most difficult to resolve. Both the British and Americans needed merchant seamen: the

British to man their navy and merchant marine engaged in a worldwide struggle on the high seas; the Americans to man their merchant marine, growing rapidly because of that struggle. In 1807, the United States needed at least 4,000 new seamen each year to enable her merchant marine to keep up with increasing demands for her supplies and the burgeoning reexport trade. The native American population could not provide enough men to fill this quota. From where would these new seamen come? From England of course. The British had a vast pool of experienced sailors who spoke English and who desired release from a hard service. By 1807, the year the impressment issue reached its zenith, probably half of the seamen in the American service were former or, perhaps, still citizens of England. This ambiguity as to their exact status related to conflicting interpretations of naturalization laws.

Impressment had been a British practice for many years. Up until the French Revolution, "recruiters" and shore patrols had practiced it on land, often kidnapping drunken seamen in waterfront taverns. Some of those unfortunates were deserters, others not. All woke up the next morning to find themselves miles out to sea aboard one of His Majesty's ships.

Given the number of seamen needed during the war and the not surprising decline in enlistments, the British Admiralty became more desperate and consequently more aggressive. It began to impress men from vessels on the high seas, arguing that it was only exercising its legal right both to seize deserters from the British Navy and to recruit English civilians.

The British resorted to this practice for two related reasons. First, they needed men. More important perhaps, taking impressment to the seas discouraged British seamen from joining the American merchant marine or other more pleasant services. Impressment on the high seas offered a visible lesson to those on your own ship of how difficult it would be to escape the long arm of British justice. And so, British vessels stopped American vessels and took from them British-looking seamen, some of whom were recent deserters, some of whom had deserted years before, and some of whom were merely former

citizens of His Majesty's empire. What right did the British have
to employ this nefarious practice without so much as allowing
the American master to present a case for his men? No right at
all except for that right accruing to the nation that rules the
seas. Actually, Americans viewed the general argument for
impressment of deserters at sea as not necessarily legal but
tolerable. What they objected to was the way it was carried out
and the many injustices alleged to have been perpetrated.

Between 3,000 and 8,000 Americans were impressed in the
years from the Peace of Amiens to the War of 1812. Most of
those men, from the American point of view, were bona fide
citizens. Impressment helps to explain why Americans were
more angry with the British than the French. Both countries
engaged in practices that violated neutral commercial rights.
Only the British carried on the humiliating practice of impressment on the high seas.

The incidence of impressment did tail off after the Battle of
Trafalgar in 1805, when the British established naval supremacy
over Napoleon. But numbers alone may not have been the key.
Sufficient Americans were impressed all through the prewar
period to keep this issue in the spotlight. Whether 1, 10, or 100
men a month were taken into the British Navy from American
ships, impressment was a running insult to our honor. No
self-respecting nation could exist for long, it was argued, unless
it could protect its citizens from attack on the high seas.

A compromise to the impressment problem was theoretically
possible. Had the United States offered to return all new or
recent arrivals from England—real British seamen—the British
might have promised to cease impressing Americans on the high
seas. What was a real British seaman? Here American and British
interpretations of citizenship differed widely. For the British,
once a British citizen always a British citizen, even if the
presumed deserter was carrying a miserable scrap of paper that
made him an American citizen. They could not trust the United
States to return all deserters, especially since the Admiralty
accepted no statute of limitations for desertion. Finally, even if
both sides adopted the American definition of citizenship,

according to Treasury Secretary Albert Gallatin, we would have had to return more Englishmen than the British returned Americans.

In 1807, the *Chesapeake* affair brought the impressment issue to a head, though the affair was unrelated to the mainstream of impressment activities. In this case, British sailors fired at and boarded an American *warship,* not a private vessel, to search for deserters. The American public was more outraged over this incident than any other during the entire period; so much so that Jefferson might have been able to push through a war declaration had he wanted one. As it turned out, 1807 was probably the best time for war since British fortunes were at a low ebb. Napoleon had established his mastery over the continent, the Spanish Empire was still intact, and Americans were united in anger. When we did go to war in 1812, Napoleon was on his way to defeat in Russia, most of his allies had deserted him, Spain was in rebellion, the Latin American states were open to British traders, and, above all, the American body politic was severely split. Furthermore, in 1812, there was no single incident or attack around which Madison could frame his war message whereas Jefferson had his Pearl Harbor with the *Chesapeake.*

Sensing the weakness of their strategic position in 1807 and nervous about the war fever in the United States, the British offered indemnities for the *Chesapeake* affair. Such an act of contrition was unusual for the Admiralty. Jefferson would have none of it unless the indemnity was coupled with a renunciation of impressment on the high seas. Later, when Jefferson was willing to accept just an indemnity, American tempers had cooled and so the British no longer had to maintain a conciliatory front. Thus, the impressment issue in general, and the *Chesapeake* case in particular, lingered on in the collective memories of proud Americans. In a real sense, considering the numbers impressed and the health of the American merchant marine, impressment was not a major issue by 1812. Symbolically, however, it was all important—the most prominent example of British violations of American sovereignty.

The other major grievance against England involved her restricted view of the rights of neutrals, an issue that was more far reaching than impressment. Up until 1805, the so-called Rule of 1756 had been virtually ignored by the British. This principle (unilaterally proclaimed by the British) declared that trade not open to a neutral in time of peace would be closed in time of war. The rule was not applied in the *Polly* case of 1800, when an American shipper was "allowed" by a British court to carry a cargo of goods from Cuba to the United States for reexport to Spain. By 1805, however, British shipping interests had become worried about the way neutral trade had expanded in apparent violation of the Rule of 1756. Because of commercial pressure, the British reversed the *Polly* decision in 1805 in the *Essex* case and made the Rule of 1756—which had never been accepted by the United States—her rule of the seas once again.

In addition, perennial problems concerning definitions of contraband, or goods prohibited for export to belligerents, and the rules of blockade surfaced with the disruption of the Peace of Amiens. Americans and other neutrals interpreted contraband in the most narrow sense and claimed that free ships made free goods. Just about anything carried in wartime on a neutral vessel, short of weapons, should be immune from seizure, or so we argued. Belligerents, in contrast, interpreted contraband as broadly as possible to deny their enemies as many supplies as possible. The most notorious example was the British inclusion of food as contraband during World War I. The contraband issue is always difficult; problems were expected here.

The British blockade was another matter. They had adhered to accepted rules up through 1806. Single ports were blockaded by the stationing of sufficient vessels to effectively seal them off, as prescribed by law and precedent. According to the traditional rules of blockade, a blockade could not simply be announced—part of a nation's fleet had to be permanently committed to the area blockaded. After 1806, the British began to adopt a different set of rules. In May of that year, in an attempt to get at Napoleon from the sea, they announced that the European coast from Brest in France to the Elbe in Germany was blockaded. Obviously, they could not blockade the entire coast. The British Navy was large but not large enough to beseige all of it. The blockade was most stringently applied on that portion of the coast west of Ostend in Belgium. Americans could trade with ports east of Ostend as long as they were not coming from a country hostile to England.

The French countered when Napoleon launched his Continental System with the Berlin Decree in November of 1806. As a consequence of the Battle of Trafalgar of 1805, Britain had swept the French Navy from the seas. Theoretically, England could blockade France but France, while dominant on land after the battle of Austerlitz of that same year, could not blockade England. Nevertheless, Napoleon did blockade England with an ingenious, and probably illegal, scheme based upon French control of most of Western and Central Europe. His Berlin Decree prohibited all trade with England and in English goods in all territories under his control. Every vessel coming from Great Britain to the continent would be refused harbor or seized.

The British answered the French broadside with the Order in Council of January of 1807 prohibiting all neutral trade between enemy ports and any other ports from which British ships had been excluded. This order was further tightened later that year when all enemy ports were blockaded and commerce with and between them prohibited unless the trader first received a license from British authorities. Napoleon closed the ring with his Milan Decree of December of 1807 toughening the provisions of the Berlin Decree. Furthermore, the French government announced, any ships arriving in Europe with a British license would be seized.

And so the neutrals, chief among them the United States, were damned if they did and damned if they did not. Britain refused to allow them to trade with the continent unless they first stopped for inspection and licensing and France promised to seize any ship adhering to British regulations. Of course, Napoleon's threat was less serious than the British since he could neither blockade England nor enforce his decrees in all of his ports. Thus, a practical option available to Americans was to accept the British rules and stay away from the continent. After all, Britain took considerably more American exports than all of the continental countries combined. To have done so, however, would have been to condone her allegedly illegal rulings, and Jefferson and Madison would not jettison the hallowed principles of neutral rights to which they held so dearly.

A CARROT AND A STICK

Confronted by the Battle of the Decrees and especially the new British aggressiveness on the seas, Jefferson had to respond. In effect, he could select from three alternate strategies. One involved the *Chesapeake* affair. At that point, he could have asked for and received a declaration of war. More people in Congress and the country at large would have followed him then than followed Madison five years later. For a brief period after the incident, he seriously considered asking for war. Or, Jefferson could have opted for turning the other cheek in exchange for peace, prosperity, and a degree of humiliation. He could have tolerated British policies, as merchants urged, and maintained a lucrative trade with Britain and her allies for the remainder of the war. (War on Britain's side, although defensible with hindsight in terms of balance of power theory, was considered out of the question.) To have adopted this policy would have meant truckling to the British Lion and a retreat before the bar of international justice, something Jefferson and Madison could never accept. Instead, the Republican leaders opted for an intermediate policy short of war that might save America's face and force the British to retract their Orders in Council. The policy of economic war that American governments practiced from 1806 to 1812 failed. This approach seemed attractive, at least in 1806. In the first place, the British had apparently bowed to an earlier threat of economic retaliation in 1794. Moreover, this policy offered a solution to the problem that pleased the greatest number of people: the doves, because it fell considerably short of real war; the hawks, because it represented an aggressive response to British provocations; and even some merchants and shippers, because it promised an end to British maritime violations. Although no one was totally pleased with this approach, few were totally displeased with it. Of course, a foreign policy that pleases the greatest number of constituents is not necessarily a wise or prudent policy.

The Republicans instituted their economic offensive (or was it a defensive?) even before the belligerents began their Battle of the Decrees. In the spring of 1806, in reaction to the *Essex* case and new impressment outrages, Congress passed the Non-Importation Act prohibiting the importation of certain British manufactures as of November 1 of that year until such time when the grievances relating to British maritime practices had been resolved. After more than a year's delay, the Non-Importation Act went into effect late in 1807, but was almost immediately supplanted by the more sweeping embargo. As it turned out, the Non-Importation Act may have been the most sensible of all of the American retaliatory acts since it complemented Napoleon's attempts to deny England markets. By the time the act became operative, however, the situation on the high seas had changed drastically. This first tentative broadside in America's economic war offered no protection to American merchantmen confronted by the Orders in Council and the Continental System.

The Non-Importation Act did not go into effect as planned in 1806 because Jefferson offered the British a carrot to go along with his stick. Almost at the same time as the British heard news of the impending act, they also learned of a new American peace overture. Jefferson dispatched William Pinkney to London to join our minister, James Monroe, for a new series of discussions about outstanding Anglo-American problems. He instructed his two diplomats to obtain from the British a treaty including a renunciation of impressment (the *Chesapeake* affair had not yet occurred) and a revision of the British interpretation of neutral rights. In exchange, Monroe and Pinkney could offer the abrogation of the Non-Importation Act and American goodwill—a one-sided proposal to say the least. This was sensed

immediately by the two American negotiators. Like their predecessors, Monroe and Pinkney ignored their instructions and
attempted to achieve a more modest but realistic settlement
with the British. The so-called Monroe-Pinkney Treaty was a
short-run, practical arrangement that could have smoothed over
relations for a few years. The settlement included modest trade
concessions from the British as well as an informal promise to
go easy on impressment, in exchange for a restoration of normal
Anglo-American trade and an American promise to refrain from
employing commercial weapons for 10 years. As might have
been expected, the British categorically refused to renounce
their right to impress fugitive sailors or to alter those naval
practices abhorrent to Americans.

Although the treaty could have played a role similar to that
played by the Jay Treaty a decade earlier—a cooling-off treaty—
the President refused to submit it to the Senate. For one thing,
Republican firebrands would never have accepted such an agreement. For another, Jefferson, who was convinced that the
British had not gone far enough in meeting American demands,
remained confident that he could get more once he tightened
the economic screws another turn or two.

The failure of the Monroe-Pinkney negotiations to produce
Anglo-American understanding may have been the major turning point of the prewar period. Nothing that occurred from
1806 to 1812 brought the two countries any closer to peaceful
coexistence. From 1806 on, Jefferson and his Republicans
placed themselves on a collision course with the British Empire.
Eschewing compromise, they demanded a full redress of grievances. To accomplish such a diplomatic victory over the British,
they unleashed a series of economic weapons based upon a
misunderstanding of international trade patterns and an over-
estimation of American economic power. By the time the
Republicans realized that they had been operating a bankrupt
policy, the years of inflammatory rhetoric and humiliation on
the seas made a return to a Monroe-Pinkney sort of settlement
politically impossible. By eliminating Monroe-Pinkney in 1806,
Jefferson severely limited his options as well as those of his
successor.

JEFFERSON'S EMBARGO

Following the failure of the British to accept his carrot, Jefferson took up the stick again. After the Battle of the Decrees, the Non-Importation Act was too mild a measure to protect a neutral who wished to maintain traditional rights in time of war. On the surface, Jefferson's next response to England and France—the embargo—was a reasonable one. To protect American vessels from illegal search, seizure, and damage, he would keep them at home and prohibit all American exports. This was the defensive side of the embargo. It had its offensive aspects as well. Not only would an embargo protect American lives and property but it would also threaten England with starvation and economic ruin. Jefferson hoped that after a few months of embargo, the British would finally realize that the Americans meant business and revoke their Orders in Council. At the outset, the President thought that his new measure would be a short-run affair. Everyone realized that an extended embargo would be self-defeating since it would adversely affect our economy. American farmers, merchants, and shippers needed the European market almost as much as Jefferson thought the British needed our products.

The embargo was not a bad gamble. In the early days of the French Revolution, when confronted with a similar threat, the British had conceded. Now facing a powerful Napoleon astride much of the European continent, they could afford even less to alienate the United States or suffer economic hardship. As it happened, the embargo failed because the British did not initially view it as a serious threat to their interests. Conversely, Americans did react to the "O Grab Me" that was allegedly bankrupting citizens involved in every aspect of overseas trade. Merchants complained bitterly that grass was growing in streets of cities along the eastern seaboard. Jefferson was left with an embarrassing problem. Not knowing how to extricate himself from the mess, he allowed the embargo to remain in effect through all of 1808, even though it seemed that the only nation it was hurting was his own. He was in a bind, self-made though it was. To have revoked the embargo would have been to admit that it was not working and that the privation and economic dislocation some Americans had suffered had been for nought. With only a short time remaining before he was to hand over the reins of government to Madison, the proud and stubborn Jefferson gave up trying to resolve his problems and began counting the days before he could escape to Monticello and peace.

The embargo failed for a number of reasons. First, and most obviously, the loss of American imports did not distress the British enough to make them renounce the privileges that came with control of the seas. Moreover, the embargo did not prohibit British imports to the United States. During the period of the embargo, England maintained her imports here at around 40% of normal levels. Even though ships carrying British goods had to leave our ports in ballast, this one-way trade proved lucrative enough for many British shipowners.

In addition, Jefferson's legislation contained a loophole. Under its provisions, American shippers were allowed to pick up cargoes they had contracted to purchase in the months prior to the embargo and they were even permitted to take American goods with them to sell in Europe in order to raise the funds necessary to pay for these contracted European exports. Of the 400 or so ships that employed this loophole, only 1% were seized by the belligerents. In economic terms, these few seizures were a small price to pay for the profitable trading deals available in a Europe at war.

What, then, can be said of Jefferson's embargo? It did head off war in 1807. On the other hand, the embargo led to unprecedented domestic political strife with the Northeast openly flouting the law when possible and even talking of secession.

By late 1808, however, the embargo appeared finally to be causing enough economic discomfort in certain financial circles to concern London. Alternate New World markets that helped relieve the slack created by the partial closing of the American market were not enough to please all British merchants and shippers. Still, by the time the embargo was voided by congressional action in March of 1809, the dislocation it had caused was not severe enough to force the British government to renounce the naval policies it had developed over the previous century. Ironically, its ultimate failure could be attributed in part to its initial limited success. When the embargo began to create a scarcity of American raw materials, prices rose so rapidly that more and more shippers were enticed to violate the law and run the embargo. Perhaps an extended embargo might have worked, but the Americans were the first to throw in the towel when they restored normal economic relations with England.

As he neared the end of his term of office, Jefferson realized that his policy had been a failure. Unwilling to admit it publicly, bereft of viable alternatives, a lame-duck President in any event, he left to Congress and his successor the task of devising new tactics in the economic war with Britain. One of the greatest of the Founding Fathers, a man who had earned his nation's devotion many times over for contributions during the last quarter of the eighteenth century, and the man who had secured Louisiana in 1803, Thomas Jefferson left the Presidency as a rather unpopular figure. No wonder when it came to choose the epitaph for his tombstone, Jefferson noted his founding of the University of Virginia, his governorship of that state, and his authorship of the Virginia Statute on Religious Freedom. He did not mention his eight years as America's third President. With barely a whimper, Jefferson left Washington in the spring of 1809, never to return. The ball was now in James Madison's court.

ANOTHER STUBBORN VIRGINIAN

In March 1809, during the waning days of Jefferson's administration, Congress finally replaced the hated embargo with the Non-Intercourse Act. This law, which prohibited all commerce with England and France, also provided for a relaxation of the ban if either or both belligerents met American objections to their decrees.

Madison was armed with this new bludgeon when he took office. His defenders argue, with some reason, that he was the unfortunate inheritor of a policy and a situation that presented him with few options. The story of Mr. Madison's War, as some have labeled it, begins not in 1812 or 1811 but in 1803 with Jefferson or even in 1792 with Washington. With the collapse of the Monroe-Pinkney negotiations, the outrage of the *Chesapeake,* and the humiliating failure of the embargo, the American government had demonstrated its inability to bring England to heel. As long as he clung to the old Republican demand for a redress of grievances, as well as a British promise to respect American sovereignty, Madison had little room to maneuver. He could have opted for more aggressive or at least effective economic warfare. Or, for a long shot, he could have sat tight with his Non-Intercourse Act and hoped for a swift end to the Napoleonic wars. Indeed, in evaluating the effectiveness of earlier Republican policies, we often lose sight of the time element. Had Napoleon invaded Russia in 1811 instead of 1812, there probably would have been no Anglo-American war of 1812. In that case, the embargo and other Jefferson-Madison policies would have appeared to have been brilliant strategems of delay that both saved face and kept us out of war. Madison was not that lucky. But he almost was.

The nation's fourth President was well-equipped for his office, and especially well-equipped for handling foreign policy. A former Secretary of State and another genuinely cosmopolitan man, he understood diplomacy and the intrigues of the Old World.

Madison was not as popular or charismatic a leader as Jefferson. He knew this and perhaps chafed at his perceived role of playing second fiddle to the Renaissance man who preceded him in the Presidency and the State Department. The three Presidents who involved the United States in international war in the nineteenth century—Madison, Polk, and McKinley—were all relatively small men who, it was alleged, spent much of their lives hidden in the shadows of bigger men. Madison had his Jefferson; Polk his Jackson; and McKinley, early in his career,

Rutherford B. Hayes and later, although this was much exaggerated, Mark Hanna. To move into the realm of the psychological, would small men who spent part of their careers as protégés of great figures express themselves through bellicosity in foreign relations?

Perhaps not in Madison's case. Cooler and less impulsive than Jefferson, Madison was not an unusually aggressive individual and he did not relish military combat. When he set us on our final course toward war, he did so with the resignation and in full knowledge that his programs for peace with honor had failed. At the same time, he did not go the last mile in his attempts to head off war in 1812. With hindsight, we can place much of the responsibility for the unnecessary War of 1812 at his doorstep.

Saddled with Jefferson's shaky policy of economic warfare, Madison was also burdened with a Secretary of State whom he despised. A domestic political embroglio forced him to name Robert Smith to the chair he himself had occupied for the previous eight years. Much to Madison's relief, he was able to fire Smith in 1811 and replace him with James Monroe. Of course, the power of any Secretary of State is set by the President, so that while Madison's problems with Smith were embarrassing and awkward, they did not weaken his overall diplomatic effectiveness. Like Adams and Jefferson, Madison was the chief diplomat of his country while the Secretary of State played a secondary role of agent and advisor.

ANOTHER BRITISH INSULT

With the air temporarily cleared by the replacement of the hated embargo with the Non-Intercourse Act, Madison set out to extricate the United States from her plight, grown more serious after the decrees were tightened in late 1808. Wishing to concentrate their efforts on Old Boney, the British also sought to reverse the deterioration in Anglo-American relations. Both sides strove for an equitable settlement of their differences. As is often the case in diplomacy, they could not agree on what was equitable.

David Erskine, a new, inexperienced, but sympathetic British minister to the United States, was instructed to try to make amends once and for all for the *Chesapeake* affair and to promise a repeal of the Orders in Council. First, the Americans had to accept the British Rule of 1756, remove all restrictions on British ships and products, and permit the British Navy to seize American ships trading with France in violation of American laws. Such terms, Erskine quickly recognized, were unacceptable to Madison. Therefore, the British minister violated his instructions and achieved an agreement with the Americans that ended the crisis for a very brief period.

Madison was unaware that Erskine was not speaking for his superior in the Foreign Office, the brilliant George Canning. The Erskine Agreement featured a reasonable settlement of the *Chesapeake* incident and a promise to revoke the Orders in Council in exchange for the lifting of American restrictions against British commerce. In one month, Madison had succeeded in doing what Jefferson could not do in five years. He had squared Anglo-American relations and called off the gods of war. Even though the impressment issue still remained to blight relations, one can imagine Madison's elation at the consummation of the Erskine Agreement. His elation was short-lived. As soon as he received word of the glad tidings of peace from Washington, Canning quashed Erskine's agreement—with good reason for his envoy had conceded too much.

When Canning pulled the rug from under Erskine and ordered the young minister home post haste, Madison was both angered and embarrassed, and most everyone else in the United States was stunned. Perhaps a more perceptive diplomat would have questioned Erskine about his instructions since it was surprising for him to concede issues that had proved intractable in the past. Conceivably, Madison and his advisors, looking for a way out of the diplomatic dead end in which they had been placed by Jefferson, eagerly convinced themselves that Erskine was compliant because the embargo and Non-Intercourse Act had worked; the British had finally begun to feel the economic pinch. This was certainly what they wanted to believe. To believe otherwise would have been to renounce the strategy of economic warfare upon which Republican foreign policy had been based since 1806. In any event, Canning's shocking action dashed all hopes for an early settlement, made Madison look foolish, and sent Anglo-American relations plummeting to a new low. Madison mentioned the Erskine Agreement in his War Message of 1812 as one of the provocations that forced him to ask Congress for a declaration of war.

A little less than a century later, the United States became involved in a similar situation. In 1902, the Senate of Colombia refused to accept the Panama Treaty negotiated by its minister in Washington. At that point in our nation's history, President Theodore Roosevelt argued vigorously that since the "dagos" in Bogota had no right to reject such a treaty, he was justified in setting plans in motion to take Panama by force. But that was a weak Colombia in 1902 and a powerful United States. In 1809, Madison had to accept the humiliation of the rejection of the Erskine Agreement and plot a new strategy to protect American honor and commerce.

A FINAL PLOY

Through the rest of 1809, Madison made little headway trying to defend our rights, and thus faced the prospect of finding himself boxed into a corner as Jefferson had been. He was stuck with the Non-Intercourse Act. Although not yet as unpopular as the embargo, the new law allowed Americans to trade with everyone except England and France. Under its provisions, however, we were suffering more in economic terms than our antagonists and our vessels were still being seized. Moreover, neither belligerent offered any indication that it was prepared to meet our demands.

Consequently, in 1810 Madison and Congress devised a new scheme to allow Americans to have their cake and eat it, too. The last in the line of economic measures, Macon's Bill Number 2, reopened trade with England and France but promised that if either revoked its decrees, we would prohibit trade with the other. The bill reversed a formula proposed by Jeffersonian diplomats in 1808 when they offered to repeal the embargo in exchange for comparable concessions.

On the surface, Macon's Bill was ingenious. Americans could again trade with France and England and also maintain their integrity by promising to cut off trade with one of the belligerents in the future. Similar to the Non-Intercourse Act in terms of its eventual threatened outcome, Macon's Bill Number 2 delayed the severance of economic relations until the Europeans decided to take us up on our offer.

How long was the new measure to remain in effect? Like other plans preceding it, Macon's Bill Number 2 was conceived to be a relatively short-run policy. Had the British and French continued their provocative behavior, the bill would have failed in its purpose since it was supposed to produce a relaxation of Europe's restrictive legislation.

Even at the time of its promulgation, Macon's Bill appeared to many to be the coward's way out. After several years of high-flown rhetoric and economic sacrifice, Madison reopened trade with his arch enemies with only a slim hope of achieving redress. Such a policy might have been practical had it been selected in 1806. Coming in 1810, after the Republicans had put themselves on record as the defenders of neutral rights, Macon's Bill Number 2 suggested to the world that the United States was just another selfish power, and a paper tiger as well, unconcerned about international law in its rush for profits from the immoral war trade. In economic terms, Macon's Bill made a good deal of sense. In terms of national and Madison's honor, to have indefinitely maintained it without any movement from the Europeans would have been insufferable.

National and Presidential honor, these slippery issues had become all important in the debate during the Napoleonic wars. From 1810 to 1812, British violations of our sovereignty on the high seas, while continuing, did not occur as frequently as they had during the earlier period. Fighting for their lives, while Napoleon seemingly held the upper hand, the British were chary about provoking the United States into open hostilities. Had we forgotten some of our old grievances and de-emphasized the need to redeem national honor and Republican face, we could have accepted an occasional seizure or impressment and counted our profits. Madison could not wipe clean the slate in such an unprincipled and materialistic manner. Macon's Bill Number 2, therefore, was a stopgap measure which, like the embargo, contained an implicit time limit.

Napoleon gave Madison the means he needed to escape from his dilemma. Perhaps the President should not have accepted such questionable means from such an unsavory character, but he was eager to grasp at any straw. When the French Emperor agreed to Macon's Bill and said he would revoke his decrees, Madison should have been suspicious of Napoleon's motives and, above all, his integrity. In 1809 and 1810, French violations of our rights were in some respects more outrageous than Britain's. Napoleon had responded to our economic offensive by seizing all American ships in French ports and allowing them to be sold at auction. The profits went to the French treasury. American sailors went to French jails, which were even worse than British jails. In general, Napoleon was more insensitive than the British when it came to dealing with Americans.

Yet, in August of 1810, Napoleon apparently made Macon's Bill a success, for he seemed to promise to stop violating our neutral rights. In exchange, one of two things had to happen— either the British had to revoke their Orders in Council and illegal blockade or the United States had to declare operative the retaliatory legislation envisaged in Macon's Bill. The first was unlikely. The second was a little more likely although Macon's Bill said that the United States would retaliate against the remaining offending belligerent 90 days *after* the other had revoked his decrees. Napoleon seemed to be saying, first retaliate against England, then I will revoke my decrees. The message emanating from Paris was cleverly ambiguous.

Madison had no love for Napoleon, whom he considered a despicable tyrant who had undone much of the good of the French Revolution. Wary of dealing with him, he saw at once the loopholes in the letter from the Duc de Cadore proclaiming the new French policy. If not read too carefully, the Cadore letter would allow the United States to save face, continue trade with the continent, and frighten the English into maritime surrender.

Realizing that Napoleon had not quite delivered the sort of declaration necessary to send the punitive sections of Macon's Bill into operation, Madison introduced legislation into Congress prohibiting British imports to the United States. While Congress deliberated, and even after the punitive legislation went into effect, Napoleon kept on seizing American ships and imprisoning American sailors. With a straight face, his emissaries politely explained that yes, the Berlin and Milan Decrees had indeed been revoked, but that American ships were violating a series of other laws unrelated to the official Continental System. Nevertheless, the deed had been done. We would have looked even sillier than we did had we opened up trade with England again because Napoleon had violated his part of the bargain. Furthermore, most Americans still considered England public enemy number one—anything serving to improve Franco-American relations only enhanced our strategic position vis-à-vis the British.

The sloppy way the Cadore letter was handled and the further public humiliation of American officials may have had some lasting side effects on American resolve and pride. By 1811, most Americans finally realized they had been deceived by Napoleon who was still doing his dirty deeds in ports under his control. Perhaps this treachery, on top of the *Chesapeake* affair and the Erskine fiasco, was the final straw. No European would trick us again, no European was to be trusted again until American honor was finally and irrevocably redeemed. So angered were some Senators at *all* Europeans that when the time came to vote for war against England, a sizable minority wanted to include France in its declaration.

A TRAGEDY OF ERRORS

The clasp of war was not completely closed when the on again-off again prohibition of intercourse with England went into effect early in March 1811. This economic offensive, based upon Napoleonic duplicity, eventually worked and forced the British to accept some of our demands. Owing to a series of untimely misfortunes, Parliament did not do so until after Congress declared war. As we look back at evidence available to Madison and his advisors, it seems clear that by the beginning of 1812, they should have realized that it was only a matter of time before the British revoked their hated Orders in Council. Why did not Madison wait them out?

First of all, William Pinkney, our minister in London, who had engaged in a lengthy series of frustrating negotiations through 1810 and early 1811, finally became convinced that he could make no headway with the obdurate officials at White-hall. Pinkney saw little likelihood that the British would even go halfway toward meeting American complaints about their prac-tices. The British were particularly difficult to deal with after having learned how Madison had used the deceitful Cadore letter to save face at home. Knowing that Napoleon had not revoked his decrees, they justifiably wondered how they could bargain in good faith with Madison's representative. And so, Pinkney departed for home in February of 1811, leaving an inexperienced chargé to look after American affairs in the British capital.

Pinkney quit his post just about the time the British began to show movement on the Orders in Council. More and more influential British voices called for a restoration of Anglo-Amer-ican trade relations. The prospect of a permanent loss of Ameri-can markets and supplies frightened some members of the business community. Had Pinkney been on the scene for only a few more months in 1811, he might have noticed this shift in opinion and then could have advised Washington that the chances for peaceful settlement had improved. Our well-mean-ing but unperceptive chargé unfortunately did not notice the changing British mood. To be sure, reports about this shift did reach the United States, but they did not bear the imprimatur of a senior American diplomat. Had Pinkney only waited the British out a little longer, there might not have been a war in 1812.

A second misfortune involved British politics. Spencer Perceval, the Prime Minister, was assassinated in May of 1812. At first glance, the tragedy should have been a godsend for the United States. Perceval was moving in the direction of a repeal of the Orders in Council at a snail's pace. His successors eventually moved with alacrity to revoke them in order to improve Anglo-American relations. However, Perceval's assassination was followed by a period of about a month when the wheels of government ground to a halt. During this time, British politicians maneuvered to find a viable coalition to run the country during the trying days of the global war that heated up in 1812. Had they selected their new government more quickly, the orders might have been revoked in May and the glad tidings would have reached Washington in mid-June, before Congress finished its deliberations on Madison's request for war.

The new British government of Liverpool and Castlereagh did repeal the orders in June. Almost immediately, a fleet of ships took off for American ports, loaded to the gunwales with products from British industry. Along with President Madison's favorite cheshire cheese, they brought with them the news that the orders had at long last been revoked. This commercial fleet became the first major prize for the Americans in the War of 1812. By the time it arrived in American waters, the two countries had been legally at war for several weeks. While the British government had been inching slowly toward the revocation of the orders, Americans had been considering an alteration in their own strategies. As Britain was moving toward peace in early 1812, the United States was moving directly into war. The British were in the dark about the speed with which we were moving because of the communication-transportation gap.

To explain this lamentable situation, we must return to the United States. It has been fashionable to say that the congressional elections of 1810 brought into power new, more bellicose Congressmen—the famed fire-breathing Warhawks—who forced the United States into war in 1812 to redeem national honor. Confident, young, and nationalistic, the Warhawks allegedly reflected the desires of a majority of their countrymen who wanted to settle accounts with the British. Thus, the explanation for war in 1812 is simple. We went to war because the hawks were less patient than their predecessors. A strong believer in the separation of powers, Madison allegedly responded to the will of Congress, believing it to be the will of the country, and asked for war in June of 1812.

The notion that the election of 1810 was a Warhawk election has been challenged. In the first place, many of those who later were counted among the hawks had not run on especially belligerent platforms in 1810. Second, those allegedly youthful hotbloods were not noticeably younger than the men they replaced. And finally, rarely have individual congressional elections turned on foreign policy issues. That many new faces came into Congress in 1811 means little once we remember that in the early days of our republic, the retirement of half of the incumbents in the House was the norm. The war cannot simply be blamed on the new crop of Congressmen of 1811.

Although a careful examination of the platforms, ages, elections, and congressional speeches does not reveal much of a difference between the Congressmen of 1811 and those of 1810, Madison apparently thought there was a difference. That is, he considered the new Congressmen to be more hawkish than the ones they replaced and considered the nation, in general, to be in a more hawkish mood. If this is the case, then the question of whether they were *really* hawkish is of little interest. Operating under the illusion that Congress was inundated with more jingoistic Congressmen, Madison felt it his duty to answer their pleas for forceful action against the British. One can understand why he might have evaluated the situation in this manner as unusually hawkish men had gained control of several important congressional committees.

But even if Madison thought that the new Congressmen were hawkish, they did not pressure him to go to war until almost the last moment in the spring of 1812. And nearly 40% of all Congressmen voted against the war resolution, while many of those who supported it did so reluctantly. Like Madison, they found themselves caught in a slow, almost inevitable drift into war and, when the moment of truth came in June, could find no other way to solve their problems save by fire and sword.

Madison was not unaware of this inexorable move toward war. When he thought it was inevitably approaching is difficult to say. We know that he implored the British minister in 1811 to press his government to settle before he was left without options. On the other hand, Madison, who did not want to go to war, contributed to the war fever by releasing documents to Congress relating to his negotiations with the British as well as letters that purported to show how the British were trying to buy Federalist support. The release of these materials excited Americans by demonstrating how unreasonably the British were behaving. Perhaps Madison felt he had to publish the documents to protect himself against the Federalist minority that contended that we could arrange a deal with England. Moreover, he did feel that the rival party was engaged in traitorous activities that frustrated Republican attempts to achieve a settlement favorable to American interests.

Although the release of the documents contributed to a more bellicose atmosphere, it does not explain how we made that large leap from economic retaliation to full-fledged war. For some reason, Americans attached a good deal of symbolic importance to the voyage of the *Hornet* which left these shores in December of 1811. The *Hornet* was to bring back the latest word on British attitudes about their Orders in Council. As the weeks went by, leaders began to suggest that if the *Hornet* did not return with favorable news, we might have to go to war. Perhaps this is the supposed incident precipitating war in 1812. The *Hornet* arrived back in late May with the inaccurate news that the British were not going to revoke the orders. At just about this time, Madison began the preparations that resulted in his message to Congress of June 1, 1812.

Prior to this point, there was no apparent consensus for war. The total embargo on British goods, announced on April 4 after a heated debate and much opposition, was interpreted by some as a measure preparatory to a declaration of war but by many others as merely the continuation of the old policy of economic warfare. After this embargo was enacted, but before the *Hornet* came home, Congress almost adjourned. Had Congressmen taken that long trip home to their various states, there would have been no war since Madison could not have reassembled them before the British revoked their Orders in Council. In those days, Presidents asked Congress to declare war and Madison would not have sent troops into battle without the approval of the legislative branch of government. If almost a majority of Congress was prepared to go home in the spring of 1812, there scarcely can be said to have been a crisis atmosphere in Washington. Thus we come back to the *Hornet's* pessimistic reports.

Reports brought by the *Hornet* convinced many people that the game had been played out. The timing was important. Madison himself later said that he would never have asked Congress for war had he known of Napoleon's defeat in Russia. Naturally, we will never know how serious he was when he offered that famous what-might-have-been. A curious bit of evidence flies in the face of Madison's disclaimers about his own hawkish spirit. The United States declared war on June 18. The ships bringing the news of the revocation of the orders arrived in late July. If he was so reluctant to go to war, why, upon hearing of the revocation, did he not merely call off the whole thing? Little blood had been shed, one of the main irritants to Anglo-American relations had been removed, and the Republican policy of economic coercion had been successful. Madison was suspicious of the way the revocation was worded and he had good reason to fear that the British might still violate our neutral rights in other fashions. Still, he could have made political gains by aborting the war. Even the most hawkish Republicans might have agreed that despite attacks from weak-kneed Federalists who wanted to surrender to Britain, their President's tough policy of economic coercion had worked with little cost in men and treasure. Why, then, did he not call off the war? The explanation for his puzzling behavior may be found in his war message itself. Perhaps Madison oversold his case when he listed all of Britain's dastardly acts that led him to suggest a vote for war.

THE CAUSES OF WAR ACCORDING TO MADISON

Madison offered Congress five specific reasons for going to war with England in 1812. Though all of them were running grievances, none was immediately pressing in the spring of 1812. If anything, the period of greatest popular outrage had passed for at least three of them. Two of them can be dismissed as hardly worth a war. The Erskine affair was a dead letter by 1812 and the British Navy's practice of hovering outside our ports and harassing merchantmen was only a minor irritant. The British had made several celebrated seizures of American ships in early 1812 well within the sight of our shores, and this brazenness angered some citizens. While Napoleon engaged in similar activities, his spoliations took place at a convenient distance from American shores and so were less obtrusive.

A third issue, the Indian menace, is more complicated. During the five years prior to 1812, the British consolidated their control of and alliance with Indians along the Canadian-American border. Such an alliance was useful to London for several reasons. First, the Indians could serve as auxiliaries in case of war with the United States, a first line of defense. Indeed, the existence of such an alliance, it was thought, might make the Americans think twice about invading Canada. London officials also feared that if they did not move quickly to line up the Indians, the Americans might attempt the same ploy. The Indians served also as a buffer between Americans and Canadians. And finally, the fur trade plus a feeling of obligation toward their charges colored British attitudes. Unfortunately for British *Weltpolitik,* some of their officials in Canada were a little too zealous in their use of the Indians as real and potential threats to the obstreperous Americans south of the border.

Those in rather remote control in London, especially in the years before the war, instructed their agents in the New World to play down the British-Indian link and, above all, to keep the "savages" quiet. They did not need another issue that might arouse the Republicans who felt personally responsible for the security of the frontiersmen. The British in London had difficulty getting their agents to accept cautionary messages. From our perspective, the British were arming and protecting their Indians, and those same Indians, from 1809 to 1811, were especially restive and frequently came into conflict with Americans. The peak of American-British hostility through the Indian surrogate was reached in 1811 with the large-scale battle of Tippecanoe, in which William Henry Harrison defeated Britain's allies led by the Prophet, Tecumseh's brother.

Undoubtedly, Madison knew that the Indians were not acting as pawns in a forward British policy. But the latest Indian "atrocities" were thought to be at least inspired by the British and so the Indian issue could be used to convince Americans once again of British perfidy. In a real sense, the battle of Tippecanoe eased the so-called Indian problem along the Canadian border. However, since the battle did occur in 1811, it was still fresh in American memories when Madison added it to his list of grievances. By itself, or even linked with the Erskine slight and the hovering complaint, the Indian menace did not justify a war. On the other hand, when linked with the remaining two of his five grievances, they did constitute a superficially strong case against London.

Madison complained about impressment first in his war message. It was the oldest and, in some respects, the most serious of all the running insults to our honor. The British had never offered the slightest bit of evidence of their willingness to renounce their supposed right to resort to that nasty practice to protect their naval supremacy. Although they were not impressing many Americans by 1812, they were still impressing some.

More important, by that date, a large number of men, perhaps several thousand, were serving in the British navy, victims of *unjust* impressment. While doves might talk about turning the other cheek in trade matters in order to maintain the large profits of the war years, there was not much in the way of compensation for impressment except to point out that quite a few sailors had been *justly* impressed. Of course, once the wars in Europe were over, the British would have had less reason to resort to impressment. Madison could not wait that long.

Finally, there were the obnoxious Orders in Council, one of Madison's major grievances and second only to impressment for most Americans. Those orders were revoked five days after the vote for war. Would the remaining four grievances, without the orders, have been enough to convince a majority of Congressmen to support Madison's request? Probably not, especially since news of the revocation might have led some to believe that the British would compromise on other issues as well. Yet, Madison's message left many things unsaid.

BETWEEN THE LINES OF MADISON'S MESSAGE

In addition to Madison's five explicit causes for war, several others weighed heavily as Congress began its deliberations. Western and southern states had been suffering from a severe agricultural depression during the years of the Battle of the Decrees. The depression set in just about the time the British issued their toughest Order in Council. To farmers and growers, the reason for their plight was clear—the British were denying them markets throughout the world. Today, we know that the causes of the depression went far beyond the Orders in Council, although they did not help things any. Remember also that the frontier was the home of the supernationalists, the hearty Republican yeomen who were most sensitive to Indian outrages. Thus, we can understand why farmers and frontiersmen were among the most enthusiastic advocates of war. Some historians point to a more nefarious reason for going to war. Hotbloods saw in a war with England the opportunity to seize Spanish Florida and

Canada. In the months before the war, there had been talk about taking Canada and Florida to extend the area of freedom. However, the desire to capture Canada and Florida—as emphasized in the so-called Expansionists of 1812 thesis—was not an important cause of war. For the most part, jingoes talked of invading the colonies to the north and the south for solid tactical reasons. Invasion of those areas, especially Canada, or even the talk of invasion, could bring the British to the bargaining table. And if the war did start, where else could the American armies attempt to bloody their foe if not in Canada? If in the unlikely event that the pitiful American military establishment could take and hold Canada and Florida, so much the better; but at bottom, for most jingoes, the discussion of American offensives related to their tactical plans for carrying out the war.

A more convincing case may be made for an underlying political cause. The final congressional vote for war was more of a party vote than a sectional vote. Republicans, even in the commercial and Anglophilic east, voted for war, while Federalists and those opposed to Madison's policies, even in areas outside of the east, voted against war. In the House, where the vote was 79–49 in favor, 17 Republicans from New England, New York, and New Jersey went against their sectional interests, or so it seemed, and joined the majority of Republicans to vote for war. Moreover, partisan clashes dominated the agonizingly long 17 days (the House took 3 days, the Senate 14) of congressional debate over Madison's war message.

The Republicans had little to commend their foreign policy since the Louisiana Purchase in 1803. They had been in power since 1801 and 1812 was an election year. For over six years, they had promised to protect American merchantmen and the flag, and they had failed miserably. Even with the recently enacted punitive legislation of 1811 and 1812, the British and the French continued their attacks on American commerce. The Republicans could not have asked for more sacrifices from the nation without some evidence that those sacrifices were producing the desired effect. In addition, the constituents of the

Republican Party, inflamed by the events of 1811 and 1812, allegedly demanded war. Therefore, to save their seats and their party, the Republicans opted for war in June. Had they not done so, they might have been replaced by even more hawkish Congressmen. Madison himself was faced with reelection. Could he have run on a four-year record of foreign policy failure and humiliation?

Though plausible, such a scenario is not entirely convincing. In 1812, the opposition Federalists were fierce opponents of war. Of whom, then, were Madison and the Republicans afraid? The Federalists could not have found a candidate to beat Madison and it was unlikely that he would have lost his party's nomination because he was too dovish. What did he have to fear in the upcoming elections? Even after making some terrible blunders as a war leader in the summer and fall of 1812, he won the election rather handily against the combined opposition of Federalists and Republican doves. The Federalists did make gains but remained outnumbered in the Senate by a 3-to-1 margin and in the House by almost 2 to 1.

Perhaps Madison feared for the cohesion of his party. Had the hawkish Republicans left the fold and formed their own faction, he would have had difficulties governing. A few more months of drift might have exacerbated the hawk-dove debate and resulted in a breakdown of the two-party system. Then Madison might have had to rule in the name of a minority party opposed by Federalists and dovish Republicans on one side and by Warhawks on the other.

Madison may not have been only acting as a self-interested partisan. More may have been at stake than just the success or failure of his party and anti-British programs. The future of the republic, or at least republican institutions, hung in the balance. Many Americans allegedly had begun to lose confidence in the ability of their government to protect them. Some were talking of secession, others of changes in the overall governmental system that seemed paralyzed, unable to protect the lives and property of its citizens even in the most rudimentary way. Had we not gone to war in 1812, and even had the British stopped

attacking Americans, the United States might have been finished, at least in the form we know her today. Some felt at the
time that she had to demonstrate to her citizens, and perhaps to
the rest of the world, that a republican system could work. And
so, fearing for the survival of the republic embodied in part in
the principles of his party, James Madison, one of the founding
fathers of that republic and one of the architects of its system
of government, had no option but to choose war in 1812.

Clearly, one can find a multiplicity of causes contributing to
our entry into the War of 1812. Some, such as the relationship
of the Orders in Council to agricultural depression, existed only
in the minds of American farmers; others, such as impressment,
represented real grievances. What remains for consideration is
the relationship between those causes and America's national
security.

NATIONAL SECURITY AND THE WAR OF 1812

For whatever combination of reasons, James Madison and his
Republicans led their nation into war in June of 1812. Did they
make the correct decision? Was America's national security
threatened enough in 1812 to justify a declaration of war
against England?

First, was the country in danger of physical attack? Could
the British have invaded and occupied our coastal cities or
swept down across our northern border, accompanied by their
ferocious Indian allies? In 1812, they had neither the desire nor
the capability to launch a transatlantic war, and they did not
display any inclination to mix with the so-called colonies in
North America just when they seemed to be getting somewhere
against the real enemy, the Emperor of France. Even in 1814,
with the war in Europe all but over and with England once
again sitting at the top of the heap of great powers, she did not
pursue an extended war in America. At least England's greatest
military leader and conqueror of Napoleon, the Duke of Wellington, did not think it advisable to mount a major campaign to
force a military breakthrough in the stalemated war. Logisti-

cally, politically, and economically, a British attack on the United States in 1812, or in years thereafter, made no sense. Additionally, Madison himself never alluded to the possibility of an imminent British invasion of his country.

It is true that England's allies, the western Indians, could have been considered a direct military threat to national security. Those Americans who lived near the Canadian and even Floridian borders would continue to feel threatened until some final solution was arranged for the Indians. Although few expected the savages to occupy Detroit, let alone the United States, their border forays were a military challenge to some Americans' security. Needless to say, our own border forays, and indeed our habitation of Indian lands, posed a military challenge to some Indians' security. But by 1811 and the American victory of Tippecanoe, that menace had been throttled. Even though the Indians might still be armed, led, and given sanctuary by their British friends, they no longer represented a serious threat to America's national security.

Looking at the more remote question of our future military security and its relationship to the balance of power on the continent, British *Weltpolitik* posed no threat to us. To the contrary, in 1812, they were leading the anti-French coalition devoted to destroying a man who had dreams of world empire, a man who thought even less of the United States than they did. Undoubtedly, we would have been safer in a world controlled by our more moderate British cousins than in a Napoleonic world. Anything contributing to a British victory would have contributed to our long-term military security. Yet we did the only thing that could have aided Napoleon: We opened a new front against the British.

If the British posed no real military threat, what about the more general economic threat of her repressive maritime legislation? What some Americans then perceived to be a serious threat was not one, in fact. Although the British Orders in Council, for example, did restrict a neutral's ͨ trade, we more than made up for this loss wit picked up as a by-product of the European wͬ who had the most to lose from the British orders, the shippers and the merchants of the Northeast and the Middle Atlantic states, were prepared to accept England's imperious behavior in exchange for the sizable profits they could realize by becoming the dominant trade partner of a major belligerent. In economic terms, then, the United States could have gotten along quite nicely with the British restrictions. If anything, after the war was over and the orders revoked, we suffered more from the restrictive British and European imperial trading systems that closed areas of the world opened to us during wartime. The economic issue really overlaps with the issue of honor, for it was through her economic offensives that Britain was thought to have assaulted American honor.

Here, we may have had the best case for going to war, especially if we argue that a nation's honor is ultimately tied to national security. Because of the British impressment of our citizens, their provocations on the high seas, the Erskine humiliation, and the general high-handed way they treated us, our honor had been challenged as had, to some degree, our sovereignty. We could not afford to allow the British to insult our flag so frequently, for such acts made the United States less of a country in the eyes of Europe. If the British and the French in 1812 were able to push us around with impunity, others would do so in future crises and we would become a defenseless pawn in the games played by continental powers throughout the world.

National as well as international respect was at stake in 1812. The United States was rent into factions. Confidence in the government was waning. Pessimists questioned whether the federal republic—weak, experimental, surrounded by enemies— could survive. The wishy-washy, no-win policy of economic offensive polarized hawks and doves. More British affronts might have led to still further divisions, internal chaos, and civil disruptions. As matters turned out, the effort to redeem our honor through war was accompanied by a good deal of these.

Be that as it may, many still subscribe to the thesis that a nation that fails to redeem its honor cannot long survive in a world of predatory powers. You must be able to bloody the bully in order to establish your right to a piece of turf in the international system, as well as your right to the loyalties and support of your own people.

This seductive line of reasoning must be examined more closely. We had put up with British provocations for 9 long years since the breakdown of the Peace of Amiens in 1803 and, for that matter, for 13 more years from 1783 to 1795. Would another year or so have made much difference? Moreover, in terms of the quality and quantity of such provocations, the American merchants had a better time of it from 1810 to 1812 than they had had from 1805 to 1809. For that matter, British activities challenging our honor on the high seas did not cease in 1815. In other forms, they irritated Americans through World War I.

Furthermore, defense of honor through war carried great risks. The entire nation could have been lost. The New England states might have seceded. Our military losses might have been much greater had Wellington decided to have a go at us in 1814. The economic dislocation might have been even more severe. In 1812, Americans *thought* national honor and sovereignty were at stake. In contrast, many other neutrals threatened by Napoleon or England accepted the slights, the limitations on their national power, and survived the Napoleonic wars none the worse for wear. Although they had been insulted and bullied, international memories are short and honor could be redeemed in other ways later.

The issue of national honor is colored by the way the United States performed in war. Had we been better prepared, we might not only have redeemed honor but also augmented national security and international respect. Indeed, had we been better prepared, the British might have come to the bargaining table in a more conciliatory mood. In other words, fighting or threatening to fight for national honor might be a wise thing to do, if you *and* your opponent think that you can win the war. Fighting for national honor when the odds suggest that the best you can do is to tie or even lose is folly.

BIBLIOGRAPHY

The best book on the War of 1812 is still Bradford Perkins's *Prologue to War: England and the United States, 1805-1812* (Berkeley: University of California Press, 1961). Thoroughly researched on both sides of the Atlantic, Perkins's book makes a strong case for Republican ineptitude in foreign policy. His earlier volume, *The First Rapprochement: England and the United States, 1795-1805* (Philadelphia: University of Pennsylvania Press, 1955), is indispensable background reading. A venerable analysis of the literature is Warren H. Goodman's "The Origins of the War of 1812: A Survey of Changing Interpretations," *Mississippi Valley Historical Review,* 28 (September 1941), 171-186. And up-to-date bibliography for the entire war is *The War of 1812 Reference Guide* (Los Angeles: John Frederiksen, 1979).

There are other sound treatments of this historiographically popular war. Reginald Horsman, in *The Causes of the War of 1812* (Philadelphia: University of Pennsylvania Press, 1962), offers many causes and is less harsh on Madison than is Perkins. Roger Brown is a prime exponent of the importance of domestic politics in the war decision in *The Republic in Peril* (New York: Columbia University Press, 1964). Julius Pratt's much older work, *Expansionists of 1812* (New York: Macmillan, 1925), is no longer taken as seriously as it once was. An especially useful article that examines the war decision is Norman K. Risjord's "1812: Conservatives, War Hawks, and the Nation's Honor," *William and Mary Quarterly,* 18 (April 1961), 196-210. Finally, in a brief essay accompanied by documents, *Madison's Alternatives: The Jeffersonian Republicans and the Coming of the War* (Philadelphia: Lippincott, 1975), Robert Rutland concludes that Madison had no other options in the summer of 1812.

In a class by itself is Henry Adams's *History of the United States of America* (New York: Scribner's, 1890). A careful account is in A. L. Burt's encyclopedic *The United States, Great Britain, and British North America* (New Haven, CT: Yale University Press, 1940).

Dumas Malone's series of volumes on the life of Jefferson must be examined, especially *Jefferson the President: Second Term, 1805-1809* (Boston: Little, Brown, 1974). Even more favorable to his protagonist is Irving Brant's *James Madison, The President* (Indianapolis: Bobbs-Merrill, 1956). Like so many authors of multivolume biographies, Brant and Malone so identify themselves with their subjects that they may lose critical perspective. Reginald C. Stuart, in *The Half-Way Pacifist: Thomas*

Jefferson's View of War (Toronto: University of Toronto Press, 1979), offers a careful analysis of Jefferson's realistic approach to the uses of coercion and limited war in international disputes.

Three specialized works on economics are Louis M. Sears's *Jefferson and the Embargo* (Durham, NC: Duke University Press, 1927), a pro-Jefferson account; Eli F. Hecksher's *The Continental System, An Economic Interpretation* (New York: Oxford University Press, 1922); and Burton Spivak's *Jefferson's English Crisis: Commerce, Embargo and the Republican Revolution* (Charlottesville: University of Virginia Press, 1979). Just when it appeared that all had been said on the War of 1812, Spivak offered a convincing new analysis of the offensive and defensive aspects of Republican economic diplomacy.

Two valuable specialized studies on the state of the economy in different regions on the eve of the war are George Rogers Taylor's "Agrarian Discontent in the Mississippi Valley Preceding the War of 1812," *Journal of Political Economy,* 39 (August 1931), 486-505 and Margaret K. Latimer's "South Carolina—A Protagonist of the War of 1812," *American Historical Review,* 61 (July 1956), 921-929.

Chapter 2

THE MEXICAN-AMERICAN WAR

As war exists, and notwithstanding all our efforts to avoid it, exists by the act of Mexico herself, we are called upon by every consideration of duty and patriotism to vindicate with decision the honor, the rights, and the interests of our country.
—James Polk, May 11, 1846—

The Mexican-American War of 1846-1848 is the most obscure of our six wars, even more obscure than the War of 1812. For our opponent, the war was far from obscure. Mexico's loss to the United States determined her future as a lesser power and dashed her hopes of challenging our hegemony on the continent. We have displayed relatively little interest in this war, in part, because it was overshadowed by that most "popular" of our wars, the Civil War. Coming only 15 years before our epic internal struggle, the Mexican-American War appears insignificant. After all, while almost one-half million soldiers perished in the Civil War, we lost only 11,000 fighting for the Halls of Montezuma. The war was also a rather unpleasant affair that we would just as soon forget. Despite Hollywood's reminders of the Alamo and brave Texans who fought for freedom against tyrannical Mexicans, those who know something about the war feel guilty over what appears to be the rape of Mexico. Congress expressed its disgust for the squalid business when, in 1848, the House passed a resolution condemning the President for provoking an unnecessary and illegal war.

Of the six wars under study, the war of 1846 is the most distasteful. In the others, we can make a case for the importance of mutual misperceptions and misunderstandings as well as the generous and humanitarian feelings of an American public misled by duplicitous politicians. In this war, we find few excuses for our leaders and fellow citizens. The war with Mexico, remembered popularly as a war fought for Texas, was in reality a war for California and territorial aggrandizement.

To a generation sickened by neocolonialist wars waged by white westerners against nonwhites, the Mexican War, with its racist overtones, appears reprehensible. This was not the case in the mid-nineteenth century when most Americans felt it their mission to spread freedom to the far corners of the globe. It was widely believed then that the inferior peoples who lost their lands, sovereignty, and treasure were contributing to the triumph of Christianity and progress. The ideology of Manifest Destiny was not just a cover story for naked aggression. Americans believed they were expanding for the entire world, for as the United States became stronger and more secure, liberty and freedom everywhere would be advanced.

To understand the spirit of the age and to revel in that spirit are two different things. We must recognize that we have a colonial legacy much like that of the French, the British, and even the Mexicans. That is the lesson to be learned here. Although we need not hang our heads in shame for the sins of our forebearers, we must acknowledge those sins perpetrated in the name of American democracy.

Our war with Mexico is also chillingly instructive for what it reveals about the ease with which a President is able to place us into a situation likely to produce a war. Through his control of the armed forces, he can appropriate the war-declaring power. Who among the Congressmen will oppose war when American boys are dying under foreign guns? Never mind the circumstances under which those boys first came under fire, the other side's justification for the attack, or the ulterior motives of the President; all are beclouded by the simple fact that American boys have been attacked. This is precisely what happened in May of 1846 when a few dissenters could not convince their colleagues in Congress to reconsider their rush to arms.

Ignoring for the moment the sordid story of the way we entered the war, the conflict with Mexico was profitable for the United States. The treaty of Guadalupe-Hidalgo that terminated the war included a final recognition of Texas annexation to the United States and the transfer of New Mexico, Utah, Arizona, Nevada, part of Colorado, and that gem of gems, California. The taking of California turned us toward the Pacific and the fabled Asian markets, the promises of which were in good measure responsible for our involvement in later wars.

THE ALAMO REMEMBERED

Even before the Mexicans freed themselves from Spanish rule in 1821, Americans displayed a lively interest in territories north of the Nueces River and west to the Pacific. The late 1790s and the early 1800s witnessed several intrigues whose ultimate purpose was to separate Spanish Mexico from her vast empire in the American Southwest. Today, it appears obvious that Mexico stood little chance of holding on to those lands in the long run. Her central government and most of her population were a rugged 600 miles to the south of Texas, communication and transportation problems were enormous, and her neighbor was a predatory power whose people viewed their imperialism as a Christian crusade.

Mexico prepared the way for her own demise as a potential great power when she allowed Americans to migrate to Texas in the early 1820s. Allowed is a mild word—she encouraged them. The land deal she offered was so attractive and the pickings so slim in the United States after the Panic of 1819 that several thousand frontiersmen relinquished their citizenship, crossed the border, and became ostensible Mexicans. But did they become Mexicans? When they entered Texas to take up their claims, they entered a virgin land, administered rather poorly by an almost invisible official Mexican presence. Despite the honorable intentions of many of the original settlers, including Stephen Austin, a clash was predictable—a clash between the independent American frontiersmen and the Mexicans whose culture had been shaped by 300 years of a Spanish rule different in almost every facet from the Anglo-Saxon experience.

After a handful of abortive minirevolts in the 1820s, the Texan Revolution broke out in earnest in 1835 with the attendant heroism of Davy Crocket at the Alamo. Given the logistic advantages that accrue to people that fight on their own soil and the general inability of the shaky Mexican regime to mount a viable counterrevolutionary effort, the Texan-Americans emerged triumphant in 1836. Independence was proclaimed and duly accepted by Mexico's leader, General Santa Anna, who had little choice in the matter because he was being held prisoner by the Texans at the time. Even before the liberated general reached Mexico City, his Congress renounced the recognition and declared Texas still a state of Mexico. From 1836 to 1848, Mexico refused to accept the legitimacy of the Texan Republic.

Despite Mexican unwillingness to view the results of the Battle of San Jacinto as final and Santa Anna's pledge to avenge his honor against the avengers of the Alamo, Texas was free. Moreover, due to a combination of circumstances revolving around the slavery issue, the annexation of Texas to the United States was not effected until 1845. Strange as it may seem, the Lone Star state operated as a separate member of the international system from 1836 to 1845. Although weak, poor, and unable to defend her vast expanse against a concerted attack from a more powerful nation, Texas was indeed independent. To the outside world, she was a backwater of civilization, the Outer Mongolia of the day. One foreign envoy was so appalled by the primitive conditions he encountered in the Texans' capital that he packed his bags and caught the first stage out, never to return.

Although annexation to the United States was the most likely option for the independent Texans, they did toy with others. One envisaged expansion south and especially west into New Mexico and maybe California. With these new territories, Texas could have become a superstate, a rival of the United States. As a slave state, she might even have been able to lure the southern states into a republic in which slavery and cotton culture could have flourished unencumbered by northerners and abolitionists. In 1841, some adventurous Texans did invade New Mexico in a vain attempt to capture the Sante Fe Trail.

Another option involved a Texas that would keep within its own territory and protect its independence by playing the role of buffer state allied with England. Anxious to break away from her reliance upon the American South for cotton, England might have protected the Texans from both Mexicans and Americans in exchange for a corner on the Texan cotton crop. Such a policy would have meshed nicely with the British desire to keep the United States relatively weak.

Although these options appeared temporarily attractive to some Texans who relished their independent status, blood and cultural ties led the Lone Star Republic to lean toward annexation to the United States. For nine years, the general reluctance of the mother country to annex a slave state and a war kept the two groups of Americans apart. However, during the waning days of the Tyler administration in March of 1845, Texas was annexed by joint resolution of Congress. Why Tyler waited until the eleventh hour and why he chose the unorthodox route of joint resolution are complicated questions that need not involve us here. Suffice to say that when James Knox Polk took his seat in the White House, he was handed Texas on a silver platter. He was also handed a host of problems and grievances involving Americans, Texans, and Mexicans that ultimately led him into a war he was not loath to wage.

THE DARKHORSE OF 1844

At the start of Campaign 44, James Polk appeared to have about as much chance of winning his party's nomination for President as did Robert Dole in 1980. Few people would have been foolish enough to lay money on Polk, even at 100-to-1 odds. A legitimate darkhorse candidate, he came from almost nowhere to snatch the Democratic nomination as well as the Presidency in 1844.

His nomination was made possible by the splintering of the Democratic Party into at least four factions. The titular leader of the party and the inheritor of Andrew Jackson's machine, Martin Van Buren, lost control because of his opposition to annexation and expansion, two issues popular with western and southern Democrats. Polk also owed his nomination to expansionist Senator Robert J. Walker's brilliant management of his campaign. When Polk arrived at the Democratic convention in the summer of 1844, he expressed the hope that he might have a chance to secure the *Vice*-Presidential nomination. He did not dream of the Presidency until the last moment. After all, he had lost his last two races for electoral office when the voters of Tennessee rejected his gubernatorial programs in 1841 and 1843. If he could not win his own statehouse, how could he expect to win the entire nation? Of course, Richard Nixon accomplished just this trick when he won the Presidency in 1968, six years after he lost the race for the governorship of California and announced that he would no longer be around for anyone to kick.

In order to accomplish his political miracle, Polk's supporters first had to push through the "two-thirds" rule denying Van Buren the nomination within his grasp under the old rules. With Andrew Jackson at home playing the sort of behind-the-scenes role played by Lyndon Johnson in 1968, and Walker wheeling and dealing at the convention, Polk secured the nomination on the ninth ballot. He then went on to defeat the Whig candidate, Henry Clay, in the Presidential contest. Like Daniel Webster and John C. Calhoun, Clay was a powerful and capable national leader who should have been President sometime between 1820 and 1850 but never quite made it. His misfortune in 1844 was to be the representative of the mysterious party whose name provokes historians to ask, "Who were the Whigs?" In addition to his party's relative weakness, Clay was hurt when he waffled on expansion and annexation. Thus, he stood little chance of overtaking the Democrats who usurped the issue of Texas and the flag. Like the election of 1920 when voters allegedly sent a message to Washington against the League of Nations and like the election of 1964 when they supposedly voted against the bombing of North Vietnam, the election of 1844 has been interpreted as one of the few national elections in our history that turned on a foreign policy issue. In that year, Polk allegedly received a mandate from his constituents to expand.

This interpretation is strained. In the first place, Polk failed to receive a majority of the popular votes. In addition, although it is difficult to determine the salient issues in Presidential elections, most likely none has ever turned on foreign policy questions. This was the case in 1920 and 1964 and in 1844 as well. Although Polk's platform was more jingoistic than Clay's, the Whig candidate was not an antiexpansionist. Further, the crucial issue for many voters was probably the tariff on which there was a clear-cut choice between the high-tariff Clay and the low-tariff Polk. If expansion was the key to the election, why was Clay able to win the electoral votes of Polk's own Tennessee, a hotbed of expansionist sentiment, and why was Polk able to win in New York, a stronghold of antiexpansionist sentiment? As in most elections, party loyalty may have been the most important variable for the vast majority of voters, with only a small minority voting on specific issues. Whatever we may think about the bases for Polk's victory, since *he* thought that voters had selected an expansionist policy, he tried to give them what they wanted. At least, such an interpretation offered him a convenient rationale for the dirty business in which he was to involve us.

At 49, Polk was the youngest man ever to assume the Presidency, a record he held until Theodore Roosevelt replaced

the assassinated William McKinley in 1901. A protege of fellow
westerner Andrew Jackson, he was called "Young Hickory" by
supporters. Any similarity between his relationship to Jackson
and Madison's to Jefferson is more superficial than real. Madison and Jefferson were equals who respected one another while
Jackson was clearly superior to Polk and both men knew it.
Polk was a much smaller man than his mentor in almost every
way, not just sheer physical stature.

For what it might be worth in terms of psychological analysis, Polk's enemies derided him as a lackey who mindlessly did
whatever his master ordered. When he was Speaker of the
House, he was treated with contempt by Representatives who
took delight in referring to him as Jackson's puppet. The degree
to which he was Jackson's man is not the issue here. Because he
had spent so many years caricatured as someone else's man,
when the time came for him to display some backbone, he may
have overcompensated with a vengeance.

In a personal sense, he was not a very pleasant fellow.
Although his diary reveals little of substance about his policies
and philosophies, it does tell us quite a bit about Polk himself.
Humorless, narrow, stubborn, self-righteous, and insensitive, he
was shrewd and clever, without being intelligent or deep. As for
positive attributes, he was a serious and dedicated President
who worked harder at his job than most of the others who
made it to the top of the greasy pole of American politics. A
relatively frail and sickly man who died within a year after he
left the White House, Polk may have worked himself to death.

He was a very strong President, perhaps the strongest up to
that time. Although Jefferson and Jackson were strong Presidents, they usually could rely upon their parties to back their
programs. With the Democrats feuding among themselves on
many issues, Polk could rarely count on an automatic majority.
Thus, he used the unwritten power of the Presidency to reward
and punish in terms of patronage and political favors to an
extent not imagined up to that point. Since he had promised
that he would be a one-term President, he was not compelled to
make the political compromises with congressional leaders

necessary to achieve a second nomination. Indeed, the fact that he had chosen not to run made him all the more powerful since prospective candidates needed his support in 1848.

In terms of his personal philosophy and background, Polk was above all a westerner. Born in North Carolina, he migrated to Tennessee, which he represented in the House from 1825 to 1839, capping his congressional career with a term as Speaker the last four years. When he deserted Washington for state politics, he was elected to a two-year term as governor of his state. But he was turned out of office in 1841 and rebuffed again in 1843.

As a westerner, Polk may have been a little more nationalistic than leaders from other sections. During the 1830s, he had been an early proponent of expansion and had accepted most of the arguments of the prophets of Manifest Destiny. He was also a staunch advocate of the Monroe Doctrine that had been all but forgotten; as President, Polk was instrumental in its resurrection.

Unlike his mentor, Andrew Jackson, he had no military or diplomatic experience. At 17, he had been too young to enter the ranks in 1812, and as a sickly youth would not have fought in any case. Coming to political maturity in the years after the Monroe Doctrine, a period when the United States turned inward and when foreign policy and international intrigues were relatively minor matters, Polk had limited exposure to foreign affairs. Without such experience, he handled himself well in his dealings with the sophisticated British, although some might think that luck had a lot to do with his diplomatic victory in Oregon. His Secretary of State, James Buchanan, did not play a significant role in Polk's diplomacy. Characteristically, the President ran the show by himself.

When he assumed the reins of government from that accidental President, John Tyler, Polk announced four major policy goals to a colleague. He promised to achieve an independent treasury system, to lower the tariff, and to secure Oregon from the British and California from the Mexicans. He fulfilled all four of those pledges. Rarely has a President been as successful as Polk in achieving his goals and rarely has a President done exactly what he said he was going to do. Clearly, then, Polk must be considered a rather special President compared to most of our compromisers and prevaricators. Yet, few experts rank him with the "greats," Lincoln, Franklin Roosevelt, and Woodrow Wilson; and more interestingly, Polk might not have been reelected in 1848 even had he wanted to stand for a second term. Perhaps the means he used to achieve his goals bothered observers. One of his biographers who ducks the issue of Polk's greatness considers him a "remarkable" President.

GREAT BRITAIN AND AMERICAN EXPANSION

Polk is all the more remarkable for the way he handled two serious crises at the same time. On the one hand, as we shall see, he had to deal with the Mexicans who were legally at war with the United States after the annexation resolution of March 1845. On the other, he was involved in a dangerous crisis with the British over the disposition of Oregon. Although it is beyond our immediate purview, we must briefly describe this latter crisis because it plays a role in our analysis of Polk's behavior in the months prior to the onset of war with Mexico.

Since 1818, the United States had been occupying Oregon jointly with the British. By the early 1840s, pressure from increasing numbers of immigrants to that territory as well as commercial interest in ports along the Pacific coast had convinced Americans that the time had come to end the unusual and, by then, awkward arrangement. Taking advantage of careless British diplomacy in Washington, Polk pulled off a coup when he ultimately obtained Oregon up to the 49th parallel, despite British claims to the area north of the Columbia river.

The timing of the Oregon affair is important. The British minister in Washington rejected Polk's first offer out of hand in July 1845 at precisely the time that the Congress of Texas approved the annexation resolution that sent Mexican and American troops rushing to their posts opposite one another along the border. Moreover, Polk's blustery Oregon message to

Congress in December of 1845, in which he challenged the British Empire by asking for a unilateral abrogation of the original 1818 agreement, was presented during a period of increasing tension in Mexican-American relations. Even more surprising is the fact that between the time Congress annulled the Oregon agreement in April of 1846 and the British accepted the 49th parallel in June, we declared war against Mexico. As it happened, everything turned out for the best for the United States. Did Polk know what sort of risks he was running? Suppose the British had decided that our war with Mexico presented them with an unparalleled opportunity to put us in our place. Not only could they have tried to occupy *all* of Oregon but they also could have helped the Mexicans to reconquer Texas and secure California.

The temporal relationship between the two crises is important for another reason. If Polk was plotting war against Mexico, as some of his critics believe he was, why did he not wait until the British situation was squared? Today, we know that war with England was a remote possibility in 1846. It may well be that Polk was more knowledgeable about this than most Americans and most Mexicans for that matter. Indeed, he may have hoped that his handling of the Oregon crisis and apparent brinksmanship would throw the Mexicans off guard—they could not have expected him to attack them when he was faced with a prospect of a two-front and maybe global war. Most likely Polk was confident from around the fall of 1845 on that he could get the 49th parallel boundary from the British who were horrified when their minister summarily rejected our first overture. Despite his talk of 50°40′ or fight, Polk expected that Congress, although inflamed in part by his own rhetoric, would ultimately accept the compromise at the 49th parallel that he knew was forthcoming. Nevertheless, Polk's management of these dual crises was extraordinary or lucky or both.

As will be the story throughout the nineteenth century, the United States and her diplomats profited immeasureably from the simple fact that we were far off the beaten track and of secondary importance to the major European protagonists. In

1846, as in 1812, the British—who controlled the Atlantic and who maintained the most extensive European interests in the Americas—simply had too many other things to worry about to risk war over what they had come to perceive as a "pine swamp" in Oregon. The period 1838-1845 was an unusually difficult one for the managers of the British Empire. They pursued a long and initially disastrous war in Afghanistan from 1838 to 1842 and a smaller Opium War in China from 1839 to 1842 (fought to make the Chinese buy British opium), Canada was restive, both England and France were involved in wars in the La Plata region of South America, the pivotal Middle East experienced a small war and a major world crisis in 1840, and affairs on a European continent split between conservative and liberal powers merited constant attention. To risk war over Oregon or California and Mexico made little sense to those who controlled the destinies of the empire. In 1814, the Iron Duke had advised against an expansion of the British military effort against a weak and disunited United States. In 1846, we were a far more powerful, resourceful, and united country, capable of administering a drubbing to the British on land and even, in a commercial sense, on the seas. Thus, the British threat was hollow as Polk suspected, if he did not know for certain. Unfortunately for the Mexicans, few of their leaders were that perceptive.

THE VIEW FROM MEXICO CITY

The Mexicans were on the defensive in diplomatic and military conflicts with their neighbor to the north. Americans had stolen Texas from them and were threatening to make off with the rest of their empire, including California. Weak, poor, unstable, yet fiercely independent, Mexico calls to mind an "underdeveloped" David confronted by an imperialist Goliath. This superficial description of the two contenders does not tell the entire story. The Mexican leaders were a proud, and to some degree, arrogant bunch who saw themselves as culturally European. They shared Europe's contempt for the United States and its institutions. This contempt, and even hatred, was exacerbated by the perpetual threat that the United States posed to Mexican sovereignty since the 1820s. With good reason, the Mexicans suspected that we would one day go to war with them because we refused to coexist with a potentially powerful rival on the continent. Not unnaturally, the Mexicans feared for the survival of their culture. They would have to face assaults from the Protestant church, secular education, and a variety of other institutions and influences that American soldiers would bring in their van. We must remember that the Mexican elite still dreamed of a role as challenger to the United States' supremacy in North America. With their foothold on the Pacific and possession of the riches of the Southwest, the Mexicans, at least on paper, had the capabilities of becoming a major power. In the 1840s, they felt that since there had to be a showdown with the United States some day, they might as well get on with it while they still had a chance.

Not all Mexicans approached war with an air of resignation. Some generals and politicians dreamed of recapturing Texas, marching through the South and arming the slaves, and finally reaching Washington which they would burn to the ground as the British had done 30 years before. Although such bravado appears absurd today, on the eve of that war, a Mexican victory did not appear to be that much of a long shot.

Unlike their clumsy rivals, the Mexicans had a professional army, trained in advanced European techniques, an army that knew how to march and look impressive on the parade grounds. But their army was a sham, poorly equipped and provisioned, and short of guns, cannons, and ammunition. There was even an occasion when a contingent of troops in New Mexico could not leave their fort to go out on patrol because they had nothing to wear. Why the Mexican generals could not or would not see through the Potemkin village they had erected is puzzling. At least many of them behaved as if they commanded a first-rate armed force.

Mexico's confidence was bolstered by her European friends. Like the Mexicans, European observers scoffed at the American military. In the 1840s, our main line of defense beyond our 7,000-man army was the militia that came out to drill on hundreds of village greens every now and then, usually ending up drunk and brawling. Poorly disciplined and untrained, these militiamen appeared to be no match for soldiers. As one British expert commented, "America as an aggressive power is one of the weakest in the world . . . fit for nothing but to fight Indians." According to a Spanish diplomat stationed in Mexico City, there were "no better troops in the world nor better drilled and armed than the Mexicans."

In addition, the Mexicans would be conducting a defensive war on their own soil (at least at first), with internal lines of communication and transportation and with a united people fighting for national survival against the hated gringo. As for us, we would be fighting among ourselves, with some sections opposing the war and maybe again threatening secession. Mexicans also thought that Americans, the most materialist of peoples, would be unwilling to conduct a prolonged war far from home, a war that might cost a good deal of money. Thus, the Mexicans expected that after a few defeats, the American armies would slink out of Mexico to confront a civil war in their own land. As for the war on the seas, Mexican and European observers had reason for optimism. Although the Mexicans had no real navy, neither did the Americans. The Mexicans thought they could outfit privateers to prey upon our large and unprotected merchant marine.

If all this was not enough to inflate Mexican confidence, they had one final ace in the hole—European support. What form this support would take was difficult to say, but few Mexicans doubted that it would play a significant role in their coming political and military engagements. It is easy to see how they could arrive at this conclusion. Since their own crisis with the United States paralleled the crisis over Oregon, the Mexicans might have thought that the threat of a two-front war would keep the United States in her place. More generally, important British and French statesmen had repeatedly proclaimed in the early 1840s that they would not look on with indifference if the United States moved to increase her territories at the expense of the Mexicans. They supported the notion of a strong Mexico to maintain the balance of power on the continent and, indeed, in the hemisphere itself. From the British point of view in particular, a powerful and friendly Mexico counterbalanced the American-held hostage in Canada.

The Mexicans made a serious miscalculation. They should have expected no more than vigorous diplomatic and moral support from the British and French. Despite the Europeans' concern with the balance of the power on the North American continent, they were in no position to come to Mexico's aid militarily and the leaders in Mexico City should have realized that. How could they have misjudged the situation so badly? In part, European ministers in their capital, optimistic about the prospects for Mexican arms, may have encouraged their potential allies a bit too much. More likely, seeing war on the horizon, the Mexicans were guilty of wishful thinking. The situation is similar to that which confronted the Spanish in 1898. Seeing that war was imminent, they too were able to convince themselves that everything might turn out for the best since they could rely on the anti-American Concert of Europe.

Granted that some Mexicans looked forward to war, that they may have appeared arrogant, and that their relationship with Europe was a red flag to us. Can they by any stretch of the imagination be blamed for the outbreak of war? To be sure, their attitude of haughty superiority contributed to the tensions of the period. Legally and morally they must nevertheless be considered the aggrieved party. Although their political system was corrupt, their politicians played on the American issue for their own political purposes, and ordinary Mexicans were cruelly treated, the fact remains that Mexico was a victim of American aggression.

As we shall see, despite our disputes over Texas and financial claims, the real issue in this war was California and the Mexican refusal to sell it. Can they be blamed for wanting to hang on to it as long as possible? What right did we have to demand that piece of territory from them? Perhaps we were exercising a sort of eminent domain, but even then the Mexicans had every right to reject our propositions. Although realism apparently demanded the sale of California and the settlement of all other issues as best as possible, in this case, the Mexicans may have been justified in maintaining a stiff front. Their future as a major power was at stake. Thinking they had a chance to beat us, they could not surrender their claims to eventual world prominence without a fight. And undoubtedly, when it came to their legal bases for war, President Polk provided them with a variety of justifications.

POLK'S PLOTS

The *Pentagon Papers* offered sufficient evidence for critics to construct more than a circumstantial case against the Johnson administration for executing clandestine operations in 1964 that would eventuate in the bombing of North Vietnam. Johnson and his colleagues had nothing on James Polk who conspired to embroil us in a war of conquest in Mexico. Although there still is a good deal of controversy about the extent to which Polk himself plotted war, it seems fair to say that he was implicated in several questionable actions in Texas and California. We do know that our envoy to Mexico reported to his new chief in the spring of 1845 that he thought it unlikely the Mexicans would part with California. It has been alleged that this information from a reliable source convinced the President to provoke a war over the Texas question that would lead to our seizure of the Mexican west. Naturally, say those who support the conspiracy thesis, while he worked on his secret plans, he publicly exhausted all options for peaceful settlement, options he knew could not succeed.

In the early days of his administration, he half seriously considered employing Indians to invade the Mexican west for us. More viable was the attempt to provoke the Mexicans into war by instigating a battle between them and the Texans. In the spring of 1845, Polk sent Commodore Robert Stockton and a fleet of gunboats to Galveston for exploratory probes. Information about the so-called Stockton intrigue comes from Texan President Anson Jones, who relished being the president of an independent country and not just another governor. Jones's account of the plot is colored by his pique at Polk and the annexationists.

That Stockton was in Texas was no secret. According to Jones, the American met several times with the commander in chief of the independent Texas Army, General Sidney Sherman. In the course of these meetings, he allegedly tried to convince Sherman to send a volunteer force of several thousand men into an area around Matamoros that had been the subject of a boundary dispute. Any skirmish that followed could have served as a pretext for the United States to come to the aid of the freedom-loving Texans who had been "attacked" by the Mexicans. The controversy over the exact boundary and the disposition of the area between the Nueces and the Rio Grande was relatively new and had not troubled the Texans up to this point. In any event, Jones and Sherman refused Stockton's overture and the plan was aborted. The story appears relatively plausible, especially considering the way Polk later escalated the border dispute into a crisis of major proportions.

Even if the Stockton story is true, it cannot be traced to Polk. If he was involved, he was prudent enough to leave no incriminating written directives. Stockton's formal instructions from Polk, which are available, offer ambiguous evidence. Concerning the possibility that the Mexicans might invade Texas, Polk told Stockton, "In the interim before annexation should any foreign power invade Texas, the Texans themselves should be encouraged to repel the invasion."

For what it is worth (and here a defense attorney's motion that the following evidence is irrelevant and immaterial would be sustained by a judge), Polk was entirely capable of such underhanded behavior. In submitting the Oregon treaty to the Senate without recommendation from him and in submitting Nicholas Trist's treaty that ended the war with Mexico in 1848 also without a recommendation, Polk displayed his penchant for refusing to take responsibility for his actions until he was certain they would be approved. In his suggestive orders to Stockton and, as we shall see, in his even more suggestive orders to General Zachary Taylor, Polk may have been trying to provoke a war without risking his honor, or, to be charitable, the honor of his office. In order to convict Polk of complicity in the alleged Stockton intrigue, however, we would have to read between the lines of his instructions to his agents and generals and that would be inadmissible in any court, legal or historical.

Texas was not the only place for such shady business. In 1845, John C. Fremont, a dashing young army officer who had married the daughter of Senator Thomas (Old Bullion) Benton, was sent with a contingent of men to scout and survey Oregon and California. Fremont arrived on the scene just as some California-Americans launched an insurrection against the Mexicans and their Indian allies. Fed up with misrule and an unbenign neglect from Mexico City more than 1,500 miles away, they prepared to seek entry into the United States. Although the story is unclear, Fremont was at least theoretically acting for Washington when he tried to take control of the local revolution. In any event, Fremont's involvement, not welcomed by all the rebels, turned what was a genuine revolt into a provocative American intervention in internal Mexican politics.

Despite Fremont's meddling, and to some degree bungling, our agents in California did help prepare the way for the transition of power that occurred in the months after the declaration of war. Although one might call such planning prudent given the clouds on the horizon, these activities again revealed the contempt Polk and his colleagues felt for Mexican sovereignty. Indeed, his shenanigans in Texas and California justified a Mexican declaration of war against the United States.

SLIDELL'S MISSION FOR PEACE

Polk's supporters point not only to the lack of direct evidence to link the White House with plots in Texas and California but also to the famous Slidell mission. According to them, only after his most generous offers were rejected by the Mexicans in early 1846 did Polk decide for war. Unlike President Madison earlier and President McKinley later, Polk did travel that last mile before he unleashed his war machine. Before this interpretation is accepted, John Slidell's mission must be examined in greater detail. Was it made only for the record? Did Polk think he could solve all outstanding Mexican-American problems, including the sale of California, short of war?

The story begins in the summer of 1845, while Polk's agents, or at least agents acting in his name, were intriguing in Texas and California. The President had received reports that the Mexicans, who were bankrupt, might at last be willing to sell their imperial birthright for a mess of pottage. And so he instructed our agent in Mexico City to ask the Mexican foreign minister whether his government would talk to an American emissary about mutual problems. The foreign minister, a moderate who wanted to settle things without a war, told our agent that his government would welcome such an emissary. But, and here is the kicker, in order for negotiations to succeed in the unstable environment of Mexico City, the Americans had to accept three preconditions.

These preconditions, duly related to Polk, were: first, the American fleet, which had been hovering off the coast of Vera Cruz through 1845, had to be withdrawn; second, the diplomat sent to negotiate with the Mexicans had to be a man "whose dignified deportment, prudence, and moderation . . . the directness and moderateness of whose proposals will tend to calm the just irritation of Mexicans"; and, finally, that he should be empowered to treat only with the issue of Texas. The first two conditions appeared reasonable. The Mexicans did not want to negotiate under the gun and they had had their fill of ugly Americans who flaunted their presumed Anglo-Saxon superiority. The last precondition, however, the most important one, apparently doomed the mission. By the fall of 1845, we would not accept any settlement that did not secure California for the United States and the Mexican leaders excluded that item from negotiation.

One can understand their position. Confronted with a domestic political crisis, they feared their opposition would seize upon any action that gave the appearance of truckling to the gringos. They might have been willing to offer a reasonable settlement on the question of Texas and might have been able to obtain their Congress' approval for such a deal. But to talk about disposing of California and New Mexico would have jeopardized the seemingly more pressing arrangement over Texas. No Mexican politician who valued his position could have sold his empire, even for American dollars.

Aware of all this, Polk proceeded to ignore two of the preconditions, which, of course, was within his prerogative. By ignoring them, he sealed the fate of the Slidell mission. It is true that he did order the fleet to quit the waters around Vera Cruz. But the man he chose for the delicate mission, John Slidell, was a most undiplomatic sort who had difficulty concealing his contempt for Mexicans and Mexican culture. Most important of all, Slidell was empowered to discuss all outstanding issues with the Mexicans, not just the Texas affair. Although he was instructed not to push too hard on New Mexico and California at first, those matters were included in his formal commission. Slidell's selection, as well as the cavalier way Polk ignored the Mexican preconditions, reflected the views of the men around Polk toward those inferior beings to the south who had erected roadblocks to American efforts to promote peace and freedom.

Finally, adding insult to injury, when Slidell arrived on the scene in December of 1845, our consul advised him that the time was not propitious for Mexican-American negotiations. If rumors of peace talks leaked out, the opposition would claim that the moderate government was preparing to surrender to the United States. Slidell was told to wait until the dust had settled from the political crisis before he waded into the scene with his portfolio of carrots and sticks. Slidell knew, or at least was told on the best authority, that if he demanded to negotiate then and there, he would receive nothing.

Undaunted, he insisted on talking to the Mexicans and, as predicted, was summarily rejected. His rejection led to a debate over the willingness of the moderates to consider talking to him in the first place. In the end, they were replaced by a more nationalist government that would have nothing to do with American peacemissions. Perhaps the Mexican moderates should never have sent Slidell packing, though they did have reason. Polk had ignored two of their three preconditions. Further, Slidell was not exactly an officially approved diplomat. That is, although he came bearing credentials as an envoy extraordinaire and minister plenipotentiary, his commission had never been submitted to the American Congress. Unwilling to publicize the mission, Polk had bypassed Congress, and so Slidell was not quite what he purported to be. That was a convenient technicality. The Mexicans sent him home because Polk ignored their preconditions.

Slidell had been prepared to make the Mexicans a generous offer. A mixed claims commission in 1840 had ruled that their government owed American citizens $2 million and the Mexicans had accepted that judgment. After four years, they still had not made the required payments. In addition, there was another $3 million or so of unresolved American claims. Had the Mexicans listened to him, Slidell was going to offer to assume all claims in exchange for a recognition of the Rio Grande boundary as well as the annexation of Texas. Further, if they would throw in New Mexico, he could sweeten the deal with an additional $5 million cash payment. And if they added the final treasure, California, they could become as much as $25 million richer. Since Polk and the American Monroe Doctrine would prohibit the sale of California to Europeans and since the Californians might declare their independence anyway, what did the Mexicans have to lose? From the North American point of view, they had little to lose and much to gain from Slidell's package. From the Mexican point of view, one could not place a monetary value on national pride.

Americans think that every nation has its price. On occasion, we were surprised when our adversaries refused to accept the dollars offered in exchange for a chunk of territory. In this case, it appears that the Mexicans should have accepted the money for California because they were not able to hold it. But by 1846, the issue had become such a volatile one and Mexican nationalism so inflamed, in part by unscrupulous politicians using it for their own advantage, that such a sale was out of the question. Polk suspected as much even before Slidell reported home empty-handed.

From this perspective, the Slidell mission appears to have been made just for the record. It was doomed from its inception. To give Polk the benefit of the doubt, we had developed a national program whose fulfillment was deemed necessary to our future security and progress. We had to capture the West Coast. Thus, Polk sent Slidell to Mexico City, knowing the odds against success, on the off chance that with the handwriting on the wall, the Mexicans might come around. If anything, then, Polk can be applauded for giving them that chance. Of course, all of the preceding presupposes the legitimacy of our claim to California, for Slidell probably could have secured Texas, the issue that sparked the war.

AMERICAN BLOOD UPON THE AMERICAN SOIL

Every American school child learns how the Mexican War began. In late April of 1846, Mexican troops crossed the Rio Grande and ambushed an American reconnoitering party. Upon hearing this startling news, the President asked for and received a declaration of war.

The real story is not that simple. After the Texans' approval of annexation theoretically produced a formal state of war between Mexico and the United States, Polk dispatched a large contingent of American troops to our new border. Under the command of General Taylor, the force took up a position at the Nueces River where it remained until the failure of the Slidell mission in early 1846. At the same time, the Mexican government dispatched a large force to its side of the border, just south of the Rio Grande River. The area between the Rio Grande and the Nueces, claimed by both sides, was not violated by either army—at first.

After the failure of the Slidell mission, Polk became more provocative. The fleet was sent back to Vera Cruz, the port of Matamoros on the Rio Grande and the Gulf was blockaded, and, most important of all, Taylor crossed the Nueces and took up a new position on the Rio Grande. According to critics, Polk had no right to send his troops into the disputed area. That action was in effect an act of war. This matter is complicated by the fact that Mexico had been legally at war with us ever since Texas had been annexed.

Critics further contend that Taylor was sent to his new position to provoke Mexicans into attacking Americans in order to give Polk grounds for war. According to them, in a brilliantly constructed dispatch that left no smoking gun for historians to discover, Polk implicitly encouraged Taylor to maneuver the Mexican army into firing the first shot.

From Polk's point of view, after the Mexicans refused to treat with Slidell, he had to take measures to secure the rightful boundary of the United States. Thus, he leaped into the breech before the Mexicans did and, theoretically (this is straining things), might have headed off war had not the Mexicans tried to push us out. To accept this line, we would have to ignore his almost obsessive desire for California. We must also remember that the boundary issue was not important until Polk made it important. It appears he made it important in order to provide the *casus belli* he needed to make off with the Mexican west.

He almost did not get his incident. With Taylor breathing down their necks, with American troops on the Rio Grande, and with their sovereignty under assault, the Mexicans refused to be provoked. Polk was stuck with an embarrassing situation since he was not able to produce the incident to make Congress declare war. Nevertheless, in the first week in May of 1846, he decided to go ahead and call for a declaration of war even without a Mexican attack. In his draft message, he planned to ask for war because of Mexico's unpaid debts and unresolved claims as well as other insults and unfulfilled obligations. In other words, he was prepared to come before Congress with a shopping list of middle-size problems which, he would contend, could only be settled by force. Like Madison, Polk had come to the end of his rope. He was going to try to obtain his war on the basis of a series of long-running disputes without the trump card of an attack on American soldiers or territory.

In an incredible stroke of luck, the Mexicans delivered his *casus belli* at the moment he was preparing to ask Congress for war. On May 9, word finally reached Washington about an incident that took place two weeks earlier. One can imagine the glee with which Polk read that a force of Mexicans had crossed the Rio Grande, invading "American" territory, encountered 60 of our soldiers (ambushed was his translation), killed 11, and took the rest prisoner. What a godsend. The incident allowed him to recast his war message in terms of a heinous Mexican attack. They had shed American blood on American soil. The Mexicans had thrown down a challenge that had to be accepted.

What would have happened had Polk delivered his message as planned in the absence of the Mexican provocation? Given the state of the nation at the time, the hostility to Mexico, and the jingoistic spirit, he probably could have obtained his declaration of war—but not without a divisive debate in Congress with a sizable minority, mostly Whigs, opposing his request. As it turned out, such a debate was impossible given the so-called offensive actions of the Mexicans. Polk had his war neat and clean.

A HURRIED DECLARATION OF WAR

The war message—hastily prepared by Polk on Saturday, May 9 and Sunday, May 10 (in violation of his no work on the Sabbath rule)—was sent to Congress on May 11. In 1812, a smaller Congress took 17 days to consider Madison's request for war with Britain. In 1846 it needed only 2. We formally declared war on May 12. How all of this came about so quickly is not a pretty story.

When news of the attack and the President's war message first hit Capitol Hill, several Congressmen expressed skepticism about the seriousness of the aggressive acts committed by the

Mexicans. Some of this represented a knee-jerk partisan response from Whigs who did not want to give the Democrats their war under any circumstance. But there were others, including Congressmen from the President's own party, who were leery about going to war over a border incident that might not have taken place on American soil. How this opposition was overridden offers a lesson in the fallibility of the checks and balances so carefully constructed by the Founding Fathers.

In response to Polk's request for war, the House Committee on Military Affairs prepared a bill that would have served a purpose comparable to that served by the Tonkin Gulf Resolution of 1964. The committee's bill ignored the issue of a legal declaration of war and merely empowered the President to take whatever steps were necessary to protect our troops and territory from attack. At the eleventh hour, a committee member attached a preamble that called for a declaration of war. If Congressmen wanted to help defend our boys, they had also to accept the war declaration. The original bill conceivably might have led to a police action and nothing more. The new bill meant full-scale war. To be fair, a declaration of war was favored by a healthy majority, made up predominantly of Democrats.

The Democratic leadership then proceeded to ramrod the bill through Congress. Polk had submitted 144 pages of supporting documents with his bill. Since they obviously could not have been analyzed quickly, they were ignored. The debate over the war measure, if we can call it that, was brief; opposition speakers were overlooked by the chair who used every parliamentary trick to stifle discussion. In defense of their actions, the Democrats argued that we could ill afford the luxury of a debate while our boys were under merciless attack from Mexicans. Each minute that went by meant further loss of American life and territory.

The vote in the House was taken on the day the bill was introduced. As expected, the Democrats were able to produce an overwhelming vote for war with 174 Representatives for, 14 against, and 35 abstentions. Although most of those in the latter two categories were Whigs, a few Democrats also refused to go along with the majority. On the next day, May 12, the Senate endorsed war by an even wider margin, 40 to 2. These votes do not reflect the magnitude of the sentiment against war. Many Whigs, and even some Democrats, were forced to vote for war because they did not want to appear to desert the boys who were defending our soil against the Mexican invaders. In terms of political fallout, the war appeared to be popular. Any Congressman who opposed war measures risked being labelled unpatriotic or even traitorous. After all, the Federalists were destroyed as a political party, in part because of their antiwar activities during the War of 1812.

The situation seems familiar. Congresses meekly approved almost all of the President's war measures for Vietnam from the Gulf of Tonkin incident in 1964 to the late 1960s. In that now-controversial incident, Congress had no choice but to take the President's word for the need to retaliate against the perpetrators of the attack on our fleet. Even with instantaneous electronic communications not available in 1846, and elaborate media coverage of Southeast Asia, Congress had no way of challenging the account offered by Lyndon Johnson. Later, when doves wanted to force the President to call a halt to the war, they could have refused to vote the necessary war credits. To do so would have meant leaving our boys defenseless against attack from the communists. Such a record would have been difficult to explain to constituents back home, so antiwar Senators continued to vote for fiscal measures that enabled the President to carry out that war.

We can sympathize with the problems Congressmen faced during those turbulent few hours on May 11 and 12. Not all were worried about partisan issues or their own political futures. Angered by the attack from the Mexicans, who were not the most popular of foreigners, most felt the time had come to teach them a lesson. Later, some regretted the haste with which they reacted to news of the crisis. We can understand their dilemma. Most of the American people whom they were supposed to represent were infected with that expansionist

fever we call Manifest Destiny. Although few openly called for
war with Mexico before May 11, the border incident was all
they needed to set out on a crusade against the backward Latins
who dared challenge the soldiers of the Lord.

MANIFEST DESTINY

Unlike the War of 1812, Americans were eager to enter the
scrap with Mexico. Would-be recruits broke down the doors of
enlistment centers in order to sign up for military service. Some
young men were even rumored to have bribed army officials to
allow them to enlist after their state quotas had been filled. One
can explain this behavior in several ways. At bottom, however,
any explanation, and indeed any general explanation for the
war itself, must take into account the extraordinary wave of
nationalism and jingoism that swept the country under the label
of Manifest Destiny.

The nature of the exact relationship between national mood
and policy in a democracy is difficult to ascertain. Perhaps, as
some cynics argue, the question is no longer a relevant one since
mood can be manipulated by Presidents. Although they must
worry about public attitudes and the general psychological state
of the nation, through clever use of electronic media and
Madison Avenue techniques, they can guarantee that their policies will rarely be at variance with the national mood. Those
who feel that we are fast approaching 1984 maintain that the
President and his analogues in other countries can now make
the public *think* that it has forced its government to do its
bidding when in reality the public is tricked into approving
policies decided upon well before the media discuss them. Be
that as it may, in the 1840s, and throughout much of our
history, national mood was in good measure impervious to a
leader's manipulatory techniques.

Does this mean that national mood developed spontaneously
in the 1840s? Those who prefer conspiracy theses contend that
although the President and his henchmen were denied the tools
available to their successors today, they still could create

national mood. According to this scenario, along around the late 1830s, the men who controlled our society—eastern bankers and merchants and maybe southern plantation owners—decided that we needed California and the Mexican West to facilitate the development of our economy. Through their control of newspapers, magazines, politicians, and even churches, they were able to sell their policies by cloaking them with Manifest Destiny. They created an expansionist mood that countenanced the forceful seizure of territories needed by the developing capitalist infrastructure.

Hard evidence for such a conspiracy is unavailable. That the mood of Manifest Destiny was used by others with baser motives is certain. But it is likely that the mood developed spontaneously as a response to the confluence of several factors which, almost deterministically, predicted an expansionist decade in the 1840s.

The United States had always been an expansionist and nationalist power. Since the 1770s, we had offered moral, economic, and political support to peoples who might join with us to forge a new republican system. In earlier periods, however, leaders were nervous about the relationship between the physical expansion of the United States itself and the survival of democratic government. For them, liberty was best protected in a small state. In terms of the examples available at the time, there did seem to be a correlation between republican institutions and small geographic entities. Our founders also worried about the relationship between expansion and the delicate sectional balance in Congress. In addition, some states' righters were leery of expansion because the more states there were, the weaker each individual state would become and the stronger the central government. Finally, as the far-seeing Thomas Jefferson pointed out in 1801, the land over which he was preparing to preside was large enough for the thousandth generation to come.

After he and his party accepted the Louisiana Purchase in 1803 and the United States gained experience in practical expansion, antiexpansionist arguments lost some of their sali-

ency. As they moved into the 1830s, Americans became more
and more certain that they had to expand in order to protect
their system. Antipathetic to democracy, the British and the
French threatened to close us in and frustrate the growth of
free institutions on this continent. Rumors concerning their
activities in Oregon, California, and Texas were grist for many
an expansionist's mill in the late 1830s and early 1840s. It was
bad enough that the continent was blighted by the existence of
Canada north of the Land of Liberty; things would become
even worse if Europe gained control of our West Coast. The
struggle to secure Oregon, for example, took on the coloration
in the media of a struggle between democrats and monarchists.
The foreign danger was a catalyst that convinced Americans
that their country had to expand before European conspiracies
limited freedom to only one small corner of the globe.

The spirit of Manifest Destiny in the 1840s could not have
flourished without a foreign threat as well as an area into which
we could expand. Although this is obvious, it underscores the
fact that the popular spirit that swept the United States during
Polk's time was inexorably linked to specific political factors.
Thus, after we had sated ourselves in 1848 and filled out our
natural boundaries, we had no place to go until changes in the
technology of transportation and communication made extracontinental expansion more practical. Manifest Destiny or an
expansionist mood had to wait 50 years before it made its
reappearance on the American scene.

Other, more general factors explain why people felt the way
they did during the 1840s. For one thing, the Panic of 1837
produced unemployment and dislocation that compelled many
to seek more fertile economic fields. The relatively empty
western lands allegedly offered a chance for a new start and
escape from failures in the East and Midwest.

Related to the Panic was the developing belief that the
United States was becoming too urban and that, as a consequence, our national character was being changed for the worse.
During the Jacksonian period, the yeoman farmer and the
frontiersman came more and more to be national mythological

heroes. With the country cooped up within its 1840 boundaries and with people deserting rural areas for the city, the fabric of the nation was threatened. The threat involved more than overcrowding and overpopulation—if the yeoman farmer disappeared from our society, we would lose those experiences that defined our unique institutions and that fostered our cherished character traits of individualism, self-reliance, and independence.

Furthermore, the threat to liberty in Europe could be partially defeated through our expansion. In the early days of the republic, we expected that Europeans would admire our model of good government and quickly cast off their reactionary systems. First, the French disappointed us. Then, when the dust had settled from the Napoleonic wars, the last remnants of the ideals of 1789 were crushed in the repression of the 1820s. In 1840, Europe appeared to be in the iron grip of despotic forces. Since the Old World was a lost cause, Americans could best advance democracy by allowing liberty-seeking Europeans to come here. We had to find land for the hordes who would quit their homelands—where else but the vast West, which, unfortunately, belonged to other peoples.

Manifest Destiny was supposedly an idealistic crusade for freedom. How, then, could Americans give land to Europeans that was taken away from those who were already here and who, theoretically, should also have been allowed the blessings of American liberty? What about the Indians and the Mexicans who were more downtrodden than most of the Europeans we hoped to attract to our refuge for democrats? This inconsistency in Manifest Destiny was more apparent than real, at least to the propagators of that creed. It was easily explained away by the concept of "The Destined Use of the Soil." That is, the Lord had provided the North American continent with the richest soil the world had ever seen. It was His will that it be used in the most productive manner possible. The Indians, who did not cultivate it, were not using this gift as it had been intended to be used. As for that minority of red men who were farmers, such as the Cherokees and the Creeks, they had been put on earth to play a certain role. When they aped the white man, they violated the divine plan.

The several thousands of Mexicans in the area we coveted proved to be a more ticklish problem. They were white, or at least part European, and they did till the soil. How, then, could we take their lands in the name of the Almighty? It was true that our Almighty was basically a Protestant deity whose mandates may not have been applicable to half-breed Catholic Latins. More likely, although the Mexicans did till the soil, they did not till it as well as we did, given our western know-how, and so they had to make way for more progressive American farmers. Though these mental gymnastics that served as rationales for expansion 130 years ago may seem absurd today, things were different then. Only a small number of uninfluential people could (or wanted to) see through them. Notions of cultural relativism rarely saw the light of day during the 1840s. Most Americans sincerely thought that everyone, including the Mexicans and Indians, would profit through the success of our experiment. Believers in Manifest Destiny, Americans were convinced that they were the people chosen to lead mankind out of darkness.

The religious flavor of Manifest Destiny blended well with the general messianic thrust of the Jacksonian period. It was a reforming era, full of new social and political movements that aimed to improve conditions and institutions in our increasingly complex society. The spirit of Manifest Destiny expressed yet another facet of a mood that one author has labelled "Freedom's Ferment."

Manifest Destiny was embraced by Americans from all sections of the country and from all stations in life. Some, however, used the rhetorically noble movement to achieve narrower goals. Oregon and California attracted them not only because they offered land and opportunity to American agriculturalists, miners, and European refugees but also because their natural harbors could be used as way stations to the fabled riches of the Orient.

American interest in the Far East can be traced to 1784 when the *Empress of China* successfully completed a long and dangerous voyage from New York, around South America, on to our West Coast, and thence to Asia where merchants traded for goods that they eventually sold at a handsome profit back in the United States. Twenty years later, when sent to chart the Louisiana Purchase, Lewis and Clark reported enthusiastically about harbors along the Oregon coast. During the early 1840s, Captain Charles Wilkes explored the Pacific coast for ports and found that at least two, Seattle and San Francisco, were suited to handle the great trade awaiting us in China and other Asian lands. Further down that inviting coast, San Diego was another excellent port.

To eastern merchants and shippers, the land that came along with California and Oregon was relatively unimportant—they wanted the ports that would give them control over the Pacific Basin. Regardless of whether the Asian trade really was or could be significant relative to our overall economy, it was thought to be in the 1840s and, indeed, for most of our history.

As for the Asian market's relationship to our entry into war in 1846, it helped keep northeastern Whigs in line, for they had to weigh their concern about war, expansion, and slavery against their desire to secure the West Coast. Needless to say, they would have liked to pick up California ports without a fight, as Polk had done in Oregon, but if there was no other way to force Mexico to give up her lands, then Whigs had to resign themselves to war.

Whigs were not alone in their economic interest in expansion. Their opposite numbers in the South saw in the fruits of Manifest Destiny the opportunity to maintain and even expand their own economic system and political power. According to nineteenth-century critics, the war was brought about by a conspiracy of the Slavocrats who hoped to use the Mexican Cession to expand their evil institution. Through the accession of new slave states, southerners would increase their power in Congress. Further, the new lands would more than compensate for the dying plantations in the Old South whose soil the cotton culture had exhausted. Thus, southerners allegedly used Manifest Destiny and the Mexican crisis for their own sectional interests.

Little evidence for such a plot exists although many southerners did support expansion because they saw it as an opportunity to improve their position in the nation. Yet even though southerners were in the forefront of those favorable to expansion, an examination of their newspapers, speeches, and votes reveals no uniformity of opinion on such important questions as war and the exact territories to be wrenched from Mexico. That some southerners, like some easterners, were prepared to use the general spirit of the time for less than lofty ends was certain. To talk about a conspiracy stretches the point beyond credibility.

In sum, wherever one looked in 1846, Americans were ready for a crusade. When Polk gave them the opportunity to fulfill the program of Manifest Destiny, they did so with enthusiasm and passion. At the start, few doubted that we were engaged in a just war, in a defensive war, in a war to defend our national security. Today, of course, as we examine the situation unaffected by the spirit of the times, we are not so confident about the justice or even the rationality of the decisions taken by Polk, Congress, and the nation in the spring of 1846.

NATIONAL SECURITY AND THE MEXICAN-AMERICAN WAR

In his war message, Polk claimed that the United States was under attack. National security had been threatened in the most direct way possible, by a frontal military assault against our territory. Polk's message must be read with a grain of salt. There was no likelihood, and almost everyone knew it, of the Mexicans launching an invasion of the United States or even of the area between the Nueces and the Rio Grande. Had Polk not pressed the boundary issue and linked it to the sale of California, our adversaries would have eventually recognized their loss of Texas. They simply did not have the offensive capability to pose a threat to us on land and they had no navy.

There is, however, another route we can take that might allow us to construct at least a marginal case for the military threat posed by Mexico. Had England and France, and not the United States, secured the Mexican West, our strategic position would have deteriorated. Although this factor might have served as a rationale for Polk and others during the period, it is unimpressive today. We had learned that British consular officials in California were urging their government to buy California before the Americans stole it. But we now know, and Polk probably knew it then, that the British Foreign Office had little interest in fishing in those distant waters which were within our sphere.

To alter the scenario a bit, had Mexico developed a stable political system, formed alliances with European powers, and populated California and the West with her own citizens (a tall order), then this potentially great power on our doorstep would have posed a serious long-term military threat. Thinking that such developments were possible given enough time, the Mexicans suspected that this was just what the United States was worried about. We wanted to deny them their rightful place in the international system.

Were we to buy this argument, we would have to accept the general notion that large powers should not tolerate the existence of potential rivals on their peripheries. Any possibility that a nearby small power might grow into a big power must be nipped in the bud. Such a static or status quo view of international relations is grossly unfair to latecomers to the race for power and influence in the international system. Must all large powers who are neighbors become military rivals eventually? Perhaps, but in this case, the chances that Mexico would have been able to fashion such a future for herself were slim. We could have afforded to wait for California to become American without a war.

As for the specific border dispute that precipitated the war, this was a matter of only symbolic importance. We were destined to gain control of the territory we wanted by hook or crook. Even had the Mexicans retained the strip of land between the Rio Grande and the Nueces, our military security would not have been weakened.

If we cannot make much of a case for the threat to our military security, what about our economic security? Many deemed the prolonged or even permanent denial of California to represent a serious blow to our economic and commercial development. Without California, we might not have become a Pacific power (perhaps not a bad thing, given the failure of the China market and our involvement in several wars to protect that phantom market). The Mexicans might have developed California themselves and even established a rival cotton culture there to challenge our dominant position as supplier to the mills of England. And finally, although this was not completely perceived at the time, the enormous agricultural riches of an irrigated California contributed significantly to our enviable self-sufficiency in foodstuffs.

Nevertheless, when we weigh the positive value of all of these riches against the negative value of a war, and then ask the question—Could we have gotten along economically without California?—the answer would have to be affirmative. Although its mining and agricultural resources were and still are quite useful to us, their denial would not have lowered our standard of living very much or have led to any more social conflict than we now experience.

The clincher must be the likelihood that all of those lands would some day become part of the United States anyway. Considering geographic factors, Mexico's weakness, and the Americans who began to trickle into her territories and who would have become a flood over the next few decades even had Mexico retained nominal sovereignty, California and New Mexico would undoubtedly have been acquired sooner or later, probably without a war. Naturally, the discovery of gold in 1849 would have complicated things considerably, but the attraction of the United States would have been too powerful for Mexico to resist. In other words, when the fruits became even riper, they would have fallen into our laps more easily than they did in 1846. It is true that few were as confident about their ultimate disposition in the 1840s as we can be today, especially considering the interest manifested in them by the Europeans. Consequently, we can understand, if not agree with, those Americans who equated our national security with the need to capture the Mexican West to guarantee economic growth.

Finally, was our honor at stake? James Polk would have us believe that it was, after the Mexicans attacked our troops. No self-respecting nation could accept without retaliation the invasion of its territory by one of its neighbors. Such a position becomes untenable when we analyze the circumstances of the so-called attack and whether we did not first challenge Mexican honor by sending Taylor to the Rio Grande before the problem involving the disputed territory had been litigated.

It is also true that the Mexicans had reneged on claims payments owed to our citizens. Though the amounts were relatively small, international law permits governments to employ martial action to obtain a redress of fiscal grievances. Some 60 years later, the Hague Court adopted the position that nations in default of their financial obligations could legally be invaded by creditor nations.

At the time, however, few Americans thought their honor was being challenged by the Mexican refusal to make payments on their $5 million debt. Polk could have obfuscated the issue for several more years without running the political risk of being accused of damaging our international prestige.

In another slight to our honor, Slidell had been sent home without a hearing. His rejection in Mexico City was nowhere near as insulting as the Erskine or Cadore deceits of the 1812 period.

More generally, we could argue that a minor state was foiling our dreams of expansion and national grandeur. As a country with great power presumptions, we could not afford to allow Mexico to refuse our generous offers. Great powers do not stand around and wait for the other fellow to act; great powers act first and resolutely to get their way. If we did not go to war with Mexico, then England and France might have gotten the idea that they could move into our hemisphere without fear of military challenge.

Some of these rationales concerning the relationship between Mexican behavior and our national honor ring true for 1846. Today, one cannot take them seriously for we were the ones who went looking for a fight. The war with Mexico appears to have been the least justifiable of all of our wars.

BIBLIOGRAPHY

The best place to begin a study of the Mexican War is David M. Pletcher's lengthy monograph, *The Diplomacy of Annexation: Texas, Oregon, and the Mexican War* (Columbia: University of Missouri Press, 1973). Critical of American imperialism, Pletcher nevertheless offers a balanced treatment of all aspects of the diplomacy of the mid-1840s. An earlier, briefer, but still important analysis is by Norman Graebner, *Empire on the Pacific: A Study in American Continental Expansion* (New York: Ronald Press, 1955). Although Graebner emphasizes the commercial interest in the West Coast, like Pletcher, he offers a multicausal interpretation.

Glenn Price, who presents evidence of conspiracy in *Origins of the War with Mexico: The Polk-Stockton Intrigue* (Austin: University of Texas Press, 1967), is not completely convincing. His short work supplants Richard R. Stenberg's "The Failure of Polk's Mexican War Intrigue of 1845," *Pacific Historical Review,* 4(March 1935), 39-68. British plots and conspiracies are examined in fine detail in the venerable, E. D. Adams's *British Interests and Activities in Texas, 1838-1848* (Baltimore: Johns Hopkins University Press, 1910).

The classic work by Albert K. Weinberg, *Manifest Destiny* (Baltimore: Johns Hopkins University Press, 1935), redundantly presents every argument used by American expansionists in the nineteenth century. More usable is Frederick Merk's *Manifest Destiny and Mission in American History: A Reinterpretation* (New York: Knopf, 1963). Merk suggests that Americans in the period were more interested in mission than in the seizure of territories. See also his *The Monroe Doctrine and American Expansionism, 1843-1849* (New York: Knopf, 1966).

Of the several biographies of James Polk, Charles Sellers's stands out. His second volume, *James K. Polk: Continentalist 1843-1846* (Princeton,

NJ: Princeton University Press, 1966), presents the most coherent analysis of his character and policies. Although Sellers does not like Polk, he does respect him.

An interesting account of the view from Mexico City is found in Gene Brack's *Mexico Views Manifest Destiny: An Essay in the Origins of the Mexican War* (Albuquerque: University of New Mexico Press, 1975).

Chapter 3

THE SPANISH-AMERICAN WAR

*The forcible intervention of the United States as a
neutral to stop the war, according to the large dictates of
humanity and following many historical precedents . . .
is justifiable on rational grounds.*
   —William McKinley, April 11, 1898—

In contrast to the Mexican War, the Spanish-American War is
one of our most popular and best known wars. Of course, it is
of more recent vintage than the first two wars examined. Many
of us can still remember veterans of '98 who paraded about on
Armistice Days. Those old soldiers fought for a new, vigorous,
and to some degree naive world power engaged in a heroic
struggle to free Cuba from Spanish oppression. Their war gave
us Theodore Roosevelt, with his sparkling teeth leading that
celebrated charge up San Juan Hill and Admiral George Dewey,
along with Gridley, effortlessly dispatching the Spanish fleet in
Manila Bay. And all of this at a cost of fewer than 1,000
combat deaths and around 4,000 deaths from disease and food
poisoning. Moreover, at war's end, we became possessors of
subject peoples (the Filipinos, Puerto Ricans, Guamanians, and
Cubans) whom we could Americanize and of new bases from
which our navy could more easily protect our merchant marine

as it spread American products, culture, and influence to the far corners of the globe. All things considered, it was a most splendid little war.

The Spanish-American War marked our emergence on the world scene as we laid claim to a chair at the table of the great powers. We had been slowly moving into their league ever since we solved our most serious domestic problem with the Civil War. In 1898, with a new navy, an incredible industrial machine, and confidence in the shape of the American Century to come, we finally proved that we belonged in the international big leagues. (In our parochial land, the big leagues are the American and National Leagues, while the old International League was only the best of the minor leagues.)

The ease with which we won the war affected our behavior and perceptions in future crises. In 1898, we took on a European state for the first time since 1812 and the final result was not close. Even though Spain was a vestigial member of the great power community living on imperial glory borrowed from the sixteenth century, and even though her army, navy, economy, political system, and insurmountable logistic disadvantages made it impossible for her to contend with us militarily, our burgeoning ego was inflated by our smashing triumph.

The story of the origins of the war, so simple in 1898, has become more complicated. Today, cynics contend that the Spanish-American War had as much to do with Cuba as the Mexican-American War had to do with Texas. Polk wanted California in 1846 and McKinley and his capitalists allegedly wanted the Philippines in 1898. Believing they were participating in a noble crusade, Americans were cruelly used by industrialists, financiers, and shippers who had their eyes on the Asian market. They were not the only ones who deceived the good American folk. Sensation-seeking publishers, led by William Randolph Hearst, sold the nation on the evil of the Spanish and the justice of the Cuban cause. Inventing stories about vile Spanish atrocities, they aroused the public and, more important for them, sold newspapers.

Even though contemporary opponents of the war made these very points, most citizens considered the Spanish-American conflict a selfless war fought to uphold international morality. For over a century, through the French Revolution and the revolutions of the 1820s and 1840s, Americans cheered European liberals who tried to cast off their yokes of oppression. Despite our passion for republican revolution, we sent them little more than good wishes and moral support. In 1898, we redeemed our pledge to defend liberty when, along with good wishes, we sent the Cubans Theodore Roosevelt and his Rough Riders. "Cuba Libre" explained how it came to be that American soldiers, sailors, and marines found themselves in the Caribbean and the Pacific involved in what by Europeans standards had to be considered a miniwar.

THE CUBAN CONNECTION

Cuba is only 90 miles from our shores. The refrain is familiar. Even in times when Cuba was not a 10-minute air hop from Florida, we treated her as if she were almost part of the United States. Attesting to the all-American character of Cuba, expansionists claimed she had been created from silt the Mississippi River carried away as it left New Orleans and entered the Caribbean. Several generations of American diplomats and intriguers tried to bring that Mississippi mud back where it belonged. Plots to buy or seize Cuba flash across our historical stage from the 1820s, through the Ostend Manifesto of 1854, and on to the Ten Years War of 1868-1878. Few in the nineteenth century doubted that some day Old Glory would wave over Havana.

Despite our exertions, Cuba, which was not for sale, remained loyal to Madrid decades after other Latin Americans threw off their shackles. For such uncommon fealty, Cuba earned the title, "The Ever Faithful Isle." Not all Cubans were proud of that record. In reality, Cuba was a restive colony kept within the empire only at great cost to the Spanish. For example, they lost an estimated 100,000 men in the bloody Ten Years War of 1868-1878. Americans were almost as deeply involved in that revolution as they were in the next. The fact that we resisted the urge to help out in the first war but were unable to remain aloof in the second illustrates the importance of national mood in an explanation of why the United States intervened in 1898.

The Cubans' last struggle against formal foreign domination began in 1895. As in previous insurrections, events in the United States helped precipitate hostilities. The Wilson-Gorman Tariff of 1894, which raised duties on sugar, threw Cuba's economy into disarray. The hard times that followed contributed to the growth of the rebel forces who were initially concerned more with political than economic liberation.

It would be interesting to discover that Americans raised their tariff to create discontent in Cuba that could lead to revolution and an eventual protectorate. Unfortunately for those who look for an overt capitalist conspiracy behind every international event, there is no evidence that this was the case.

In a military sense, the revolution that began in 1895 was almost a carbon copy of the revolution of 1868 and, for that matter, of Fidel Castro's revolt against Fulgencio Batista in the 1950s. Inadequately armed and poorly trained in conventional warfare, the rebels conducted a guerrilla war, attacking remote posts, burning cane fields, and generally trying to disrupt Cuban economic and political life so much that the rotting colonial edifice would fall by itself. Striking from their mountain retreats, the rebels hoped to make staying in Cuba so costly to the Spanish that they would grant full autonomy, at the least, and maybe independence. When the rebels burned cane fields, they also irritated American owners who, they hoped, would force Washington to intercede.

Those engaging in guerrilla wars do not adhere to Marquess of Queensberry rules of fair play. Counterrevolutionary force always seems to be more brutal than revolutionary force. The Spanish-Cuban War was no exception to the rule. Although government operatives may not have been more brutal in the qualitative or quantitative sense, either their atrocities were more widely publicized or outsiders tended to consider atrocities committed in the name of national liberation to be different from atrocities committed to suppress freedom. In any event, the Spanish prosecuted their war against the rebels in a manner which should seem familiar. Since as Mao reminds us, the guerrillas are fish and the peasants water, the Spanish tried to dry up the lakes by removing the peasants from restive districts. In order to identify the rebels, deny them cover, intelligence, and supplies, and to establish "free-fire" zones, the Spanish forcibly transported whole villages from the countryside to concentration camps. After such a relocation had been completed, the Spanish Army fired at anything that moved in the cleared area.

Many peasants, moved to those camps for their own safety, perished behind the barbed wire. They did not die from Spanish torture or purposeful mistreatment, although there was some of this, but from sickness and plague. The living conditions were so abysmal and the sanitation procedures so crude that the camps became breeding grounds for all sorts of communicable diseases. A few years later, the same thing happened to Boers under British care in South Africa. To the horror of liberals in both England and America, thousands died in British concentration camps from 1899 to 1902 because of primitive sanitary engineering. The widespread death, suffering, and inhumanity in the Spanish camps in Cuba outraged Americans who came to think, through the assistance of their friendly tabloid, that the Spanish were deliberately setting out to murder the native population. To make matters worse from a public relations point of view, the architect of the Spanish military policy was General Valeriano Weyler, a man who had earned the sobriquet "Butcher" during the Ten Years War.

The Cuban rebellion was a godsend to American journalists who were completing the transformation of their newspapers into vehicles for mass audiences. Competition was fierce and headlines—"Extra, Extra read all about it, Spanish Sink Maine!"—sold newspapers. For a generation whose senses were not constantly stimulated by radio, television, movies, and *Playboy,* lurid descriptions of the scandalous behavior of the

Catholic Spaniards, who apparently spent considerable time ravishing demure Cuban virgins, made for exciting reading. That the Spanish might have ravished a maiden or two was possible, but give the yellow press one real ravishing and it invented scores of others. We now know that unscrupulous reporters and editors provoked their own incidents and fabricated stories out of whole cloth in order to coop rivals.

The journalists were aided by the Cuban Junta, an international organization that raised funds, ran guns, and served as a public relations agency for the rebels. It provided American newspapers with the latest news from the front, all of which turned out to be favorable to the cause of Cuban independence. Aside from such quasi-legitimate activities, the Cuban Junta also bought American journalists who, unbeknownst to their editors and readers, planted stories about Spanish inhumanity. Needless to say, with this double-barrelled barrage from Hearst types and the Cuban Junta, Americans received a distorted view of the events and issues in the Cuban rebellion. On the other hand, perhaps there was only one view to be seen in this case, the view of a colonial people fighting for freedom.

Though newspaper barons and the Cuban Junta aroused the American public, we should not overemphasize their role in bringing us into the war. Their messages were read and accepted because Americans in the mid-1890s were receptive to them. Twenty-five years earlier, albeit with a less developed yellow press, many of those same messages fell upon deaf ears. Despite what we may think about the awesome power of the media and Madison Avenue, they still cannot unilaterally create a national mood; we must be ready for their messages. In the 1890s, Americans were ready to become interested in the messages appearing daily in their press—they were itching to go on a crusade or an adventure, or both.

THE EXPANSIONIST IMPULSE

In those allegedly Gay Nineties, many Americans were in an ugly mood. Why they became jingoes in the 1890s and not the

1880s or the 1900s is a complicated question. In order to offer even the most tentative answers, I will discuss a variety of factors that came together to give that decade its distinctive character.

First of all, and this was mostly of symbolic importance, the American frontier was perceived to be disappearing. In 1890, the Census Bureau announced that it could no longer draw a line from Canada to Mexico to demarcate a continuous frontier area. Although much land remained unoccupied, arable land was disappearing. Frederick Jackson Turner, the great historian, called attention to this fact when he presented his Frontier Thesis in 1893, a natural corollary of which pointed toward expansion. If, as Turner argued, the frontier had been instrumental in defining our unique character and institutions, we had to find ourselves a new frontier or stagnate in our cities. While Turner himself did not urge extracontinental expansion, others who read his epochal paper did. Both Theodore Roosevelt and Woodrow Wilson were concerned about the implications of his analysis.

More important than this ethereal intellectual construct was the nature of economic conditions in the 1890s. Although the period from 1865 to 1900 was seen popularly as a boom period with Carnegies, Rockefellers, and Harrimans building a mighty industrial machine, it is more accurately depicted as a series of crises in the midst of a boom. We experienced a turbulent depression in the 1870s, a major recession in the mid-1880s, and what was perceived to be the most serious depression in our history from 1893 to 1896. These hard times, especially the depression of the 1890s, contributed to the development of the expansionist mood in several ways.

According to economists of the period, depressions were caused by overproduction. Industrial capacity was expanding more rapidly than the domestic market and so, periodically, supply exceeded demand, factories had to close down, people were thrown out of work, and the economy fell apart. Such instability was unnecessary, or so it was thought. If we could only find places to dump our surpluses, factories could work around the clock; the economy could perpetually flourish.

Unfortunately, we were not the only people looking for new markets. Our quest brought us into conflict with Europeans who already had a corner on most of the world's trade. Thus, we had to develop a large and efficient merchant marine, a modern navy to protect that merchant marine, and bases, coaling stations, and even an isthmian canal to safeguard our commerce and security. This program did not necessarily envisage the taking of formal colonies except insofar as an island or two might provide a useful entrepôt on the way to China, the "greatest uncut commercial melon of them all." Many important business leaders, who considered foreign markets a panacea, used their influence to see to it that the government and its military, diplomatic, and consular services assisted their new outward thrust. It is difficult to separate our commercial offensive from diplomatic intrigues, alliances, and perhaps even wars.

More generally, the depression of the 1890s produced a "psychic crisis" in our society affecting all Americans. Spokesmen for the rich and the poor confronted one another across rhetorical barricades, armies of unemployed marched on the nation's capital, and millions suffered ignominiously and anonymously as it appeared that the country was disintegrating. A foreign danger or the opportunity for national adventure might have been just what the doctor-psychiatrist ordered for the sick and disillusioned country. A little war would provide the means for the nation to release its tension safely, to forget its own troubles, and to rally around the flag in a therapeutic orgy of patriotism. American leaders did not consciously use the foreign danger to divert attention from internal problems. Yet the psychic crisis of the 1890s made Americans more eager to accept some glamorous, exciting, national adventure presented to them by their leaders and media.

The widespread support for some sort of expansion was more than just a negative response to our psychic crisis. During the 1890s, important thinkers in the Anglo-Saxon world had become convinced that Anglo-Saxon institutions and civilization represented the apogee of man's evolution from the primeval ooze. The whole world was going Anglo-Saxon or as Theodore

Roosevelt said, "the Twentieth Century will be the century of the men who speak English." It was thought that we could best assist the natural, but slow development of an Anglo-Saxon world by taking up the white man's burden and leading the heathen out of the shadows of darkness. Imperialism, that word conjuring up such pejorative images today, was considered to be merely another way of doing the Lord's work. It was our duty to go into the tropics, capture natives, and teach them the Bible, western manners, and good hygiene. In that way, they would become better people (maybe even people who would consume our products) and we would fulfill our mission. As in the 1840s, many reformers were imperialists who saw little difference between fixing up domestic society and fixing up the world.

Some expansionists were more concerned with *Weltpolitik* than saving souls. The advocates of a "Large Policy" for America, men like Theodore Roosevelt, Admiral Alfred T. Mahan, and Henry Cabot Lodge, were generally unaffected by economic or spiritual considerations. They argued that we were entering the arena of the great powers whether we liked it or not. The communication and transportation revolutions had transformed the oceans from barriers into highways. The question could no longer be *whether* we should play the great power game, but *how* we would play it. At the turn of the century, we had to begin to play it according to the rules of the established great powers, all of whom owned empires and large military establishments. In the cutthroat international system in which survival of the fittest was the rule and war was endemic, we had to develop a mighty empire along with its trappings—or face possible extinction.

Most everyone then—businessmen, realpoliticians, reformers, missionaries, and the general public—was receptive to the idea of expansion. Though a small minority advocated the taking of whatever colonies were left in Asia and Africa, the majority of Americans considered the aping of European forms of imperialism distasteful. There was no argument, however, over the need for the United States to spread its benevolent system and cornucopia of products to all peoples. Everyone agreed on a general strategy—expansion. Tactical questions involving colonies and other tools used to facilitate expansion were left for the events themselves to decide. Such was the national consensus when the Cuban insurrection broke out in 1895. It was Spain's misfortune to be in the wrong place at the wrong time in our history.

MADRID, HAVANA, AND WASHINGTON

The Spanish government was not unaware of the mismanagement, corruption, and neglect that led Cubans to take up arms in 1895. Anticipating a new revolt, it began to modify the most objectionable of its practices in 1894. But colonial bureaucracies worked slowly and the Spanish colonial bureaucracy perhaps the slowest of all. It was one thing to recognize the problem and quite another to move the reforms from drawing boards in Madrid into operation in Havana.

The revolution began as a new government was coming to power in Spain. The government was led by Antonio Cánovas del Castillo, a familiar figure on the Spanish political scene. This conservative prime minister, who was in charge during the crucial years from 1895 to 1897, was a corrupt, self-seeking courtier who owes his place in history, if any, to his legendary amatory exploits. Bereft of a coherent program for Spain and her colonies, Cánovas tried to retain his office and little more. As for Cuba in particular (he also had to deal with a revolt in the Philippines), he hoped that his civilian administrators would appease moderate Cubans with a few reforms while his military chiefs crushed the rebels. He was more interested in the latter than the former.

The token reforms offered the rebels were too little too late, although even in 1897, Cánovas might have been able to end the war with a promise of autonomy for Cuba within the empire. To many in Spain, autonomy was synonymous with independence. If autonomy came would independence be far behind? Any politician who talked of such a drastic concession might have lost his office or worse. Cuba had become a matter of honor to Spanish elites who refused to surrender that last reminder of the glories of Philip II to scruffy guerrillas and greedy Americans. The Spanish government approached the problem of Cuba as the Mexicans had approached the problems of Texas and California 50 years earlier. Although hanging on to that ungrateful colony could lead to war with the United States, what politician would be courageous enough to surrender Spanish patrimony, even if he knew it was the only rational thing to do?

An anarchist assassinated Cánovas in August of 1897, four years before William McKinley met a similar fate. Few mourned his passing. Cánovas's regime was replaced by a Liberal government which, in the past, had appeared soft on the Cuban issue. Although the new prime minister, Praxedes Mateo Sagasta, hoped to achieve an equitable arrangement with the rebels, he would not grant them full autonomy let alone independence. Further, the Liberals bitterly resented American meddling, especially our gratuitous offers to serve as ultimate arbiter of the dispute.

Why did not the Liberals, whose hearts seemed to be in the right place, tidy things up more sensitively and speedily? First of all, and here we can think of contemporary analogies, they thought they owed something to thousands of loyalists in Cuba who might be slaughtered in a bloodbath when the rebels came to power. When, in January of 1898, rumors reached Havana suggesting that Madrid was ready to concede autonomy to the rebels, loyalists staged a series of violent antiautonomy riots. In addition, a sudden, and perhaps humiliating, peace would have been a direct insult to the Spanish Army, no mean force in the nation. From 1895 to 1898, over 50,000 soldiers had lost their lives trying to snuff out the insurrection. Could a Spanish government have allowed brave boys to die in vain? When Sagasta finally recalled "Butcher" Weyler in late 1897, the general was greeted by cheering crowds on his return to Spain. Finally, and most important, the Liberals shared the Cánovas government's conviction that in terms of national honor, Cuban independence was too heavy a price to pay for peace.

The Spanish were in a terrible bind. They could not subdue the rebels and they would not accept their demands. The longer they fought on, the more difficult it became to make peace short of independence. They also had to develop a policy acceptable to the champion of the rebels, the United States. They handled this problem in a way that would only exacerbate the already tense relations between the two countries. To American demands for peace and reform, they made a variety of promises and predictions, few of which were ever followed up. They could only temporize so long. At a certain point, the Americans had to lose faith in the Spanish ability or willingness to terminate the war in Cuba. Although by the end of 1897 it appeared that the rebels would not be soon pacified (despite confident talk from generals about light at the end of the tunnel), and although they would not voluntarily lay down their arms without independence, and although Cuba was becoming more and more an economic and political liability, and although American intervention was becoming more and more likely, the Spanish stubbornly hung on in a suicidal fashion. Like the Mexicans of the 1840s, they thought they still might have an ace up their sleeve—support from European great powers.

A NEW HOLY ALLIANCE

The year 1898 was a banner one for European plots and intrigues. The capitals of the Old World buzzed with rumors of an Anglo-German alliance, an Anglo-French war in Africa, and, of interest to us, a new continental alliance to put the United States in its place, once and for all. The European powers, especially Germany and England, were concerned about our unparalleled economic growth and bumptious diplomacy. During this period, their journalists began writing about an "American Menace" featuring the aggressive Yankees, backed by their powerful new navy, roaming the seven seas to steal European markets. As shown in our victorious diplomatic stand-down with England over the Venezuelan boundary in 1895, we were beginning to lay claim to the paramount role in the Western Hemisphere that had been ours, only rhetorically, since 1823. The idea of an anti-American concert lingered on through the early twentieth century. As late as the summer of 1914, Germans and Englishmen talked of an informal alliance to combat the pernicious Monroe Doctrine.

Although sentiment counts for little in diplomacy, we must also remember that many European leaders disliked the United States. To them, our culture was crude, materialistic, and singularly unaesthetic—we were pushy brutes who challenged the spirituality of European civilization. Conversely, while Spain was not exactly the most popular or influential European power, she was a monarchy under attack from republicans in the New World. Kaiser Wilhelm II, one of the few ruling heads who still talked of the divine right of kings, wanted to leap to Madrid's defense. Supported at least emotionally by his Catholic parties and his Navy and Colonial Leagues, he felt the Cuban issue might provide an opportunity to tender the upstart United States a lesson. He also felt that since the Americans were giving signs of moving into the British orbit, their defeat would enhance Germany's position vis-à-vis her chief rival in Europe. Given the delicate nature of Anglo-German relations in early 1898, the knight errant in Berlin was restrained by cooler heads in the Wilhelmstrasse who pressed the Austrians to broach the subject of continental assistance to the Spanish queen-regent in distress.

Emperor Franz Joseph, that incredible figure who occupied the Hapsburg throne from 1848 to 1916, was related to the Spanish queen and so appeared to be a legitimate organizer of an anti-American league. Austria-Hungary, Italy, and Spain had only recently been allied in a Mediterranean Agreement the shortsighted Spanish had allowed to lapse in 1895. Spain was on the fringes of the Triple Alliance and could have been of strategic value in case of war with an England perched precariously on the Rock of Gibraltar. Thus, the Austrians went from capital to capital trying to interest others in the plight of their Spanish cousins.

The French, who expressed interest in helping out, feared that an anti-American demonstration would propel Washington into London's open arms. Such a development would have been highly undesirable for France with the Fashoda crisis in the offing in 1898. Nicholas II of Russia, no admirer of republics, was attracted to the Austrian proposals but he also had to think twice since, at that moment, he was launching some risky Asian ventures. In the end, the only power, if we can call him that, who did anything to help the Spanish was the Pope, who asked McKinley to be moderate in his dealings with Her Catholic Majesty.

In one futile gesture, the European ambassadors in Washington went to see McKinley, five days before he asked Congress for war, to plead for a delay. This demonstration made for the record took the form of a request, not a demand. As had been the case all through the nineteenth century, no European nation was willing to extend itself by challenging the United States unless it was certain that all were prepared to do likewise. Even had they been able to get together, they could have only threatened and blustered. None would risk ships or men given the fluid situation on the continent, the primary theater.

Once again, we had Britain to thank for this situation. Her navy still controlled the Atlantic. No one could aid Spain without approval from England, the one power disinterested in starting up with us. The great Anglo-American Rapprochement, which was to leave an indelible mark on the twentieth century, was in the process of formation. Given a perceived confluence of interests between U.S. and her own foreign policies, England sat on her hands in 1898. Her helpful behavior in this crisis was remembered in the following years when it was her turn to subdue an unruly colony in South Africa. On the popular level, our sympathy went out to the Boers who were fighting against British colonialism. But American statesmen, grateful for British support in 1898, maintained a scrupulous neutrality, and thus further solidified the entente that was to flourish under the patronage of Theodore Roosevelt and William Howard Taft.

Not surprisingly, the Spanish came up empty-handed in their quixotic search for European assistance. Although they should not have expected any other response from their ungallant friends, like the Mexicans 50 years earlier, they grasped at any straw. Poorly protected by their rotting fleets and overextended armies, they had to face the bristling United States by themselves. As the Cuban war dragged on, the odds that Spain could avoid such a one-sided contest grew longer and longer. For much of the period from 1895 through 1897 (with time out for the campaign of 1896), Cuba was the most exciting issue in American politics.

THE CUBAN FEVER

The widespread and contagious Cuban Fever, as it was called, spawned many American statements of support for the brave opponents of Spanish tyranny. In the early months of the war, the A.F. of L., the Sons of the American Revolution, Civil War veterans groups, Protestant church organizations, hundreds of local and national politicians, and many thousands of ordinary Americans first warmly applauded the Cuban insurrection and then, more ominously, demanded that their government do more than just cheer for the rebels. After the first hero of the revolution was reported to have been killed under a flag of truce in 1895, 1,200 Americans stormed the Cuban Junta's recruiting office in St. Louis pleading for a chance to get at the Spanish bounders. Although few wanted their own country to enter the war then and there, citizens demanded recognition of Cuban belligerency, permission to send arms and supplies to the rebels, and a policy of official hostility to the Spanish.

From the Spanish point of view, gun-running to Cuba was not very neighborly. As in the period from 1868 to 1878, and in countless other Caribbean revolts, for financial and sometimes political reasons, Americans brought guns, ammunition, supplies, reinforcements, and a variety of other things to rebels dependent on these illegal lifelines. Although President Cleveland did his best to prevent filibustering, the Caribbean was a large sea, we had a long coastline, and only so much navy to go around. Madrid recognized our difficulties in enforcing neutrality, but with good reason accused us of the most serious sort of interference in their internal affairs.

Grover Cleveland, a lame-duck President, was plagued by the Cuban Fever during his last year and a half in office. He was especially worried about being forced to recognize the belligerency of the Cuban rebels. Such an announcement would have jeopardized our neutrality because it would have legitimized American assistance to the insurrectionists. During our own Civil War, the Union was outraged when the British recognized the belligerent status of the Confederacy. Responding to public pressure, Congress passed a joint resolution favoring the recognition of Cuban belligerency in April of 1896. Cleveland refused to implement it.

While offering lip service to the goals of Cuban freedom from 1895 to 1897, he and his Secretary of State were no friends of the rebels. They privately maintained that a free Cuba would be a chaotic place, an easy mark for some European nation more powerful than the Spanish. Even without a challenge to the Monroe Doctrine, a free Cuba would become a haven for intriguers who had made neighboring Haiti and Santo Domingo such unstable and violent places. McKinley later employed a comparable line to explain why it would be dangerous to free the Philippines.

More immediately, those with financial stakes in Cuba, the planters and merchants, opposed the rebel movement and were supportive of the Spanish government with which they could do business. Although nothing ever came of it, Cleveland even toyed with the idea of helping the Spanish to pacify their island.

To be fair to him, he contended he could not recognize Cuban belligerency because we had to maintain our neutrality in case we were able to bring both sides together for impartial mediation. A premature recognition of Cuban rights would have made our mediation unacceptable to Madrid.

As the months went by, as the intensity and brutality of the war increased, and as growing numbers of Americans called upon Cleveland to do something, he became more and more exasperated with the Spanish. His exasperation did not stem from any love for the rag-tag guerrillas. He was upset because the clumsy Spanish could not suppress their little revolt. By the time he left the Presidency, Cleveland was fed up with the Spanish whose inefficient policies had created a political issue that added to his woes during the depression year of 1896.

Had Cleveland stayed on through 1898, he probably would have done pretty much what McKinley did. American policy from 1895 through 1898, despite the change in parties in 1897, can be viewed as a continuum as we became progressively angry with the Spanish and sympathetic toward the rebels. Although the sentimental McKinley talked a little more about atrocities and was more interested than Cleveland in finding a solution acceptable to the Cuban people, there was no clear break between the official policies of the Cleveland and McKinley administrations.

A SECOND LINCOLN

In the days before he assumed office, William McKinley was hailed as a second Lincoln. A giant would again walk the halls of the White House (figuratively speaking for McKinley was a short, chunky man who looked more like Napoleon than Lincoln). McKinley did not come close to greatness in his Presidency. One of his sympathetic biographers agrees but points out that the tragic hero was planning dramatic new programs for his second term that was cut short by an assassin's bullet in 1901.

McKinley came from a relatively poor family from Ohio, a state that played a role in the nineteenth century not unlike that played by Virginia during our early years. His education was interrupted by the Civil War, one of the most profound events in his life during which he experienced war firsthand: a bloody heart-wrenching war pitting American against American. McKinley's experiences at the front, which he talked about frequently in later years, colored his notions about the efficacy of war as a means of solving disputes. Only after he convinced himself that he could save more lives by going to war in 1898 than by remaining at peace was he able to lead his country into another battle.

The Civil War shaped his life in a practical way as well. A good soldier who rose from commissary sergeant to staff officer by war's end, McKinley caught the eye of fellow Ohioan General Rutherford B. Hayes, who was elected President in 1876. Hayes supported McKinley's political ambitions after the latter read law in the late 1860s. Entering politics in Canton, McKinley held a congressional seat from 1877 to 1883 and from 1885 to 1891 when, after a third gerrymandering of his district, the Democrats succeeded in retiring him. It was not for long though, for he won the governorship of Ohio in 1891 and was reelected in 1893.

Like Polk, who also spent his political life in the House of Representatives and state politics, McKinley had no real diplomatic experience. His most important substantive interest in the House was the tariff which did relate to other countries, but it is doubtful that McKinley ever gave foreign affairs much thought. Moreover, as Polk had grown to political maturity during the diplomatically quiet years from 1825 to 1840, McKinley developed during the even quieter years of the 1870s and 1880s when foreign policy was obscure and unimportant.

As a professional politician, he was a smashing success. Congenial, patient, sympathetic, yet shrewd, he was the sort of fellow whom everyone liked. He appears even more admirable when we consider his private life. His wife was sick through most of their marriage, and perhaps mentally unbalanced, his two daughters died at an early age, and he faced personal bankruptcy in 1893. Through it all, he maintained a cheerful demeanor that struck his friends as most remarkable.

He weathered his many personal storms so well because of a deep commitment to his God whom he often called upon for guidance in matters of state. Today, we would probably greet such public religiosity with skepticism. In the 1890s, not only was McKinley's faith believable to many but it was also seen as genuine. That is, when he announced that the Lord had advised him to take the Philippines in the summer of 1898, he was convinced that he had received divine inspiration. Naturally, the fact that one professes to act in the name of the Lord is no guarantee of righteous behavior. It is important, nonetheless, to understand that for the majority of Americans, McKinley was the moral leader of the nation. His honesty, sincerity, and generosity were virtually unchallenged.

McKinley's religiosity does not seem to mesh with his political career. He was an extremely partisan leader in an extremely partisan age. Today, we are amused by broadsides warning that the security, stability, and even survival of the nation depended upon the victory of the Republican Party. Yet many intelligent and sophisticated people accepted this line. Theodore Roosevelt, for example, was always a firm believer in the superiority of the principles of the Republican Party. We must remember that the Spanish-American War came on the heels of one of few allegedly, ideological Presidential campaigns in our history. Never mind that William Jennings Bryan, McKinley's Democratic rival, was a conservative fellow. At the time, the majority of voters believed that McKinley and his Republicans stood for the American Way under assault from Bryan's armies of have-nots, the poor, socialists, and radicals. McKinley's constant concern for the future of his party did not necessarily represent narrow partisanship. For many Americans, my party right or wrong was synonymous with my country right or wrong.

Although a strong political and moral leader, McKinley has been considered a weak President. Such a characterization is not fair. Compared to Theodore Roosevelt and Woodrow Wilson, McKinley looks weak; compared to his post-Civil War predecessors, he appears vigorous. In the late nineteenth century, most American politicians accepted congressional supremacy. McKinley, who did assert himself on occasion, may be said to have been among the strongest of the weak Presidents.

He appears to have been weaker than he was because of his fabled reliance upon Ohio businessman Mark Hanna, head of a sprawling company that has produced several generations of influential Republicans. According to critics, McKinley made nary a move without the tug on his strings from the puppet master behind the curtain. Hanna was a political genius whose wealth and connections contributed to his friend's success. However, in their personal relationship, McKinley was the equal if not the superior to Hanna. Of course, the fact that so many contemporary observers perceived their respective roles in a different light must have had some effect on the President who may have felt the need to be more assertive.

He had no trouble asserting himself in his Cabinet since many of its members were almost senile. Among the most doddering was his Secretary of State, John Sherman, who left the Senate to make room for Hanna. Sherman was replaced in 1898 by William Day who in turn was replaced, after the war was over, by John Hay, one of our most famous Secretaries of State. McKinley was little concerned about the effectiveness of his Secretary of State since he planned to make the important decisions himself. He had the wisdom to select Stewart Woodford, a perceptive and sensitive man, for the Madrid ministry. Enjoying the confidence of his hosts, Woodford kept McKinley well-informed about the labyrinthian complexities of Spanish politics.

Upon taking office, the President sent a personal envoy to Cuba to survey the situation. The story his agent brought back, a story of death, destruction, and protracted conflict, worried McKinley for both personal and political reasons. In his first official statement on Cuba in May of 1897, he temporarily assuaged moderate hawks by asking for an appropriation of $50,000 for the relief of Americans who had suffered losses during the revolution. Privately, in late June, he urged the Spanish to offer meaningful reforms to the Cubans and to end the war quickly—he and the American people would not tolerate much more bloodshed and violence. This was the first of several private messages McKinley sent to Woodford for transmission to the Spanish government. Through 1897 and on into the early part of 1898, his dialogue with the Spanish was private for the most part. He did not speak out on Cuba because he hoped to remain above the domestic debate and also because he felt that such a delicate problem was best handled through diplomatic channels. Noble though such sentiments may seem, his virtual silence on the Cuban issue through March of 1898 allowed less honorable figures to fill the foreign policy information-education vacuum.

The Spanish replied to McKinley's first warning and plea in late August, almost two months after they received it. Throughout this crisis, their diplomats rarely moved with speed to respond to him. Such nonchalance was not due entirely to sloth. Since McKinley's interventions were very difficult to handle, his opposite numbers in Madrid hoped to delay as long as possible the moment when they had to convey a reply they knew would be unsatisfactory. In the case of his first message, they told him to mind his own business and order would soon be restored. Further warnings and threats were met in November by a promise from the Queen of sweeping reforms and peace. Temporarily satisfied, McKinley told the nation in his State of the Union Address late in 1897 that he was pleased to see that the Spanish appeared to be moving toward peace, but he included in his conciliatory remarks a veiled threat to the effect that they had better be serious. Alas, the Queen never effected her promised reforms. By the end of that year, after nine months of dealing with Madrid, McKinley had good reason to question Spain's credibility as well her ability to terminate hostilities in Cuba.

REMEMBER THE *MAINE*, TO HELL WITH SPAIN

As the insurrection dragged on into 1898, Spanish-American relations continued to deteriorate. Yet war appeared to be far off until two incidents forced McKinley's hand. The first incident, the less important of the two, involved the purloined de Lôme letter. Enrique Dupuy de Lôme, the Spanish minister in

Washington and a die-hard supporter of a Spanish Cuba, was
furious with McKinley whom he considered foolish and inept.
In a private letter to a friend in Havana, he referred to the
President as "weak and a bidder for the admiration of the
crowd." Most likely, hundreds of dispatches and letters sent out
from scores of legations each week contained language much
stronger than de Lôme's but his fell into the wrong hands. A
rebel agent intercepted it in a Havana post office and sent it to
William Randolph Hearst who published the offensive letter on
February 9.

De Lôme's resignation did not appease Americans who rallied
around the President. Bryan and his friends might refer to
McKinley with scurrilous language, but not a foreigner. As one
bit of doggerel threatened,

> Dupuy de Lôme, Dupuy de Lôme, what's this I hear of you?
> Have you been throwing mud again, is what they're saying true?
> Get out, I say, get out, before I start a fight.
> Just pack your few possessions and take a boat for home,
> I would not like my boot to use, but—oh—get out, de Lôme.

By itself, the de Lôme affront was not that serious but it came
only a week before the major incident of the prewar period, the
sinking of the *Maine*. The *U.S.S. Maine* had been dispatched to
Havana harbor in January for a so-called goodwill visit and also
to provide refuge for Americans who might have to flee in a
hurry. Or at least that was the story we gave the Spanish. Even
though they correctly interpreted the visit of the *Maine* as an
attempt by the muscle-flexing United States to pressure them,
the Spanish did not take official umbrage at her presence. By no
stretch of the imagination can the dispatch of the *Maine* to
Cuba be compared with the dispatch of General Taylor to the
Rio Grande in 1846.

On February 15, the *Maine* blew up and 260 American sailors
lost their lives. Almost everyone in the United States assumed
that the Spanish were responsible. Although at the time we had
no evidence of their culpability and although naval officers on

the scene cautioned against jumping to conclusions, few doubted that Madrid had perpetrated the deed. No evidence was needed for who else could have done it?

One can now think of several explanations for the still-unsolved mystery of the *Maine.* She might have suffered an internal explosion caused by a faulty boiler or a careless smoker. A preliminary Spanish investigation reported that the explosion was of internal origin. An American board of inquiry, following on the heels of the Spanish board, determined that the *Maine* had experienced some sort of external damage. Someone or something had blown her up, she did not blow herself up. Still, there was no reason to reject summarily the Spanish claim in February of 1898 since the assessment of blame for the explosion was obviously a tricky technical problem.

Even if our board of inquiry's report, made public on March 28, was correct, could not the *Maine* have been blown up by *agents provocateurs* from the rebel camp who wanted to enrage Americans? Or perhaps it was blown up by a crazed loyalist who had no relationship to Spanish authorities in Havana? Or finally, the *Maine* might have collided with a mine that had broken loose from its moorings in Havana harbor. If it was a mine, then the explosion was an accident and certainly no direct fault of the Spanish.

The accident thesis is most credible today since the crime, if that is what it was, is still unsolved. Is it not likely that someone, somewhere, by now would have made a death-bed confession or released documents to implicate human beings in the incident? Does not the absence of one shred of evidence over 80 years after the act strengthen the case for an accident? In 1898, contemporary observers were unable to make such a judgment. Nevertheless, had they stopped to think about it, a Spanish attack on the *Maine* was illogical.

The last thing Madrid wanted was to provoke a war with the United States. The blowing up of the *Maine* was about the only thing they could do to guarantee such a war. They had no conceivable strategic or tactical reason to attack the vessel. We had many more ships where the *Maine* came from and many more able-bodied seamen eager to avenge the deaths of their comrades.

Few in this country accepted Spanish denials of misbehavior. The President himself, the moral leader of the nation, who should have known better, and probably did, went along with the crowd that thirsted for Spanish blood. McKinley argued that anything that happened in Havana harbor was ultimately Spain's responsibility and that the sinking of the *Maine* demonstrated the sort of chaos that flourished under Spanish misrule.

We did not go to war over the sinking of the *Maine.* While shocking and outrageous, the incident did not have the effect of Pearl Harbor or the Rio Grande attacks. But it was the last straw for Americans and McKinley. In the days following the sinking, the demand for retribution guaranteed that any decision for war with Spain would be a popular one. We can only feel sorry for the Spanish (if we can feel sorry for anyone fighting a counterrevolutionary war) who did not know how to atone for their alleged attack upon the U.S. Navy. Undoubtedly, they lost any confidence they might have had in the fair-mindedness of American leaders who allowed their public to believe such a far-fetched story of Spanish adventurism.

The question of our fair-mindedness, however, should not have affected their response to our secret offer to buy Cuba forwarded to Madrid in the wake of the *Maine* affair. McKinley was willing to pay the Spanish $300 million and was prepared to throw in a few million dollars worth of gifts for the negotiators. Although the Queen was attracted to the proposition, no Spanish politician would touch the ignoble deal. And so the stage was set for McKinley's ultimatum to Madrid. Refusal of the ultimatum meant war, a war Sagasta knew he could not win. The Spanish were led to believe otherwise. Because of the exigencies of domestic politics, Sagasta had not informed them of the seriousness of their predicament and, if anything, inflated their confidence in the ability of their armed forces to handle the United States.

McKINLEY'S ULTIMATUM

On March 27, 1898, McKinley gave the Spanish one last chance to tidy up the Cuban mess according to our wishes before we tidied it up for them. On that day, he issued an ultimatum he did not expect would be accepted.

First, he demanded that the Spanish close their concentration camps, launch a relief program, and treat Cuban noncombattants with decency.

Second, he demanded that the Spanish arrange a six-month armistice during which time they and the rebels would negotiate a peace.

Finally, and this third point was not as clearly drawn as the first two, if the belligerents did not resolve their dispute by October 1, the end of the six-month armistice period, the Spanish had to accept the arbitration of the United States.

On the face of it, we can sympathize with the Spanish who could ask in whose name and with what legal authority did the United States make such demands upon another sovereign state? What went on in Cuba was an internal Spanish matter. As we have learned, to talk about legal bases for international behavior is sophistry. We were 90 miles from Cuba, intensely interested and involved in the insurrection, and had the army and navy to back up our interest. That was all we needed to issue such an ultimatum. The Spanish government knew we meant business and that we were itching for an opportunity to bloody our shiny new swords. It also expected to come out on the short end of a war against the United States.

On April 1, the Spanish agreed to offer more relief and reform to the Cubans and to end reconcentration, a partial response to McKinley's first point. Three days later we told them that this was not enough. With unaccustomed speed, they offered a dramatic concession on April 9 when they agreed to our demand for an immediate armistice. They never did get around to replying to our demand for American arbitration after October 1. They could read between the lines. American arbitration meant Cuban independence. Why would the rebels negotiate in good faith if they knew that after October 1 William McKinley would decide their fate? Given the widespread support for Cuban independence in the United States by 1898, for any American arbitrator to grant the rebels less would have been difficult.

The Spanish acceptance of parts of McKinley's ultimatum represented a victory for the United States. Having received affirmative responses to two out of three of his demands, and not having received a definite rejection of the fuzzier third, McKinley could have waited out Madrid. Although Minister Woodford was not sanguine about the prospects of the Spanish acceding completely to McKinley's ultimatum, he urged the President to give them a little more time. McKinley and the rest of the nation were too impatient for such restraint. In terms of the historical record, then, even if we argue that the Spanish never would have accepted American mediation, we looked a little too eager for war. We did not give them enough time and, even more damning, McKinley was apparently unmoved by Spain's concessions on his first two points.

He prepared his war message on April 6 after receiving the first concession but before receiving the second one. The message itself was presented to Congress on April 11, two days after the armistice ultimatum had been virtually accepted. The content and tone of his message demonstrated that the President was no longer interested in the ultimatum.

If anything, the Spanish embarrassed McKinley by appearing conciliatory. He was able to rationalize ignoring their concessions by convincing himself that they had not gone far enough and that, in any event, they would never grant Cuba independence. In his message, McKinley outlined the horrors of the insurrection, Spanish outrages perpetrated against Americans and their property, the disruption of Cuban-American commerce, and how our strategic position was being undermined by the turbulence in the Caribbean. Only in the last paragraph of his address, in a matter-of-fact way, did he inform Congress that the Spanish had accepted some of his demands. Not many heard that part of the speech so carried away were they with his call to arms. Had he begun with a careful discussion of recent diplomatic events, Americans might have responded differently to the crisis. Instead of headlines screaming "President Asks for War" the headlines might have been, "Madrid Closes Camps and Accepts Armistice." Why did the usually temperate McKinley behave in such an unreasonable way when he transmitted his message to Congress on April 11?

McKINLEY'S DECISION

McKinley's decision to go to war in 1898 is more difficult to explain than Polk's but easier to explain than Madison's. We do know that the domestic political debate over Cuba had gotten out of hand. McKinley's Olympian silence through early 1898 had allowed jingoes to capitalize on the *Maine* and other atrocity stories. Eager for a campaign issue after their bitter defeat in 1896, Democratic defenders of Cuban liberty demanded to know why McKinley and his party were not doing more to alleviate Spanish oppression and brutality. Although sophisticated polling techniques were unavailable to them, both Democratic and Republican politicians realized that the public thrived on such rhetoric. Unless McKinley made some dramatic move, the Republicans would have been left holding the bag as opponents of Cuban freedom. So many Republicans jumped aboard the Democratic war wagon that Congress might have even declared war without the President asking for it.

A partisan politician and firm believer in the superiority of the principles of the Grand Old Party, McKinley had to protect his flanks. Congressional elections were only seven months away. As he confided to a friend, "If peace negotiations had been prolonged, the Republican Party would have been divided, the Democrats would have been united, nothing would have been done, and our party would have been overwhelmed in November." Did McKinley go to war to save the Republican Party?

There are two issues here, both of which can be interpreted in a manner generous to McKinley. Convinced that Democratic programs would be disastrous for the country, he had to save the Republicans at the polls by allowing them to ride the crest of the wave of pro-Cuban sentiment. In addition, and this was not articulated at the time, a congressional declaration of war without a prior Presidential request could have set a dangerous precedent. Such rationales can be developed for almost any sort of partisan behavior. They must be looked at skeptically.

The matter of causation here is much more complicated than the relationship of party considerations and elections to the Cuban insurrection. Playing no mean role in shifting the congressional balance toward war was Senator Redfield Proctor, a respected leader who toured Cuba in early March. In a major address on March 17, Proctor told his colleagues what he had seen. Many in the hushed audience were moved by his depressing picture of destruction and chaos on that unhappy island. No jingo, although a quiet expansionist, Proctor suggested that something had to be done to end the bloodshed and, as far as he could see, the United States was the only likely peacemaker. Many Congressmen, as well as other influential Americans uncertain about intervention, were allegedly pushed over the brink by Proctor's sober account.

Proctor was not enough for everybody, especially an unsentimental business community without which a President would probably not make a major foreign policy decision. McKinley was especially beholden to the eastern establishment of industrialists and financiers who had bankrolled his campaign against the "socialist" Bryan. From 1895 through 1897, business leaders were predominantly on the side of the doves. Indeed, whenever rumors of interventionist programs were reported in the media, stock market averages tumbled. Businessmen had cogent reasons to oppose American involvement: 1897 was the first year of full recovery from the crippling depression of 1893; exports were booming again; and most segments of the economy were performing well. A war might have threatened this new stability and endangered our merchant marine. In addition, it was widely believed that war would necessitate huge federal expenditures and thus an expansion of our currency. Since the supply of gold was limited, the government might have had to begin coining silver again—silver being anathema to the gold bugs of Wall Street.

Not everyone in the business community was dovish. From the start, a small minority of American businessmen wanted Washington to do something about the war. Those who had a financial interest in the war-ravaged Cuban economy urged Cleveland and McKinley to intervene—but not on the side of the rebels. Americans had invested around $50 million in Cuban properties, and those who owned sugar plantations were especially concerned about the guerrillas' pyromania. The total trade between Cuba and the United States amounted to $100 million a year, a not insignificant amount. Some in the rebel leadership appeared to be rather radical in their approach to future Cuba-American financial ties. Following the nationalist program of the martyred José Marti, these leaders threatened not only to win independence from Spain but also to throw American capital out of their country. American intervention before independence was achieved might guarantee the more exploitative development of a "free" Cuba. Still, since the number of influential businessmen involved in Cuban enterprises was relatively small, their voices were drowned out by the rest of their colleagues who demanded a hands-off policy, at least until 1898.

In March of 1898, after the *Maine,* prominent members of the business community began to come around to the idea that some sort of intervention in Cuba would not be a bad idea. Their about-face can be attributed to several fast-breaking events. First (and leaving aside the fact that they were human beings who were affected by Proctor's report just like everyone else), the Anglo-American Arbitration Treaty of 1897 underlined the growing friendship between the two English-speaking nations and thus served as a symbolic protection for our ships in case of war with Spain. Second, the discovery of gold in Alaska meant that the war could be financed with gold—there was no reason to bring silver or inflation into the matter. Finally, and most important, as the nation teetered on the brink of indecision in the winter of 1897-1898, the business community did not know which way to leap. War would seriously affect their plans for production, plant expansion, marketing, and a host of financial considerations that had to be settled quickly. Many businesses had already delayed making those decisions for an inordinately long period of time. Tired of treading water, they decided that we had to get on with the war so they could plan for the coming year.

Was this shift in business attitudes instrumental in McKinley's ultimate decision? Although we will never know for certain, some things are clear. Obviously, a conservative President could not have moved into war unless he knew the industrial barons were in his corner. An anxious McKinley asked an agent in New York to survey business opinion in the weeks after the *Maine*. On March 25, the President received the telegraphed report, "Big corporations here now believe all would welcome it [war] as a relief to suspense." McKinley sent his ultimatum to Spain two days later. Circumstantial evidence, yes, but we must consider it in trying to explain McKinley's behavior in late March of 1898.

The role of the business community may not be that nefarious. This case demonstrates that it could not control the public through its alleged domination of politicians and mass media, for when it reluctantly opted for war, the community appeared to be reacting to independent political and public pressure. Crude Marxist models of decision making in a capitalist polity would seem to be invalidated, at least in this instance.

And so we are brought back to the public and the politicians, infected with nationalist fever, who propelled McKinley, along with the businessmen, into war with Spain. It might well have been that McKinley and his Wall Street allies had the power to keep us out of war but did not use it. McKinley especially appears to have abnegated his role as leader when he allowed hotbloods to distort the issues and inflame the public. Those who defend his decision contend that he had no other choice.

He had to respond to the public's demands. Nevertheless, by not educating and informing the public in 1897 and early 1898, he closed off his options, unless he was prepared to face defeat in the congressional elections in November.

From his point of view, this was not necessarily an undesirable way to run the nation. Talking often of the need for leaders to respond to the voice of the people, McKinley claimed that none of his major decisions was made until he listened to his constituents (as well as to the Lord). For example, he decided to take the Philippines only after he "felt" a groundswell of support for such an action. This is not much of a defense. In early 1898, the people had been misled by demagogues and sensation-seeking journalists who filled the gap McKinley vacated. When he finally entered the picture, he had no one to blame but himself for the shrill war hoops that compelled him to ask for war.

We can see how a sensitive man might have convinced himself that the people and their representatives were correct and that war, even for those who remembered the carnage of the 1860s, was an appropriate response in April of 1898. Had the United States not gone to war to end the Cuban-Spanish contest (a war to end war), more Cubans and Spaniards would have been killed, more children orphaned, and more homes and villages destroyed. McKinley's decision for war, supported by almost all Americans, was based, at least in part, upon humanitarian considerations.

CONGRESS DISPOSES

In his message on April 11, McKinley did not quite ask for a declaration of war against Spain. He merely outlined the intolerable situation in Cuba and requested the powers necessary to terminate the insurrection on a basis favorable to both Cubans and Americans. Theoretically, we did not have to go to war against Spain in order to accomplish this feat. Some of McKinley's advisors, as well as Congressmen, thought that we might somehow land in Cuba, establish ourselves between the

contending sides, and enforce a cease-fire. In military and politi- ·
cal terms, such a plan would have been more difficult to
accomplish than the parting of the Red Sea.

The resolutions Congress passed on April 19, in response to
McKinley's message, offered the Spanish a final opportunity to
escape war with the United States. They merely declared that
Cuba should be independent, that Spain should withdraw from
the island, and that the President could take the necessary
military and naval measures to accomplish those feats.
McKinley signed the resolutions on April 20 and sent them
along to the Spanish with a deadline of April 23. If they agreed
to pull out by that date, McKinley would not launch hostilities.
According to international mores, no self-respecting power
could have afforded to surrender to our demands. Spain did not
honor McKinley's new ultimatum with a reply. On April 25,
Congress declared that a state of war had existed between the
two countries as of April 21.

The original resolutions were approved overwhelmingly by
the House by a vote of 311 to 6 and by the Senate, 68 to 21.
The difference between the number of dissenters in the two
houses, a difference comparable to that seen in 1812, demonstrates the closer relationship between the Representatives and
their jingoistic constituents.

Little is to be learned from an analysis of the party break-
downs on the war resolution. McKinley's request was not met
with partisan haggling. Indeed, 19 of the 21 Senators who voted
in the minority in the Senate were Republicans. More interesting and suggestive was the battle over the Turpie Amendment to
the war resolution that recognized the independence of Cuba.
McKinley and his congressional allies defeated the amendment
by arguing that it would have been improper for us to recognize
the rebels as the government of Cuba before free elections had
been held. We would recognize Cuban independence once the
war was over and the citizens of Cuba were able to vote for
their representatives. To allay suspicions that we coveted Cuba
for ourselves, the administration supported the Teller Amend-

ment calling for the ultimate recognition of Cuban independence and renouncing American interest in taking the island.

We recognized Cuba as a sovereign nation in 1902, four years after the end of the war, but only after the Cubans included the onerous Platt Amendment in their new constitution. Several features of that amendment, which was not freely accepted, made the island a protectorate of the United States. Considering this outcome, as well as our hesitancy to endorse Cuban independence in 1898, one might question the selfless nature of our entry into war. We can argue, as the Republicans did, that the Platt Amendment was crammed down the Cubans' throats for their own good—politically inexperienced, they needed our benevolent protection from foreign interventions and violent revolutions. Naturally, since Cuba lay astride the sea-lanes to our proposed isthmian canal, it was in our interest that she remain stable, quiet, and pro-American. The latter criterion seemed threatened by nationalist reformers in the rebel van. The fact that we did not just take Cuba, as Americans had urged throughout the nineteenth century, astonished Europeans. Perhaps we were not as naive as cynical imperialists thought. A protectorate may have represented the best of all possible worlds. We were free from daily responsibilities and expenses of running a colony while the Platt Amendment protected our strategic and economic interests.

We will never know whether McKinley and his advisors were planning a protectorate status for Cuba when they defeated the Turpie Amendment. If they were, then our entry into war must be cast in a different light. Compelling evidence of such prescience on their part has yet to be discovered. Moreover, his strange performance in the Philippines suggests that strategic planning was not one of McKinley's long suits.

A PLOT TO TAKE THE PHILIPPINES?

The defeat of the Turpie Amendment was not the only funny business in the story of our entry into the war. Returning briefly to our discussion of the economic milieu of the mid-1890s, we know that American businessmen were searching for foreign markets, especially in the Pacific. China, that huge commercial prize, lay open to any aggressive trader who possessed ships and way stations to the Orient. We had secured the northern link to the Orient in 1867 with the purchase of Alaska (the Aleutian chain extends far out into the Pacific) and Midway Island, and we finally annexed Hawaii during the Spanish-American War, along with Guam. None of these bases could compare in strategic importance with the Philippine archipelago, only 400 miles from China. In a coincidence almost too good to be true, the Spanish faced colonial insurrection in the Philippines from 1896 through 1898. Although they succeeded in buying off its leader in 1897, the revolt still smouldered in remote islands as the Spanish prepared to do battle with the United States in the spring of 1898.

Add to this background the role played by arch-expansionist Theodore Roosevelt, then-Assistant Secretary of the Navy, and you have the makings of a first-rate conspiracy. In the weeks before the outbreak of war and, conveniently, during a period when his sick and addled superior was away from his desk, Roosevelt issued secret orders to the commander of our Far Eastern fleet, Admiral George Dewey, to attack the Spanish fleet in the Philippines if and when war was declared. Dewey did his job well and easily sunk most of the shabby Spanish fleet. When the war ended, we retained the Philippines as a colonial possession, a status she enjoyed until 1946. Superficially, we seem to have a case of déjà vu. The Spanish-American War seems to be a simple story of a war over Cuba (Texas) to get the Philippines (California).

Would that we could explain the war so neatly. Under close scrutiny, the story just does not hold up. Roosevelt's famous secret orders were not that secret. They were approved both by the Secretary of the Navy upon his return to the department and by President McKinley and his advisors in the White House. The securing of Manila Bay had been an integral part of the Navy's contingency planning since 1897—it was not Roosevelt's idea at all. Tactically, Dewey's attack made good sense, especially since the Navy knew it could gain an easy victory and some glory. Although there was no chance that the Spanish Asian squadron could make it around the world to help out in the Caribbean, it could have attacked our Asian commerce. Prudence called for the destruction of the Spanish fleet in Manila Bay.

As noted by those alleged expansionists, Admiral Mahan and Henry Cabot Lodge, our interposition in the Philippines could be used as a bargaining chip in the peace negotiations. Dewey's victory increased the pressure on Madrid to accede to American demands in the Caribbean before they lost everything. Well into the war, neither Lodge nor Mahan supported the idea of the permanent retention of the Philippines.

If there was some plot here, the conspirators were adept at obfuscation. For example, official records suggest that for two to three weeks, Washington had no Philippines policy. Dewey's naval victory was not immediately followed up by an attack upon the colony proper. He controlled Manila Bay while Spanish administrators went on about their chores in Manila itself, unhindered by the Americans with whom they were officially at war. When an occupation force was finally dispatched from the United States, its commander was not given his orders until almost the last moment. McKinley apparently could not make up his mind about the exact role he wanted our troops to play. Similarly, by the time McKinley got around to issuing instructions to his peace commissioners concerning the Philippines, they were already in Paris. In addition, those instructions kept on changing, as first he told them to bargain for Manila, then a few weeks later for Luzon, and finally for the whole archipelago. If there was a conspiracy afoot, McKinley went to incredible lengths to cover his tracks.

Moving back in time a bit, no evidence exists to show that officials in the State or Navy Departments had designs on the Philippines before 1898. Furthermore, an examination of the newspapers and magazines of the prewar period reveals that few journalists ever wrote about the Philippines, and those that did discuss the obscure islands were unaware of any conspiracy to make them American. This lack of journalistic interest was maintained until Dewey's victory when people began to say to themselves, "Hey, wait a minute, it looks like we can have the Philippines." Such a prospect then became attractive to businessmen, strategists, and missionaries who had not given the idea any thought until our navy created the power vacuum in the Pacific.

To those who believe in the relative omniscience of their government, as well as in its byzantine plans and conspiracies, such lack of foresight seems incredible. But that is apparently the way it happened. We went to war over the Cuban issue. In the process, we discovered that we could also pick up an Asian colony that had not even been a gleam in McKinley's eyes on April 11, 1898. To believe otherwise, we would have to accept the existence of a major conspiracy in which the President and his agents successfully hid the truth from historians who were fooled into thinking that we naively blundered into the Philippines. Interpretations of McKinley's motivations in the spring of 1898 must affect the analysis of the relationship between our entry into war and national security.

NATIONAL SECURITY AND THE SPANISH-AMERICAN WAR

The Spanish-American War may be one of those wars that resists an analysis based upon a national security framework. If everyone from the President down to the public initially conceived of the war as a military mission of mercy, then any discussion of its national security implications should be irrelevant. Yet we argued earlier that the only justification for going to war is a threat to national security. Consequently, we must determine if we were threatened in 1898.

Did Spain pose a direct military threat? Although once war had broken out, a few nervous inhabitants of eastern seaboard cities girded themselves for an assault, Spain posed no danger to our territories. Her navy was rotting, her army was little better, and both faced enormous logistic disadvantages. Furthermore, with our emerging friend England the gatekeeper of the Atlantic, Spain was unable to round up allies.

It was true that even before the war started, the Spanish were responsible for attacks on Americans and their properties in Cuba. That is, the rebels, whom they were unable to control, burned cane fields and occasionally injured our citizens. Clearly, we cannot equate such disturbances in a foreign country, albeit one close to our shores, with a military attack upon the United States.

On the other hand, the threat becomes a bit more ominous when we examine the long-range strategic picture. Continued Spanish control of an island so close to our prospective isthmian canal, coupled with their friendship with unsavory members of the Triple Alliance, suggested that some day in the not-too-distant future Cuba might have fallen into the hands of a formidable opponent. Had Germany come over to give the Spanish a hand, perhaps in exchange for a naval base, our strategic position could have been weakened. To make this argument more contemporary, Fidel Castro posed no real military threat until powerful friends equipped him with missiles to reach our shores. At that point, according to crisis managers in the Kennedy administration, Cuba became an imminent threat. Of course, such a demarche was unlikely at the turn of the century given the European powers' proclivity to tread lightly in the Caribbean. Even blustery Kaiser Wilhelm II had come to respect the inviolability of the Monroe Doctrine.

As for economics and national security, some Americans were hurt by the Cuban-Spanish struggle. Cuba was our most important Latin American trading partner. Her war disrupted normal commerce and sugar production. Nevertheless, in terms of our overall economy, the loss of the Cuban market was of only marginal importance. In fact, we probably would have done better in economic terms with a Spanish Cuba than with a truly independent Cuba.

More generally, few American businessmen doubted that we had to expand externally in order to solve our economic problems. Such expansion called for the control of all areas adjacent to our proposed canal. Turbulence in the Caribbean might have ultimately affected foreign trade that was deemed necessary to our national survival. Such an argument makes little sense today and, even during the period, advocates of intervention did not use it. The relationship between a rebellion in Cuba and world markets was too tenuous to be taken seriously.

The question of honor and prestige is more complicated. Since Americans abroad were being assaulted, McKinley had to show that he could protect his citizens, as well as his navy, from the ravages of war. However, as we have seen, the most serious attack on our honor, the sinking of the *Maine,* may not have been of Spanish origin, and certainly was not considered by other nations to have been an insult. In any event, since we entered the war primarily to free the Cubans, the issue of our defense of property and international rights was a subsidiary one.

In a broad sense, we had recently laid claim to dominance in the Caribbean and Latin America north of Venezuela. Allegedly, the eyes of the world were on us, our new navy, and our industrial machine. Did we have the will to use them or were we all bluster and paper bullets? Perhaps the great powers might have given some thought to challenging our rights here had we not shown them that we meant business when we booted Spain out of the hemisphere.

Such a rationale for our entry into the war sounds plausible, except for the fact that few Europeans looked at us in that fashion in 1898. Our reputation would have suffered little had we somehow stayed out of the Cuban affair. After all, we had made our point with the British in 1895 in Venezuela; that vigorous diplomacy served notice that we could assert ourselves and get away with it. To the Europeans, our great white fleet and steel production spoke more eloquently of our power than any little war we might have fought in Cuba.

Nonetheless, it is clear that questions of honor, prestige, and even mission justified the war not only for the United States but for Spain as well. The *International Herald Tribune* told its readers on September 27, 1898, as the war came to an end:

> The object of every war by a Republic should be, not war for its own sake, but the promotion of liberty and a satisfactory peace on that basis at the earliest moment. The fate of the war has been hard for Spain but she has met her fate bravely. When her fleet was either destroyed or badly damaged, the outcome was clear. *Her honor is saved.* Peace can now be formally declared [italics added].

BIBLIOGRAPHY

For a broad introduction to the era, Ernest R. May's *Imperial Democracy: The Emergence of America as a Great Power* (New York: Harcourt Brace Jovanovich, 1961) has stood the test of time. Several years later, the same author imaginatively employed theories of opinion analysts to explain how it was that the nation went to war in 1898. In *American Imperialism: A Speculative Essay* (New York: Atheneum, 1968), May argues that a temporary breakdown in elite consensus contributed significantly to the McKinley administration's decision for war. H. Wayne Morgan's *America's Road to Empire: The War with Spain and Overseas Expansion* (New York: John Wiley, 1965) is a valuable, brief synthetic work. A study critical of McKinley and our entry into war is Walter Karp's *The Politics of War: The Study of Two Wars Which Altered Forever the Political Life of the American Republic (1890-1920)* (New York: Harper's, 1979). Karp maintains that McKinley and the Republican Party carefully planned the entry into war for domestic political purposes.

One of the first products of the University of Wisconsin's revisionist school, and one of the best, is Walter LaFeber's *The New Empire: An Interpretation of American Expansion, 1860-1898* (Ithaca, NY: Cornell University Press, 1963) which stresses the perceived needs of American capitalists as the prime cause of expansion and intervention in the 1890s.

A companion volume that concentrates on Asian markets is Thomas J. McCormick's *China Market: America's Quest for Informal Empire, 1893-1901* (Chicago: Quadrangle, 1967). Critical of American expansion but not as monocausal is David Healy's *U.S. Expansionism: The Imperialist Urge in the 1890's* (Madison: University of Wisconsin Press, 1970). An older, oft-cited work is Julius Pratt's *Expansionists of 1898* (Baltimore: John Hopkins University Press, 1936) that concentrates on Hawaii and the Philippines.

For the Cuban background and especially an interpretation that emphasizes United States fear of Cuban radicalism, see Philip S. Foner's *The Spanish-Cuban-American War and the Birth of American Imperialism* (New York: Monthly Review Press, 1972). The best account of the background of the taking of the Philippines is in John A.S. Grenville and George Berkeley Young's *Politics, Strategy, and American Diplomacy: Studies in Foreign Policy, 1783-1917* (New Haven, CT: Yale University Press, 1966). Another debunking study is Lewis L. Gould's "The Reick Telegram and the Spanish-American War: A Reappraisal," *Diplomatic History* 3 (Spring 1979), 193-200. Gould does not accept the legend of the Wall Street turnaround in March of 1898 and its alleged impact on McKinley.

For McKinley, indispensable is the fine review article by Joseph A. Fry, "William McKinley and the Coming of the Spanish-American War: A Study of the Besmirching and Redemption of an Historical Image," *Diplomatic History,* 3 (Winter 1979), 77-95. The most readable biography is Margaret Leech's *In the Days of McKinley* (New York: Harper's, 1959) which hails McKinley as an underestimated heroic figure. Almost as favorable is H. Wayne Morgan's *William McKinley and His America* (Syracuse, NY: Syracuse University Press, 1963).

Chapter 4

WORLD WAR I

But the right is more precious than peace, and we shall fight for the things which we have always carried nearest our hearts—for democracy, for the right of those who submit to authority to have a voice in their own Governments, for the rights and liberties of small nations.

—Woodrow Wilson, April 2, 1917—

From a European perspective, our first three international wars were minor affairs that took place on the periphery of the global system. Our participation in World War I was quite another story. To be sure, our human and material losses paled before those of the main belligerents. They wasted an entire generation of young men in trench warfare in the west and massive battles in the east. During the final year and a half of the conflict, we did send to the continent over 2 million soldiers who helped win the day on the Western Front. "Lafayette we are here," shouted the cocky American doughboys as they disembarked at Le Havre, prepared to save the Old World from Prussian autocracy as well as its own follies. Later, battle-hardened veterans of the American Expeditionary Corps complained, "Oh Lafayette, we've paid our debt, for Christ's sake send us home." The disillusionment that followed the peace to make the world safe for democracy was intimately related to the manner in which we entered the war and to our general misconceptions of the issues at stake in Europe from 1914 to 1917.

Today, the story of our entry into World War I seems less interesting and certainly simpler than the story of our entry into World War II or the Southeast Asian quagmire. Almost forgotten are our disillusioned soldiers as well as the revisionists of the 1920s and 1930s who excoriated Woodrow Wilson and his friends for leading us into an affair which, they contended, was none of our business. Such a memory lapse is understandable. After a second generation of American boys met the Germans in France in 1944, few doubted the wisdom of our participation in the earlier war—had we only done a better job of applying the coup de grace to German militarism in the fall of 1918.

In his Second Inaugural, Richard Nixon referred to our four great wars of the twentieth century, each of which, he claimed, was fought to defend others against aggressors. Obviously, many listeners were troubled about the linking of the two world wars and the Korean conflict to the counterrevolutionary war waged in Southeast Asia. But most would have applauded had he singled out World War I as one of those good old-fashioned struggles between the forces of light and the forces of darkness. Any doubts we may have had about our entry have been packed away in our old kit bag.

It is unfortunate that earlier controversies spawned by our participation in the first of this century's wars to end war are no longer salient. A careful study of our behavior from 1914 to 1917 helps make understandable our subsequent behavior from Pearl Harbor to the 38th parallel.

The Great War (none were so pessimistic to call it World War I until the onset of the Second Great War in 1939) was one of the most significant events of the century. Despite the launching of the atomic age in 1945 and the ensuing Cold War between the world's first superpowers, as well as the technological and anticolonial revolutions speeded by World War II,

World War I may have been an even more dramatic historic watershed. The earlier war demolished the *ancien régime* that had been running things since the Congress of Vienna, ushered in the three "isms" that mark our age—communism, fascism, and anticolonialism—and, above all, catapulted the United States to preeminence among nations. By the time World War I had ended, Hapsburgs, Hohenzollerns, and Romanovs had been dethroned and even the victor nations had suffered unprecedented physical and psychological damage, while the United States emerged virtually unscathed, wealthier, and more powerful, if not wiser. Indeed, one might argue that the American Century really began in 1918, even though Henry Luce and the rest of the American establishment did not acknowledge that fact until 1941—and by then "our" century was almost over.

The story of our entry into World War I is, above all, the story of an American President to whom the right was more precious than peace. Woodrow Wilson is considered to be one of our greatest leaders, an acknowledged source of inspiration to such disparate successors as Herbert Hoover, Franklin Roosevelt, and Richard Nixon. In the minds of most Americans and a large number of Europeans, Wilson still represents the best in the American tradition of fair play and justice for all white peoples.

Many lessons can be learned from the investigation of the prolonged public and private disputes about neutrality policies in World War I. Once again, the ways in which domestic politics impinged upon the construction of a prudent foreign policy underlined the inherent weaknesses in the diplomacy of a democracy. And, as in the other wars, but maybe more so in this case, the public, which could not grasp the complexities of international relations, became easy prey for native conmen and foreign propagandists. Finally, this extended world crisis enhanced the powers of the President to define the issues in any foreign policy debate, to dominate congressional opponents who attempted to defy him, and to carry on a secret diplomacy worthy of a Metternich or a Bismarck.

The analysis of this war will be more complicated than that of earlier wars. Naturally, we will be interested in whether Americans belonged in the war, but we will also be concerned with the ancillary question, did the United States enter the war for the correct reasons? Moreover, since the crucial issue here was neutrality and since our leaders claimed that they were neutral, we must study how the belligerents viewed our behavior, whether the United States was as neutral as possible, whether a policy of strict neutrality was desirable, and, finally, how our interpretation of neutral rights affected our entry into the war. All of these questions are related to the story of the origins of World War I and so it is to the famous historiographical morass that we must turn before moving on to purely American considerations.

GERMANY, ENGLAND, AND THE
ORIGINS OF WORLD WAR I

Few historians subscribe to a unicausal interpretation of the causes of World War I and they do not point their fingers at one power as the major initiator or aggressor. Instead, they choose to emphasize the tightly bonded alliance system, the relationship between the prestige of those alliances and national power, the almost autonomous manner in which the general staffs carried out their war plans during July of 1914, the perceived competition for world markets, nationalism in the Balkans, and arms races. Although some historians judge certain nations to have been more culpable than others, few of the major actors have escaped blame for the unprecedented global conflict launched after the Guns of August had sounded.

At the time, most Americans did not view the outbreak of war that way. Since Germany had crossed the Belgian and French frontiers first, and since Germany was the unquestioned leader of the Central Powers coalition, she *appeared* to be the aggressor. Such an analysis came easily. Germany had a reputation for arrogance, militarism, and aggression, with the legacy of Bismarck and the leadership of truculent Kaiser

Wilhelm II, who seemed to live only for his army and his growing navy. That other nations mobilized before the Germans and that mobilization was an offensive act were not considered by most American observers. Their designation of Germany as the villain of the piece was unwarranted although understandable. That designation made it all the more likely that Germany and the United States would eventually come to blows. Yet, perhaps war was inevitable, given the way both countries developed during the latter part of the nineteenth century.

Like the United States, Germany was a relative newcomer to world power. Unified in 1871 by the brilliant Bismarck, Germany constructed mighty industrial and military machines which, by the turn of the century, had surpassed those of France and were beginning to challenge Englands'. Germany's drive to supplant England as the leader of Europe, a drive that also threatened to upset the delicate balance of power on the continent, was the primary cause of Anglo-German hostility. In 1914, the two powers were not involved in territorial conflict. Although the French and the Germans clashed over Alsace-Lorraine and the Austrians and Russians over the Balkans, German and British forces did not face one another across any hostile border. Undoubtedly, the stereotypical strutting Prussian was not a sympathetic figure. One can nonetheless feel sorry for the Germans who saw themselves engaged in legitimate economic and diplomatic offensives in the tropics.

Of all states, the new major power in the West should have empathized with the German parvenu. Indeed, one opportunity to head off general European war involved a concert of the old powers to combat the "American Menace." Even as late as the spring of 1914, some European diplomats talked of a rumored British-German alliance against the aggressive Americans. The two rivals might have buried their hatchets not in themselves but in a United States perceived to be the greatest threat to European civilization.

Americans knew little about this fantastic scheme to resurrect Czar Alexander's Holy Alliance. For them, the world situation seemed clear-cut. By 1914, we had learned to live with our arrogant British cousins who had dominated the Atlantic and the southern portion of our hemisphere since our earliest days. But not so with the Germans. Like the British, we also feared German naval and economic growth that challenged our interests in the Caribbean and Latin America. While British competition was accepted as a *fait accompli,* this new rival worried those few Americans who gave world politics much of a thought during the halcyon days of the Progressive Era. For those who did, Germany was a potential foe as was Japan in the Pacific. Conversely, England—our enemy in the War of 1812, Oregon and Mexico, the Civil War, and other crises during the nineteenth century—was almost a friend.

The year 1914 marked the hundredth anniversary of the termination of the War of 1812—the hundredth year of peace between the two quarreling but kissing cousins. Those who planned the celebrations and pageants in 1912 and 1913 had no idea that they would experience a situation that would turn out to be almost a replay of the prelude to the War of 1812.

This time, however, although the British played their usual role on the high seas, the Kaiser's adoption of Napoleon's role offered new twists. Moreover, this time the United States went to war against England's enemy. Finally, whereas in 1812 the Anglo-American skirmish was of marginal significance to the rest of the world, in 1917 our entry into World War I was instrumental in turning the tide against the Germans and winning the war for the British and their friends.

Unlike James Madison, Woodrow Wilson was on center stage throughout the period and, of course, on into the period of the peace conference. It is fitting that we begin our analysis with that most complex individual and especially powerful President.

THE SCHOLAR PRESIDENT

Woodrow Wilson is considered a great President. Although he guided important Progressive legislation through Congress during his first administration, he is remembered most for his war leadership and sponsorship of the League of Nations. Similarly, the claims to greatness of Lincoln, Franklin Roosevelt, and even Truman may relate to their successful management of major wars. Perhaps one cannot become a great President unless he faces a serious military crisis. Had Charles Evans Hughes won the election of 1916 and then had he successfully led the United States through World War I, he, and not Wilson, might today be considered *the* great President of the period.

Even without World War I, Wilson might have achieved greatness. He was without question a superior man, one of the most intelligent and sophisticated thinkers we have ever had in the White House, the first intellectual our system had catapulted to national leadership since the Jacksonian "revolution" of the 1820s. Wilson had spent the better part of his life in universities, first studying law, then, after an unhappy hiatus as a lawyer, back to study for a doctorate, then on to university teaching at Bryn Mawr, Wesleyan, and Princeton, and finally to the presidency of the latter. His academic field of expertise, American government, was tailor-made for his later career as a politician, and his most important book, *Congressional Government,* was a major text during the latter part of the nineteenth century.

Unfortunately for the reputation of college professors in government, Wilson's celebrated tactical blunders in foreign policy lend credence to the view that those who spend their lives in academic ivory towers know nothing of the realities of politics and diplomacy. It is true that as an expert on American government in the pre-World War I era, he could not have been expected to know much about foreign policy since we barely had one. In one of his texts, for example, he devoted 13 times as much space to the Interior Department as to the State Department. Still, Wilson calls to mind the stereotype of the allegedly fuzzy-brained, idealistic, and ultimately unknowledgeable professors who pass themselves off as experts on the real world of which they have never been a part.

His effectiveness may also have been weakened by the arrogant way he treated ordinary politicians, including Congressmen. He found many of them to be petty, partisan, and, above all, quite a cut below him intellectually. Of course, he had every reason to feel superior to them in terms of his intelligence as well as his personal and public honesty. Since he found it difficult to conceal his contempt for their capabilities, when the time came to compromise or to deal with them at least temporarily as equals, communication was problematic.

Even more important in limiting his effectiveness was Wilson's spirituality. More than most politicians and diplomats, Wilson's behavior was guided by what he felt were moral principles that had universal applicability. Once convinced of the rectitude of his policies, he could become incredibly stubborn, unwilling to yield to contrary arguments. Furthermore, Wilson was an ardent champion of Christianity. His father was a minister, his mother the daughter of a minister, and most of his formative years revolved around an ascetic religious life. Unlike the stereotypical prodigal minister's son, Wilson adhered to the straight and narrow. Although he was never ordained in a formal sense, he did indeed follow in the footsteps of his father as a minister without the cloth, a politician-preacher to a congregation of millions. His missionary work was admired in many quarters. Americans and others throughout the world felt that Wilson was the one leader whom they could trust. Unlike his colleagues among prime ministers and presidents, he seemed to be concerned with international justice.

Much has been written about Wilson's conception of foreign affairs. The so-called realist school of critics of American diplomacy consider Wilsonianism—a combination of idealism, moralism, and legalism—to be the cause of many problems. Wilson's defenders maintain that their man's association with idealism has been overdone. From their perspective, Wilson was an intelligent diplomat who was sensitive to the nuances of the international system and who well-understood the games played by crafty Europeans. In fact, Wilson's critics from the left claim that his idealism was a cynical cover for a program devoted to making the world safe for laissez-faire.

A most complex man and a most complex subject, he was certainly inexperienced in international relations when he assumed the Presidency in 1913. As he told a friend, "It would be the irony of fate if my administration had to deal chiefly with foreign affairs." To be sure, Wilson had traveled to Europe on many occasions and had occasionally written about the state of the world, but he was not as experienced a diplomat as Theodore Roosevelt or even William Howard Taft.

A keen student of the American system, Wilson recognized that because of our emergence to world prominence, the powers of the Presidency had been greatly enhanced. While he shared responsibilities with Congress on domestic matters, the Constitution made the President dominant in foreign policy. Wilson used these implied powers time and again from 1914 to 1919.

In the more philosophic sense, Wilson believed in the Progressive dream of a democratic world. The fact that all nations would eventually adopt a democratic system, as they seemed to be doing in Russia, Germany, and even Turkey, augured well for international peace for he felt that democratic states were inherently peaceful. Wilson's view of foreign relations was colored by his conviction that ordinary people did not want war. As the people became more and more powerful, they would pressure their representatives to settle international disputes at the conference table and not on the battlefield.

Wilson hated war. Although he was to say that the right was more precious than peace, he was a profoundly spiritual man who leaned toward pacifism. Though he did believe in just wars, compared to Theodore Roosevelt, Wilson was a dove. Roosevelt and some of his friends believed that war was endemic to the Darwinian nation-state system and, to some degree, even good for the race. Wilson disagreed and hoped to reform the system so that international conflict could be settled in the same Christian, rational, nonviolent way as was domestic conflict in the United States.

When he first heard that world war had broken out in August of 1914 he was heartbroken. He was upset about war in general and the fate of his good friends, the British. Like almost all of his colleagues in the American establishment, Wilson was strongly Anglophilic. He once remarked that he would have preferred to have been the Prime Minister of England than the President of the United States, so great was his admiration for her system of government and culture. The Germans, for Wilson, lacked spirituality. He was personally offended by the manner in which the war had begun, with the Germans invading neutral Belgium while their Chancellor casually remarked that the treaty guaranteeing her neutrality was a "scrap of paper."

By October of 1914, as Wilson's initial shock wore off, he reconsidered his emotional response to the news of war. He soon stated privately that while he was no supporter of Prussian *Weltpolitik,* the European system, more than any individual nation, "caused" the war. That system had produced arms races and alliances that fostered nationalism and irredentism that inevitably had to explode into war. Thus, Wilson decided that it was his duty to mankind, as well as to his own nation, to make the postwar world a safer place. Although he never relinquished his plans to reform the system, by the time he brought the United States into the war, he had returned to his original position on the Germans as the prime culprits in the tragedy. He then deluded himself and others into thinking that the first step to sweeping reform would be the elimination of evil Prussians from the international system. It appears that the Wilson of August-October 1914 and February-April 1917 was not as sophisticated as the Wilson of the middle period.

The Great War was not Wilson's only foreign policy problem. After a relatively quiet four years under William Howard Taft, all hell seemed to break loose in Latin America and it was there, as well as in Europe, that Wilson cut his teeth as a maturing statesman. Despite his earlier castigations of dollar and big stick diplomacy and his promises in his Mobile, Alabama, address to be a good neighbor, Wilson found it necessary to send American troops into Santo Domingo in 1914 and 1916 and Haiti in 1915. The Haitian intervention was longer and bloodier than anything in which Roosevelt and Taft had been involved. The Caco War, which smouldered in the Haitian bush for six years, was an ugly little counterrevolutionary war, obscured by more significant events in Europe.

Wilson and his aides also had to keep their eyes on China. The Europeans were far too busy in the Great War to concern themselves with their Chinese interests which were taken care of by their new Entente ally, Japan. Take care of things the Japanese did, as they marched into the vacuum left by the European belligerents, not only in the German sphere of influence in Shantung but in other areas as well. From early in 1915, when Japan issued her 21 Demands that threatened the sovereignty of the new Chinese Republic, until November of 1917, when the Lansing-Ishii agreement papered over the Japanese-American dispute in China, Asian affairs demanded attention from the President who longed to concentrate on his Progressive reform program.

All of these were small potatoes compared to Wilson's several dangerous Mexican escapades. He was deeply involved in the Mexican Revolution, a massive social upheaval that began in 1910 and did not run its course until 1920. In April of 1914, Wilson sent marines into Vera Cruz in an attempt to destroy a Mexican leader whom he did not like (and, to be charitable, who was not a very likable sort in terms of the future of Mexican reform) and, in March of 1916, he again invaded Mexico against the wishes of a new leader with whom he had affected a rapprochement. This latter invasion involved a massive punitive raid led by General Black Jack Pershing, soon to command the American Expeditionary Force in France. Pershing, along with 5,000 soldiers, raced back and forth across northern Mexico trying to find Pancho Villa and his band of "cutthroats" but Mexico was a pretty big place and all Mexicans looked alike. On several occasions, Pershing's forces clashed with Mexican troops that had been sent north to protect their country's sovereignty from the American invaders and the two nations teetered on the brink of war as late as the summer of 1916.

Clearly, even the Mexican affair was a minor one compared to the stupendous events of World War I. Nevertheless, we must not lose sight of the fact that the United States had grown so dramatically since her last war that her new worldwide interests played a role in the way she perceived and reacted to events on the continent. Although Wilson was a most powerful and active President, he had, to delegate some responsibility in this increasingly complicated business of running American foreign policy. The manner in which he delegated those responsibilities and the individuals involved became almost as controversial as the policies themselves.

PRESIDENTIAL ADVISORS

Like most strong Presidents, Woodrow Wilson was his own Secretary of State. His assumption of this role was all the more understandable when we consider the man who held the office during the first two years of his administration. That old war horse, three-time loser for the Presidency, William Jennings Bryan was rewarded for his faithful service with the post of the President's first minister. Bryan, who may have had his heart in the right place when it came to peace, had not the foggiest notion about international relations.

Despite foreign travels, his life had been spent grubbing about in domestic politics. Characteristically, Bryan astounded the diplomatic world with one of his first pronouncements, the banning of alcohol from American diplomatic receptions.

Despite his naiveté, or maybe because of it, Bryan was the most genuine neutral in Wilson's Cabinet. He saw little difference between the British and the Germans and, above all, felt we had to maintain a strict neutrality lest we be pulled into a conflict that was none of our business; a Middle American isolationist, perhaps, but an honest man who found Wilson's neutrality skewed in one direction. Because of Bryan's lack of sophistication about worldly matters and also because of his opposition to official neutrality policies, the President delegated little authority to the Great Commoner, who, in any event, resigned over the *Lusitania* issue in June of 1915. Instead, Wilson relied heavily upon a man who held no mandate from either the people or Congress, Colonel Edward Mandell House.

Colonel House was Woodrow Wilson's Henry Kissinger. To put it another way, Henry Kissinger was the latest in the modern line of powerful Presidential advisors, the first of whom was probably Colonel House. Harry Hopkins, Sherman Adams, McGeorge Bundy, and Walt Rostow played comparable roles under Franklin Roosevelt, Dwight Eisenhower, John F. Kennedy, and Lyndon Johnson, respectively. A Texas-style colonel, House met Wilson first in 1911 and almost at once became his closest confident. Wilson bypassed the State Department to use his personal advisor without formal portfolio for delicate missions abroad. On those missions, House talked with kaisers and prime ministers as if he were their equal or at least a person of exalted official status. But he had none and for this reason, among others, was attacked by the press and later by revisionist historians.

The trust Wilson placed in his advisor was extraordinary. The House-Wilson correspondence reveals that when the colonel embarked for trips to Europe, he took few written instructions. Moreover, while abroad, unlike most diplomatic agents, he frequently did not wire back for guidance or even attempt to keep the President informed about his progress. Wilson was confident that his friend would respond just the way that he would have responded had he been there.

House, who was probably more pro-British than Wilson although not as much so as Wilson's second Secretary of State, Robert Lansing, was a controversial figure. He was responsible to no one but the President. Whereas the Secretary of State was responsible to Congress and its prying committees, House owed nothing to them. Herein lies an important constitutional question that has still not been resolved.

Can we accept the employment of essentially private executive agents such as Colonel House and Henry Kissinger (from 1969 to 1973) in a democracy? Does this practice not suggest the secret diplomacy of some nineteenth-century monarch and does it not violate the spirit of our Constitution? On the other hand, when we elect a President, we also tacitly accept his entourage and all of his friends who might influence him. Surely, we cannot claim the right to monitor those who advise the President. The issue of Colonel House and his successors is a complicated one. In terms of historiography, House played an important role in the 1920s and 1930s when Wilson was criticized for allowing his pro-British advisors to lead us into war.

That almost everyone around Wilson was pro-British goes without saying. His diplomatic corps, especially his ambassador in London, Walter Hines Page, was wholly sympathetic with the British position. Wilson was well aware of the Anglophilia of the American establishment. Although some of his decisions appeared to be unjustifiably pro-British, they were not influenced by his friends' pro-British inclinations but by the needs, as he saw them, of national security. It may well have been, however, that the Anglophilia of the establishment was important in the development of American opinion from 1914 to 1917.

AMERICANS RESPOND TO THE GREAT WAR

On August 4, 1914, after the feverish diplomatic and military maneuvers of late July had produced a real world war, only a handful of Anglophiles such as Theodore Roosevelt called for immediate American entry. Even Roosevelt adopted a more pacific position once his instinctive enthusiasm over the prospects of fighting in another splendid war had waned. Most Americans advocated neutrality because the events on the continent seemed unrelated to our security. This did not mean that we did not have our favorites in the military contest just as we had our favorites in the last world war, over a century earlier. But such favoritism would not get in the way of legal neutrality, or so we thought.

When the war began, the vast majority of Americans, perhaps as many as 80%, were at least mildly favorable to the British cause. Despite a heavy dose of history lessons castigating tyrannical George III as well as the bullies of the seas of 1812, the British were cousins who practiced a sort of democracy, albeit with a distasteful admixture of royalty and snobbishness. They seemed to represent better our sort of people than did the Germans. Leaders in every field—business, media, education, and government—were strongly pro-British. It was bad form among the elites to harbor pro-German sentiments. Thus, most Americans were at least mildly pro-British while their leaders were staunch supporters of their friends in England when the war began. Such an array of support for the British proved important when the President promulgated his patently unneutral neutral policies.

A large minority of nonestablishment types, made up for the most part of hyphenated-Americans, was strongly pro-German. Most of the eight million or so German-Americans could be found in the pro-German camp. Kaiser Wilhelm was no Hitler for them, while British policy seemed to be devoted to denying Germany her rightful place in the sun. In 1914, unlike 1939, little stigma was attached to rooting for the Germans.

The Irish-Americans, if anything, may have been even more Anglophobic. In the months preceding the outbreak of war, the perennial Irish question had again reached a crisis with an Anglo-Irish war on the horizon. World War I was a godsend to Irish patriots; a German victory could lead to Irish independence. The Germans themselves were involved in Irish intrigues providing aid, comfort, and supplies to Irish rebels.

Jewish-Americans formed a third bloc that was, by and large, pro-German. Jews were violently anti-Russian. The first part of the twentieth century witnessed an increasing Jewish, and American, hostility toward the cruel anti-Semitism of the Czarist regime. In 1911, Jewish pressure was successful in forcing Washington to abrogate the Russian-American commercial treaty. In addition, although it may seem hard to believe today, Germany was a refuge for Jews from Eastern Europe and also a center for Reform Judaism, a branch of the faith with influential followers in the United States. While Jews were not as numerous as the Germans or the Irish here, they did wield considerable influence in several important states where they clustered.

Finally, in terms of ethnics who were supporters of Germany, we can include the Scandinavian-Americans who also hated Russia. Their hatred stemmed from fears of Russian expansion into Scandinavia. Such expansion was considered to be a possibility by newspaper editors in Sweden and the United States. Again, although Scandinavian-Americans did not constitute a particularly large group, they were politically powerful in several key midwestern states.

In all, 20% or more of the American population, almost exclusively hyphenates, hoped for a German victory. At the start of the war, they were far more passionately dedicated to their cause than was the rest of the mildly pro-British population. Can a minority shouting loudly drown out a relatively passive majority? Such often appears to be the case in a democracy. In World War I, things were complicated by the powerful and interested Anglophilic elite sitting astride the relatively silent majority. Through its virtual monopoly of the media, in which it attacked real and alleged German atrocities, it helped convert many mildly pro-British supporters into enthusiastic wavers of the Union Jack as the war moved through 1915 and 1916. By the beginning of 1917, most Americans were prepared for a crusade against the Germans who increasingly came to represent the enemy.

During the 1930s, it was fashionable to say that Americans reached this peak of anti-German frenzy because of insidious British propagandists who spread the germs of hate. To be sure, the British ran a well-oiled, sophisticated propaganda outfit with a news service subscribed to by hundreds of newspapers, an elaborate speakers' bureau, and a variety of other overt and covert agencies, sometimes assisted by the American Secret Service, that helped get the British message to the American people. They were not alone. The Germans also tried to make friends and influence people although they had a much more difficult time of it. In part, they were handicapped by the lack of allies in the media. Of course, the British had many more real atrocities with which to work than the Germans who did invade Belgium and use the submarine. As one pro-German remarked on the growing pro-British sentiment in America, "Had the Germans only taken the ordinary route to Paris." Finally, speaking the American language both figuratively and literally, the British were better able to cater to our whims and prejudices than the alien Germans.

Without modern polls and survey data, it is difficult to determine the influence of rival propagandists on Americans from 1914 to 1917. Most likely, they did not enjoy as much success as was thought during the revisionist 1930s. The British efforts probably helped make those who were mildly pro-English more so and German efforts may have helped keep their supporters in line. Although a small percentage of Americans in the middle—the "don't knows" of a survey—may have been swayed by one propagandist or another, the majority of Americans did not need foreign agents to convince them of the justice of the several causes. They saw the stories of the submarines and they had images of historical England and historical Germany, images that tended to weigh heavier than anything they may have heard from propagandists. Undoubtedly, the pro-English biases of the media helped them along, although not enough to blame the outpouring of anti-German wrath in 1917 on American journalists who were connected to British propagandists. But we are getting ahead of the story. When the war began, just about everyone, including the President and his advisors, was committed to a policy of neutrality. Proclaiming neutrality was much easier than constructing a policy that was genuinely neutral.

A NEUTRAL'S LOT IS NOT A HAPPY ONE

To define and maintain one's neutrality in 1914 was a messy business. At best, international law is a hodgepodge of mutually exclusive treaties initialed by some nations. At worst, it is an anarchic domain in which each nation's interpretation of those treaties, as well as court cases and historic precedents, is its own international law. In few areas is international law as ambiguous as in neutrality law. We saw something of this in 1812. The problem did not improve with age.

In 1856, following the Crimean War, the major powers drew up a treaty redefining neutrality, contraband, and blockade.

Between that time and 1914, sweeping changes in weaponry, transportation, and communication systems made a good portion of the mid-nineteenth century codes irrelevant and outmoded. In order to bring them up to date, most of the important nations met at London in 1909 to construct a new set of naval neutrality laws. The treaty they drafted was ultimately unacceptable to England since it was biased in favor of neutrals and belligerents with small navies. The London Treaty's definitions of contraband were so rigid and the freedom given to neutrals to trade with belligerents so liberal that the ruler of the seas could never have lived with the document, even though it was ratified by other nations. In 1914, England, the number one sea power, was prepared to enforce its own historic neutrality laws, the London Treaty to the contrary notwithstanding.

Leaving aside the issue of the specific body of neutrality laws to which a neutral might appeal for guidance and support in August of 1914, there were two very general ways in which neutrality could be defined. A neutral could try to maintain the strictest possible legal neutrality by using treaties, conferences, and precedents to establish a posture acceptable to its own international lawyers and, it hoped, to the international lawyers in the belligerent camps. According to such a scenario, Woodrow Wilson should have secreted himself in his ivory tower surrounded by the appropriate legal texts. From that lofty perch, he should have handed down his decisions, irrespective of their impact on the outcome of the war or even on American security. That is, if he received a report that belligerent X violated law Y, his law books would suggest a course of action and that would be that.

On the other hand, a neutral could try to be fair to both sides by refraining from adopting a policy that upset the military balance. A neutral could act neutrally, in a legal sense, and in so doing ruin one of the belligerents. For example, in 1914, had Wilson demanded that the British behave themselves, and had the British refused, as was likely, he could have severed the Anglo-American trade link and the Germans might have won the war. In that case, Wilson would have been strictly neutral, but terribly unfair. Is a neutral responsible for the consequences of its neutral behavior?

Everything the United States did, whether in accordance with international law or not, had to affect the outcome of World War I to some degree. Perhaps prudent neutrals should call in their ships and stay out of the way of the belligerents until a war is over. This is what Thomas Jefferson did in 1807. Such behavior is not only economically unwise but also unneutral and unfair. When the war began, the British had every reason to expect to trade with the United States. Their naval and economic plans were predicated upon such a trade. Had we closed our ports and factories to them, we would have changed the rules in the middle of the game and thus would have been guilty of behaving unneutrally and unfairly.

Woodrow Wilson apparently tried to be both neutral and fair to both sides, or at least, to balance the two aspects of neutrality so that we did not influence unduly the belligerents' chances on the field of battle. There is a third element in neutral policy that may be the most important of all. It is possible that in its attempt to be neutral and fair, a nation might end up destroying its own security or economy. Faced with irritating nonlethal violations to neutrality but a prosperity dependent on an acceptance of those violations, what should a neutral do? During the Napoleonic wars, most of our merchants made money despite an occasional illegal seizure. As we have seen, it was in our immediate economic interest then to accept British assaults against our honor. Though such behavior would have been unfair to Napoleon, it would have kept us out of the war and economically healthy. It seems sensible for a President to choose security and prosperity over neutrality—if the choice is ever that clear. Unfortunately, it never is, and so Wilson ended up declaring his absolute neutrality and then proceeded to bend international law to protect the economy.

When the war began, questions of neutrality were not thought to be very important, despite the precedent of the War of 1812. Everyone expected that the new world war would be a short one. When Wilson issued his neutrality proclamation in which he promised that the United States would be "neutral in thought as well as action," it appeared to be a relatively simple thing to do. Few Americans expressed concern about the relationship between our neutrality and possible involvement in Europe's latest folly. While it was going to be difficult to remain neutral in thought, to remain neutral in action was going to be easy since the war would be over before the snow flew.

WILSON DEFINES AMERICAN NEUTRALITY

The President's first neutrality policies appeared to be eminently fair. Although he did not weigh them on the scales of justice, his actions approximated a rough balance between the British and the Germans.

Thus, for the Germans and against the British, Wilson refused to speak out on the alleged German atrocities in Belgium. No matter how much he abhorred the attack on the peaceful neutral and no matter how much he hoped that the Germans would behave with uncharacteristic decency, he felt that it would have been unneutral of him to say anything about the matter in public.

Moreover, when American manufacturers began to export submarine parts to Britain, Wilson ruled that such shipments violated the spirit of the law that prohibited a neutral from selling whole vessels to a belligerent. Finally, Wilson's policies concerning those vessels in the German merchant marine trapped in our waters when war began were favorable to Germany. First, he ruled that they could obtain American registry. Second, he tried, albeit unsuccessfully, to have Congress appropriate funds to purchase the vessels for the American merchant marine. Both measures would have increased the number of neutral vessels plying the Atlantic and thus the number of merchant ships that might have been able to make it through the British blockade. Three small items, no doubt, but they did demonstrate an initial attempt to be fair to Germany.

On the other hand, the British received benefits from Wilson's early neutral policies. For example, when requested by the Germans, among others, to demand that England adhere to the Treaty of London of 1909, a treaty favoring nations without a navy, Wilson categorically refused. On several occasions, he asked the British to accept the treaty their diplomats had signed but which Parliament had quashed in 1911. When they balked, he pressed them no further.

He also ruled that the presence of two German-owned wireless stations in Sayville, New York, and Tuckertown, New Jersey, violated the neutrality provisions of the Hague Convention of 1907. For the duration, the American government operated those stations. Since the British had severed the Atlantic cable to Germany, the seizure of the German stations was a blow to their private communications system here. Secret orders to their American operatives had to be sent via Stockholm and Buenos Aires. The more circuitous the route, the more likely British intelligence would pick up the scent.

On balance, these five early neutrality decisions were more favorable to German interests than to British. Nevertheless, all could be defended on the grounds of legal neutrality. Of course, it was relatively easy to be strictly neutral on these issues for none related to vital American interests. When neutrality and national interest clashed, the story was not the same.

In August of 1914, Secretary of State Bryan proudly proclaimed a new policy. Heretofore, neutral bankers, including Americans, had financed the war efforts of belligerent nations. Now Bryan announced that American citizens would be prohibited from making loans or extending credits to belligerents. As he pointed out, "money is the worst of all contrabands because it commands everything else." A noble sentiment, it astonished more practical men who could not understand how the United States could throw away an opportunity to make money. As the war dragged on through the fall of 1914, the worse things became for the Europeans, and the better they became for us. When the war began, we had been in a serious recession, spiralling downward toward a depression. With the war orders of August, September, and October, our economy came to life. We found ourselves in a boom and the longer the war went on, the richer we became. There was a catch to this immoral business. The British, our chief customers, were fast running out of cash. We soon discovered that they would not be able to buy our goods indefinitely unless we resorted to that old, if seamy, practice of extending credits and loans. Faced with this development, Wilson forgot our high-minded pronouncements. In October of 1914, he permitted Americans to extend credits to belligerents and in September of 1915 permitted loans. Thus, the orders continued to come and our economy boomed.

This very important issue raises several questions about our neutrality. Obviously, Wilson put his foot in his mouth when he had his Secretary of State attack money as the worst of all contrabands, since only two months later, he had to take the lower ground in order to maintain prosperity. Wilson had no other choice in this case, but after this turnabout he could not claim he was neutral. He was the one who had earlier defined the extending of loans to belligerents as unneutral. This is not to say that his ultimate policy was unwise; merely that Wilson himself established the context in which that policy would be judged. No one would have considered us any the less neutral had we countenanced loans from the start. The minute we adopted our new and unprecedented policy toward loans, our later reversion to the old definition jeopardized our claims to neutrality. It was true that the original ban related to a practical problem, the fear of a flow of gold to Europe during a time of economic malaise. However, Bryan did not say anything about this when he offered his "worst of all contrabands" statement.

American bankers extended some $2 billion in loans to the Entente side and only $27 million to the Germans. Our financial community did not loan money to England just because its members were pro-British. Bankers are unsentimental about investments. London was the center of the financial world where we had been accustomed to deal in the years before the war. Moreover, the British, who were buying things here, needed money far more than did the Germans who were relatively self-sufficient. Even had the Germans wanted to purchase

American wares, they met difficulties transporting their goods across an Atlantic patrolled by the omnipotent British Navy. Finally, the bankers, who considered a British victory more likely than a German victory, were reluctant to advance credits and loans to a regime that might not survive the war. For whatever reasons, the flow of money to Britain *appeared* to be unneutral since it was not matched by a comparable flow of money to Germany.

There is a final and more sinister interpretation of the significance of the loans for our eventual entry into war. According to revisionists, in 1916 American bankers began to worry about a massive default. If England lost the war, and by 1916 she showed no signs of being able to win it, their money might be lost. Thus, so goes the argument, through their influence in Washington, in the media, and in every walk of life, the bankers created an interventionist climate. Although Wilson began his Presidency as an enemy of finance capital, he had made his peace with Morgan et al. by 1915. After Bryan resigned over the *Lusitania* incident, Robert Lansing became Secretary of State. Lansing, who was closely connected to Wall Street (as was his father-in-law, John Foster who was Secretary of State from 1892 to 1893 and his nephew, John Foster Dulles), supposedly represented the bankers' interests in high policy-making circles. The plot is simple: The bankers loaned money to Britain, Britain looked like she was going to lose, so the bankers forced us into war to protect their investments.

Simple but wrong. Whether the bankers were wholeheartedly for war in 1917 is not the issue. Did they want to go to war because they feared for their investments? The evidence, and especially the logic of the situation, would suggest that the answer to that crucial question is a definite no. Although a banker might be Anglophilic, he generally would not loan money to a British friend unless that loan was secured with blue chip collateral. And if there was anything the British had, it was blue chip collateral. In the United States, for example, British investors owned a good deal of our railway stock. Moreover, they guaranteed most of their loans with properties in Canada,

Australia, India, and other colonial territories which would have been secure for American creditors even had Germany won the war. The bankers did not worry about getting the bulk of their money back plus a healthy return. Yet even without the bankers' plot, the story of the loans and the Wilson administration's contradictory pronouncements in this realm remains one of the major issues in our neutrality policy.

Wilson did not break with precedent when it came to the arms trade. In previous wars, neutral munitions makers had sold weapons of war to belligerents and, indeed, this seemingly immoral, if profitable business continues. Americans were permitted to sell arms to all comers after August 4, although they stood a chance of losing their goods either to British surface vessels or the submarine, depending upon the ultimate destination of those lethal shipments.

Why did Wilson allow traffic in arms but initially not in money? A most difficult question, for what is the difference between supplying cannons and supplying money to buy the cannons? If anything the former seems more immoral than the latter. Nevertheless, leaving aside the boost the war gave to our armaments industry, one can apply a peculiar sort of moral calculus to the arms trade. Had Americans been prohibited from selling arms to belligerents, a belligerent that was more poorly armed and therefore (perhaps) more pacific prior to the war would have been penalized. Given precedents, belligerents had every reason to expect they would be able to augment their arsenals with purchases from neutrals. In the years prior to the war, although the British may have worried about the growing disparity between their land armaments and those of the Germans, they felt they did not have to participate fully in the tension-producing arms race since their control of the Atlantic guaranteed a steady flow of supplies from the United States if war came. Somewhat convoluted reasoning, yes, but the arms trade was at least legal in terms of international law. It only seems ironic juxtaposed with our original holier-than-thou approach to the money question.

There is another problem here. Almost all of our arms went to the Allies. Of course, throughout the war, the British needed munitions more than the Germans. All the same, we did have many weapons the German General Staff would have loved to buy. Unfortunately, Germany had no safe way of transporting this contraband across the Atlantic—the British had swept the German Navy and merchant marine from the seas and threatened to seize neutral vessels that tried to run their blockade. In the end, we supplied a good portion of the arms used by one side to kill the other side, even though we did it neutrally.

During the 1930s, revisionists and isolationists strongly criticized the immoral arms trade in which Americans made fortunes providing the materials for British young men to slaughter German young men. The attacks on the "Merchants of Death"— the cruel American capitalists whose profits dripped blood— seem quaint today. In recent years, governments, not just private individuals, have trafficked in arms for political and economic reasons. France, the United States, England, Russia, Israel, China, and every power with an arms surplus has given arms to client states or sold them to ordinary customers with the face-saving proviso that they be used for defensive or collective security purposes.

Finally, in this catalogue of complex and ambiguous neutrality policies, we come to the most controversial issue of all, our acquiescence in the British mining of the North Sea. The sowing of mines in areas which belligerents wished to deny to other belligerents or neutral contraband carriers was common custom by 1914. No one questioned the legality of mining—under certain conditions.

The Germans were the first to employ mines in World War I when they scattered several off the British coast that ultimately destroyed some vessels. This initial German use of mines was later cited by the British to justify their own overuse. They argued, "the Germans started it, didn't they?" But the British mining did not compare to the German since the British mined the North Sea. A little bit of mining in a harbor or an important channel was precedented; the mining of an entire sea was not.

The British mining of the North Sea made it impossible, for all intents and purposes, for vessels to reach German ports without first stopping off in England for inspection and sailing instructions through the mine fields. The Germans protested immediately. According to them, the mining represented an illegal blockade. In addition, after the British tightened up their contraband lists to include food items, the Germans stated that the North Sea mining snatched milk and bread from the mouths of their babies and women. Although the Allies did try to starve civilians, this latter claim was something of an exaggeration since the Germans did not want for food until 1918.

Behind the German protest was their proclaimed inability to see any moral or legal difference between mining and submarines. If one was acceptable, why not the other? Both the mine and the submarine struck by surprise, both could be just as fatal to the victim and, if anything, the submarine commander exercised more discretion than the mindless mine. Mines sunk hospital and passenger ships, submarines selected merchant and war vessels for destruction. Why was Wilson tough on submarines yet soft on mines? Other neutrals, especially those who bordered Germany and the North Sea, were not at all happy with the British tactic.

Wilson considered the mining of the North Sea to be within the letter, if not the spirit, of the law, whereas many aspects of submarine warfare were, for him, illegal. More important and certainly more practical, few Americans lay at the bottom of the North Sea, victims of British mines. The mining of the North Sea was so effective, compared to the submarine blockade of the Atlantic, that captains were unwilling to venture into its waters without first stopping off in England. As a result, the British mines rarely killed or maimed. On the other hand, at no time was submarine warfare so effective that it scared neutrals and merchant ships away from the Atlantic run to Britain. Through the spring of 1917, a neutral vessel carrying contraband stood a very good chance of making it to England unscathed. Consequently, shipowners from neutral countries put up with the risks of an occasional sinking, along with the attendant loss of life, in order to reap the benefits of the Atlantic war trade. Had the submarines been more effective, had the odds of getting across the Atlantic been longer, fewer neutrals would have dared ply the war zone and thus fewer American travelers would have been killed by German torpedoes. The relative ineffectiveness of submarines meant that some Americans and other neutrals were going to end up at the bottom of the Atlantic while few would be claimed by British mines.

On the North Sea affair, our logic appeared questionable when we drew the distinction between a mine and a submarine. At the time, our policy seemed sensible, legal, and practical. One can only sympathize with the Germans whose misfortune it was to be forced to rely upon a weapon that the rest of the world considered immoral, especially when it was used effectively.

In order to assess Wilson's definition of American neutrality, we have to ask several questions. Was he neutral or, more likely, was he as neutral as possible? Was he as fair as possible? Did his neutrality policy affect our entry into war?

As to the first, when we review Wilson's early actions and then compare them to the confusing precedents of international law, we must conclude that Wilson was generally neutral, at least in a legal sense. Only when he chose to alter traditional policy on loans can we fault him, but even there our eventual policy of permitting the loans was within the letter of international law.

But were we fair to both belligerents and did the application of our neutral policy help shape the outcome of the military battles on the continent? Clearly, the impact of our neutral policies was more damaging to the Germans than the British. For example, by accepting the mining of the North Sea as well as the British refusal to sign the London Treaty of 1909, we contributed to the establishment of British naval supremacy. One can imagine a German victory resulting from the following scenario. We insist on a revocation of the mining program and adherence to the London Treaty. The British refuse, and we counter with a severance of economic relations. Such an action coming in 1914 or 1915, when the British desperately needed our supplies, might have weakened the Allies sufficiently to insure their loss.

To look at things another way, we appeared to be hurting Germany by not hurting England. It was far easier for us to hurt England than Germany for Germany's main strength lay in her land forces, while England's lay in her navy. German activities on the European battlefields did not involve any violation of our neutrality, whereas everything that happened on the British-controlled seas was of vital importance to us. Had we made too many rulings against Britain, we could have caused her to lose the war. But by ruling against Germany's ancillary power *under* the Atlantic, we only made it more difficult for her to win. Thus, although Wilson was not as fair as he might have been, his activities did not upset the balance to a significant degree.

Wilson's neutrality and relative fairness does not tell the entire story. All through the war, he insisted that he maintained a scrupulous and impartial neutrality, even when it came to American interests. As we have seen in his early decisions, the Germans had every reason to suspect that he had been less than fair to them or, at least, more than fair to England. His neutral policies, especially those involving the Atlantic link to Britain, created an environment in which the Germans could not believe American protestations of good faith. Although their violations of our neutrality eventually led us into war against them, they felt they were merely righting the balance Wilson had tipped toward Britain from 1914 to 1917. If such an interpretation does not appear justified from the preceding catalogue of early neutrality policies, it should become so as we consider our specific reactions to British and German maritime policies.

HIS MAJESTY'S NAVY AND THE
RIGHTS OF NEUTRALS

Both the British and the Germans violated our rights. The former's disregard of international etiquette led to severe tension. The latter's led to war. On the surface, this situation seems unfair since the quantity of British violations greatly outnumbered the German. The respective quality of the two sorts of violations was quite another story.

The British assaulted neutral rights in many ways. First of all, they engaged in illegal searches and seizures, a perennial habit of the British Navy. According to our (and most neutrals') interpretation of the law, the British continually transcended the bounds of legitimate belligerent rights. For example, a belligerent warship was supposed to make its search for contraband on the high seas—it could not order a ship into port unless it had good reason to suspect that the ship carried contraband that could only be detected through the use of X-rays or other devices. The British did not think twice about forcing a neutral to England.

Or to take another example, shiploads of minerals on their way to Italy (before Italy was in the war) and meat to Holland were seized as contraband on the grounds that those items would *probably* have ended up in Germany through overland transshipment. Never mind that the British could not prove such an allegation. They claimed to know where those materials were going.

The contraband question itself became a bitter issue of contention between America and Britain as the war progressed and the Admiralty's list grew longer and longer. By late 1915, just about everything the Germans might have wanted to buy from us was considered contraband and liable to British seizure. The prohibition of food shipments to the Central Powers was especially rankling.

The British also violated our neutrality every time they rummaged through mail bags on board ships they were searching. The interception of American mail headed for German territories was a breech of international law. Some American businessmen even claimed that the Admiralty, acting for British businessmen, was engaged in industrial espionage unrelated to the war effort. Similarly, on occasion, German citizens were removed from American vessels in contravention of international law.

Furthermore, the British displayed American flags on some of their merchant vessels in order to deceive submarines. We were prepared to accept the limited use of this *ruse de guerre* as we had in the past, but the British overdid it and thus dangerously frustrated German submarine commanders who could not distinguish between a real and a bogus American ship.

The British also violated the spirit of our neutrality by "hovering." Their warships lay about a few meters beyond our three-mile limit, waiting to pounce on suspected contraband carriers. It was one thing to try to find your prey in the middle of the Atlantic; it just did not seem sporting to snatch them up so easily, within sight of our shores.

Finally, in the summer of 1916, the British adopted a policy which, according to Wilson, was the "last straw." They published the names of American companies still trading with the Central Powers and prohibited Allied businessmen from trading with them or carrying any of their products on their vessels. A limited blacklist drawn up earlier had been kept private. Now, the British published it, thereby attacking our freedom to engage in trade with both England and Germany. (Interestingly, in 1941, even before we were at war, Franklin Roosevelt issued a comparable blacklist of American firms trading with the Axis powers.)

By 1916, then, we had compiled a full bill of grievances against the British. Despite all of these provocations, we did not break relations with them for several good reasons. Above all, they were sensitive to our situation and knew exactly when to tighten their screws a turn or two. Their violations grew incrementally and almost imperceptibly. They often timed the announcement of a new, tough Admiralty ruling to coincide with a submarine outrage. American front pages featured the gory story of a sinking while the financial pages noted in a small box the addition of some new vital material to the contraband list. By the time the submarine incident had dropped from the front pages and Americans turned their attention to something else, the new British ruling was a *fait accompli.*

Had the British offended us in 1914 the way they finally offended us in 1916, we probably would have threatened to break relations with them unless they ceased and desisted. Such a threat could not have been ignored in 1914. At that time, they relied upon our goods, especially foodstuffs, more than they did two years later when their empire took up the slack. Recognizing this factor in 1914, the British tread cautiously, violating our neutrality in ways calculated to result in little more than verbal slaps on the wrist from Washington. By 1916, however, we needed them almost as much as they needed us. Their war trade had pulled us out of depression. Had we threatened to sever relations in 1916, they might have called our bluff, secure in their belief that at the last moment we would not have sacrificed our economy on the altar of Jeffersonian moral outrage.

Wilson did not take the British policy lying down. From the start, he and the State Department protested against each perceived violation of our rights. As the months passed, these protests increased in vigor and volume. It was said that Wilson had written so many protests that the White House had run out of stationery. In 1916, he even gave serious thought to retaliatory commercial legislation. During the six months prior to the German declaration of unlimited submarine warfare on January 31, 1917, Wilson was far more worried about British behavior than German. The Germans had temporarily curbed their submarines while the British were becoming increasingly feisty. A change of government in London had brought men to power who were not as willing to put up with Wilson's constant complaining. The mood in England became ugly as many argued that while they were suffering unprecedented hardship defending democratic ideals, the United States, enjoying profits from the war trade, complained about obscure legal issues. As tempers rose in both Anglo-Saxon countries in 1916, Wilson appeared to be as neutral, or at least as anti-British, as he had been since the start of the war.

At the same time, Wilson had to worry about the Republicans; 1916 was an election year. His reelection appeared to be a long shot since he won in 1912 because the Republicans ran two candidates against him—Taft and the Progressive Roosevelt. In 1916, a reunited GOP standing behind Charles Evans Hughes prepared to reestablish its position as the majority party. Had Wilson called for the British to halt their violations or else, and had they refused as they would have, we might have been thrown into a recession and Wilson would have been thrown out of office. Many more Americans would have been angry about a depression than his failure to prosecute vigorously our legal case against the British. After all, none of the British actions cost one American life.

From the German point of view, American behavior toward Britain was intolerable. As we will see, we treated German maritime infractions in quite a different way indeed. For practical reasons, Wilson could not have threatened to sever the British-American trade link although only that threat early on might have produced some movement from London. At the same time, he continuously held out the threat of a diplomatic break and worse over the heads of the Germans. But what could Wilson have done and to whom did he owe his prime loyalty— international law or the security and economic well-being of his country and, perhaps, his and his party's political well-being? In an earlier period, Jefferson and his colleagues chose the higher road of international law and morality with disastrous results. Wilson, who sounded rather Jeffersonian in his protests to the Germans, adopted the Federalists' policy of accepting British violations, albeit with the firing of a series of paper broadsides, in order to maintain our prosperity. The maintenance of the British-American trade link coupled with Wilson's insistence that he was a genuine neutral made his policy appear both inconsistent and biased against Germany. Moreover, it was the sinking of American contraband carriers—carriers accepting British "tyranny"—that eventually brought the United States into the war in the spring of 1917. One can only wonder if the generally pacific Wilson ever conceived of his options as dichotomous: continued prosperity but the likelihood of eventual war with Germany or depression and no war. Most likely, his choice was never that clear-cut but he did know that he ran the risk of war so long as he did not maintain an even-handed approach to the two key belligerents. In any event, our unwillingness to demand more from the British weakened our case against the Germans. We can understand their impatience with what they thought to be a hypocritical Wilson for when it came to German violations of American neutrality, the President went beyond the sending of nasty notes.

SUBMARINE WARFARE

The Germans never had the opportunity to violate our rights in the British manner. Although their navy was the second largest in the world, it was no match for the British. Except for the Battle of Jutland in 1915, it remained virtually inoperative throughout the war. From the German point of view, this waste of a splendid navy was a shame because the insular British were far more vulnerable to naval blockade and even starvation than were the autarchic Germans. The Kaiser did have some submarines.

Germany was a latecomer to submarines. Prior to the war, the British were ahead of them in that esoteric branch of naval weaponry. Nevertheless, the Germans did possess a few U-boats which they dispatched after August 4 to make what mischief they could. As things turned out, those initial forays worked so well that the German Admiralty began to think that the war on the seas could be successfully waged even with its surface fleet bottled up.

Unfortunately for the Germans, the submarine was not covered by existing maritime law. Up to the fall of 1914, submarines had never been used the way the Germans proposed to use them. Consequently, there was no body of international precedents, let alone law, to which a neutral or belligerent could turn for guidance when it prepared a case for or against the submarine. With little to go on, Americans and other neutrals, as well as the gleeful British, had to adapt the rules for surface vessels to the submarine—and this was absurd. According to traditional practices, when a captain desired to search and maybe even destroy a contraband carrier, he hailed the offending ship, boarded her, and, before dispatching her to the bottom of the sea, adhered to a series of humanitarian rules that guaranteed the safety of crew and passengers. For example, the belligerent captain was supposed to take the crewmen of the doomed ship on board his own craft, or at least allow them time to take to lifeboats. This was the way civilized belligerents behaved on the high seas. Even the British generally followed such regulations.

Try as it might, a submarine could not behave as a surface vessel. In the first place, it was most effective below the water. Thin-skinned and poorly armed, it was a sitting duck for the cannons of a merchant vessel or even for some bold captain who chose to use his ship as a battering ram. When submarines adhered to naval etiquette and surfaced to warn the enemy, as they sometimes did, much of their tactical advantage was lost. A submarine had to strike by surprise to maximize its strategic strengths. Moreover, its miniscule size precluded its picking up survivors clinging to the flotsam and jetsam of what was once their ship. For these reasons, the submarine was considered by many to be an immoral weapon.

Who is to say what is an immoral weapon in war which is itself immoral? No matter how ridiculous it may seem to distinguish between lethal weapons, we label some as more moral than others. For example, most nations agree that dum-dum bullets, poison gas, and atomic bombs are immoral weapons. That is, it is legitimate to kill and maim your enemies with rifles, machine guns, mortars, bombs, or just the simple bayonet, but not with gas or dum-dum bullets. The atomic bombing of Hiroshima and Nagasaki appears to many more immoral than the firebombing of Tokyo that preceded those attacks. Yet, more people died in firebombings than in atomic bombings. Illogical, perhaps, but the whole business of making rules for sportsmanlike war is illogical.

From the American point of view, when the submarine operated effectively—striking merchants by surprise—it operated immorally. When the Germans formally announced their submarine policy to the world in February of 1915, Wilson cautioned them that they would be held to "strict accountability" for violations of neutrality. He never used that phrase with the British.

Civilians in German ruling circles worried about how the submarine would affect neutral opinion and, in the American case, behavior. Those civilians, who throughout the war steadily lost their limited power to the military, contended that unrestrained use of the submarine would lead not only to the weakening of the German cause in the eyes of the world but also to the conversion of neutrals into belligerents. Time and again, the generals and admirals countered such warnings with purely military arguments concerning the numbers of ships they could sink and the relationship of submarine warfare to the battle on land. Unlike their civilian critics, they paid scant attention to the middle- and long-range political ramifications of their shorter run strategies. This debate between those with a military perspective and those with a political-diplomatic perspective is not unusual.

Despite the caution of much of the civilian leadership, the German government issued its first formal submarine warfare declaration on February 4, 1915. As of February 18, the waters surrounding England would be considered a war zone in which U-boats would strike at all enemy merchant ships. Neutrals were warned to keep their people and products off those ships. While the Germans promised to try to avoid mistakes, the fact that British ships often ran neutral flags would make it difficult for them to distinguish between genuine neutrals and camouflaged enemy vessels.

Over a month passed before an American ship or citizen was lost to the submarine. We enjoyed this brief honeymoon because the Germans tried to avoid offending us, and also because they had only 20 submarines or so to patrol the huge expanse of the war zone. In late March, the inevitable occurred and Leon C. Thrasher, an American citizen, went down with the British steamer, *Falaba*. The debate in Washington over responses to the Thrasher case is interesting, especially when we compare it to the next and more famous case, which was, in a legal sense, almost identical. Prepared to issue a firm protest, Wilson was temporarily talked out of it by Secretary of State Bryan who argued that we would appear unneutral because we had been tolerating British violations of our neutrality. Before the Thrasher case had been settled, the *Lusitania* was sunk.

Not just 1 but 128 Americans went down with the luxury liner that lost 1,198 passengers and crew on May 7, 1915. There was absolutely no doubt that the famous vessel had been a victim of a U-boat and, to make matters worse, the insensitive Germans decorated the young commander for his accurate marksmanship. The *Lusitania* was the *Chesapeake* of World War I and even more. Its sinking was the incident that most inflamed German-American relations from 1914 to the early part of 1917 and it colored all future dealings between the two powers. The dispatching of the passenger liner to the bottom of St. George's Channel was considered by almost all Americans to have been a barbarous and inhuman act; more barbarous and inhuman than the Thrasher case because it involved multiple deaths. Although Wilson had contemplated ignoring the Thrasher incident, the enormity of the so-called crime of the *Lusitania* had so outraged the population that Wilson the politician had to respond with force or else be considered a weak President who could not defend our right to travel unmolested on the high seas. Even had politics not been an issue, Wilson was personally offended by the *Lusitania* sinking.

Sensing the magnitude of the crisis, the Germans constructed a defense for their action. They pointed out that the allegedly peaceful passenger vessel had been carrying contraband in the form of munitions. Indeed, they contended, that was one of the reasons she sunk like a stone in only 18 minutes. Moreover, had the submarine surfaced to warn the *Lusitania's* passengers, it would have been crushed into matchsticks by the giant vessel whose captain was under orders to ram submarines. And in any case, noted the German Admiralty, the *Lusitania* was armed. Her armament, plus the legal relationship of all vessels in the British merchant marine to the Royal Navy, made the *Lusitania* little different from any other ship of the line.

The question of the arming of the *Lusitania* is one that has intrigued several generations of investigators. Germany claimed that a large "thing" covered by a tarpaulin was on one of the decks, guarded night and day. When the official British divers went down to examine the wreck of the *Lusitania,* they reported, not surprisingly, that no such object was to be found. In recent years, more impartial investigations have concluded that the liner was not armed.

The Germans went even further. They maintained that the British wanted the *Lusitania* sunk in order to strain German-American relations. At least, its captain behaved incautiously when he refrained from taking maneuvers recommended to vessels trying to elude U-boats. The German commander likened the *Lusitania* to a sitting duck almost asking to be sunk. Although this allegation is difficult to swallow, the *Lusitania's* captain did exercise poor judgment when he charted a peace-time approach to Ireland.

Finally, the Germans pointed out that they did not strike by surprise. They had warned Americans through public advertisements of the danger of travel on the *Lusitania.* Therefore, any passengers who refused to heed the warnings took their lives in their own hands.

Though Bryan did not accept all German explanations, he did feel that Wilson should consider them before rushing to judgment. His was a minority view in the Cabinet as well as the country at large. Wilson maintained that nothing the Germans could say would ever convince him that a belligerent had the right to sink a passenger vessel. In addition, and here was the clincher, if we were ever going to have a say in the way the peace was structured, we had to defend neutral rights and international law. If he bowed to German brutality here, Wilson argued, no one would listen to our plans for a just peace at war's end. We could not allow the Germans to weaken our prestige.

When asked by Bryan and others why he did not try to keep his countrymen out of the dangerous war zone (something done in the 1930s), Wilson insisted on our traditional right to travel on belligerent passenger vessels. During presubmarine days, such travel had caused few problems. To relinquish our rights would have been tantamount to surrendering a portion of our sovereignty; no nation could maintain its prestige by abnegating its solemn obligations to its citizens and the international community. Yet, had we kept Americans out of the war zone there would have been no war with Germany. Wilson later said the right was more precious than peace. Perhaps, but though we may agree on what he meant by peace, the right is more difficult to define.

Bryan registered his dissent on the *Lusitania* matter in a most unusual fashion--he resigned from the Cabinet. He felt he could be more effective fighting Wilson from the outside than in a Cabinet in which he was constantly ignored. We can sympathize with this simple man who may not have understood all the implications of power politics but who, in his own way, tried to lead America toward even-handed neutrality. He appears an even more tragic figure when we consider the way the President earlier had transferred almost all important foreign policy functions to Colonel House and Bryan's underling in the Department, Counselor Lansing.

When Bryan left the Cabinet, guileless neutrality lost a powerful spokesman. His replacement, Robert Lansing, was more pro-British than Wilson and far more of a realpolitician than the Great Commoner whose political career had ended.

With Bryan out of the way, Wilson issued a strong protest over the *Lusitania* and demanded indemnities, an acceptance of guilt, and promises to refrain from such practices in the future. The Germans moved slowly to meet some of Wilson's demands. While claims and counterclaims were shuttling across the Atlantic, a new crisis arose over the sinking of the *Arabic,* a British liner, and the 2 Americans among the 44 passengers who went down with the ship.

The uproar in the United States was predictable with memories of the *Lusitania* horrors still lingering. Going beyond his formal instructions, the German ambassador to the United States told Wilson that his government repudiated the *Arabic* attack (which had been, in fact, a mistake), agreed to pay indemnities, and promised that such things would not happen again.

The Germans behaved cautiously through the remainder of 1915, but in early 1916, they began to heat up the submarine war again, albeit doing their best to strike at targets considered legitimate by Wilson and the neutrals. Nevertheless, on March 24, 1916, the *Sussex* was attacked and Americans suffered casualties. Given the apparent violation of earlier *Arabic* pledges, some of the President's advisors called for a severance of German-American relations. Not prepared for such a drastic step, Wilson gave the Germans one last chance.

The Germans responded with the *Sussex* Pledge, in effect giving us one last chance. They promised not to sink vessels without warning and to provide for the safety and security of passengers inconvenienced by the submarine, but these concessions were made conditional upon British acceptance of neutral rights. Wilson was pleased with the *Sussex* Pledge except for the condition and told the Germans so. The matter of the British violations of neutrality was left dangling. When the Germans later violated their pledge in February of 1917, they claimed they were acting legally because the British had not halted *their* illegal activities. Wilson did not accept that explanation.

We probably would have avoided war had Wilson kept Americans out of the war zone. Such a statement raises several questions. Should he have tried to avoid war? Could he have avoided war? For the time being, let us argue that the avoidance of war was in the national interest. How then could Wilson have kept Americans out of the war zone? The means were available in the Gore-McLemore Resolution of February 1916. Bryanites and Congressmen who felt that obstinate insistence on our rights would eventually force Germany's hand introduced a resolution to prohibit Americans and their goods from entering submarine-blockaded waters.

The President mounted a vigorous campaign against the bill. He did not want Congress tying his hands. The Gore-McLemore Resolution became a constitutional issue for him since it represented an attempt to undermine his ability to conduct foreign policy. Although a careful reading of the Constitution, as well as the comments of the Founding Fathers, suggests that such a congressional initiative was in order, the President thought otherwise. His successors have reacted in much the same way to congressional attempts to maintain the checks-and-balances system.

When it came to the substance of the issue, Wilson contended, as he had before, that we could not afford to truckle to the submarine. Our national honor, international law, and especially the need to maintain our prestige in the days to come all militated against a cowardly abnegation of our obligations.

This was not the only way to save American lives. Some suggested that it would be more dignified merely to ban all armed ships from our ports. According to the rules of neutrality, offensively armed ships—warships—were not allowed in neutral waters, but defensively armed ships—merchants with cannons—were. Had we barred the armed merchants, then German submarines in the Atlantic might have been able to safely surface, warn the contraband carrier that her time was up, allow passengers to take to lifeboats, and then, and only then, blow her out of the water. Some European neutrals under German guns did adopt this policy.

Any decision barring armed ships from our ports would have favored the Germans since it would have made a submarine's job easier. Nevertheless, during the early days of 1916, Wilson toyed with the idea. In the end, he decided against this modification of our policy on the grounds that it would be unfair to the British. Although the proposed rule was legal, it might have altered the balance on the high seas and thus the course of the war. More important, Wilson toyed with this measure at precisely the time that Colonel House was in London on his promising House-Grey mediation mission. To announce the new armed-ship policy at that juncture, it was thought, would endanger the delicate negotiations. True enough, but then why was the measure not considered again after the British finally decided to reject House's proposal? The *Sussex* Pledge of May 1916 did make the issue temporarily irrelevant, but what appeared to be a good plan in January would still have been a good plan in May.

Clearly, we did possess options that might have kept us out of war. We should be able to understand the Germans who thought that we behaved unfairly and did not exhaust all possibilities for compromise through the various crises. We can also understand, if not accept entirely, the Kaiser's complaints about our unwillingness to keep Americans out of the war zone:

> Humanity in Wilson's head means unlimited possibilities for real or hypothetical citizens of the USA to cruise about on hostile and armed merchantmen whenever they like in the war zone. Should these partially paid protections to British ships by chance be killed or wounded by us is inhuman. But sending millions of shells and cartridges to England and her allies to kill and maim thousands of German soldiers is not inhuman but quite proper because very lucrative. To insult, hamper and illtreat all the small neutrals because they wish to remain neutral is perfectly right as well as the trampling under foot of all international law and abrogating the London and Paris declarations which leaves the sea helpless, open to British piracy, that is quite admissible because done by England. The British threaten the hunger war against all noncombattants women and children in Central Europe is absolutely not inhuman in Wilson's eyes and quite right. But that Germany should by all means possible parry this diabolical plan and the practices of England to put it into execution even at the expense of some American passengers who have no right to get in its way—that is inadmissible and very wrong in the eyes of Wilson and most inhuman. Either starve at England's bidding or war with America. This is in name of Wilson's humanity.

BUMBLING SPIES

U-boat commanders were not the only ones who contributed to Germany's ill fame in America. Her spies and saboteurs also were responsible for the deterioration of German-American relations. During wartime, a neutral expects that his soil will be used by rival spies and intelligence agents. Hollywood's images of Lisbon, Istanbul, and Bern during World War II readily come to mind. A little bit of hanky-panky can be tolerated, especially if it is carried on quietly and with discretion. During World War I, the Germans not only transcended the bounds of normal intrigue but also had the misfortune to get caught at it.

In several well-publicized affairs, German officials were discovered with incriminating documents revealing their attempts to organize strikes among munitions workers, to buy or blow up factories, to embroil the United States more deeply in the Mexican crisis, to destroy Canadian Great Lakes canals, and to subsidize newspapers and journalists. The British, who were engaged in comparable activities, were able to elude detection in most cases. We know now that Treasury officials charged with maintaining surveillance of foreign agents were more zealous in their pursuit of German than British spies. It was also true that the Germans were incredibly clumsy. One of the Kaiser's bumbling spies fell asleep on an elevated train in New York and lost his briefcase stuffed with secret documents to a light-fingered agent. Another, who fell in love while on vacation in Maine, told his patriotic American girl friend about his exploits as a secret agent.

Once again, we can sympathize with the Germans to some degree since our country was turning out many of the weapons the Allies used to kill their countrymen, and almost all the media was pro-English. How else, except by buying newspapers, could they get their message to the American people? The Germans did make it worse by usually confessing their sins once confronted with the evidence—"I did it for the Kaiser and I'm glad"—or words to that effect. Even the Austrian Ambassador, Count Constantine Dumba (there was no end of puns about his name), admitted his involvement in sensational intrigues. Thus, all of these incidents helped convince Wilson, and especially the American public, that Germans were not very honorable.

WILSON AS MEDIATOR

There is another element in the story of our entry into World War I. We have already seen how Wilson was worried about British violations of our neutrality, angered by German submarine warfare, and nervous about our economic and his political prospects. In addition, from August of 1914 to January of 1917, he worked on a variety of proposals to end the war. Although these proposals constitute a separate strand in the story, and an important one at that, we must not lose sight of the fact that they were intimately related in time and space to the other strands.

Behind Wilson's mediation proposals was a desire to make a peace that would contribute to the restructuring of the international system. In order to eliminate the revanchist spirit that had so much to do with this and earlier wars, the President worked for a peace without victors. Although he was in sympathy with British *Weltpolitik* and hoped that the Allies would administer a modest drubbing to the undemocratic Germans, the chief element of his peace featured an equitable redrawing of European boundaries so that neither side gained territory at the expense of the other. Some in Wilson's entourage who were not averse to seeing a big British victory did not allow their emotional attachment to the mother country blind them to practical problems. As Colonel House noted, the destruction of Germany would create a power vacuum in Central Europe into which would march the Russians (the Czarist and not the Communist variety—yet). From our point of view, a Central Europe dominated by a relatively strong progressive Germany was a saner place than a Central Europe controlled by the Czar.

Our first attempt at peacemaking was a dud. During the initial weeks of the war, Bryan blundered about with a rather embarrassing public peace proposal and after this failure, despite his commitment to a just peace, the Secretary was shoved into the background and Wilson and House handled the peace offensives. When the Germans failed to take Paris and finish off the war in a few weeks, action on the Western Front bogged down into almost four years of trench warfare. Both sides constructed elaborate trenchworks from the English Channel to Switzerland and, from the fall of 1914 to the spring of 1918, they moved little from those original positions. The massive offensives launched by one side and then the other resulted in millions of casualties and meaningless exchanges of 10 or 20 miles of territory. There were no breakthroughs, despite the promises of the generals. For all intents and purposes, the war in the west, the major front, was a stalemate. Wilson should have had a relatively easy time as mediator once the outlines of the struggle became clear to the belligerents. To the contrary, even after the rival generals proved to be impotent against the respective defensive positions, after they sent their men out, time and time again, to hurl themselves suicidally on the enemies' machine gun nests, Wilson did not come close to stopping the carnage.

We can understand his failure. In the first place, the war in the west was not quite a draw, at least on paper, since the battlelines were drawn well within French territory. By breaking into France in August of 1914, the Germans had won the first round. Consequently, even though the French threw them back short of Paris, their initial gains suggested they were winning. And if they were winning, why should they make a peace on the basis of a draw? Had the Germans been repulsed on the French border and had the trenches been dug along the frontier, the war might have been easier to terminate on the basis of *status quo ante bellum.*

Moreover, generals on both sides stubbornly insisted that a breakthrough was just around the corner, their next offensive would work, and that their opponents would be forced to sue for peace. Both camps argued that if the war ended in stalemate, there would be no real peace—merely an armistice. The conflicts that caused war to erupt in August of 1914 would still be there, festering close to the surface of international politics. All those conflicts purportedly could be resolved with just one breakthrough. And so the generals were repeatedly given another chance.

Finally, as the war developed into a total war, the belligerents became prisoners of their own propaganda. Although the British and Germans did not really care for one another when the war began, they did not hate one another. After all, they were united by the vast family of Queen Victoria. Willy (Kaiser Wilhelm II) and Nicky (Czar Nicholas II) were nephews of the late Edward VII. But as the war dragged on and the generals called for the second and third sons of their citizenry and the government demanded more hours in the factory and higher taxes, the respective leaders had to offer something to their suffering populations. That something turned out to be participation in a noble crusade to topple the Satan in Berlin (or London, or Paris, or St. Petersburg) from his throne. What began as a traditional balance-of-power war was converted by propagandists into a holy war against anti-Christs. After a year or so of telling your people that they were engaged in a struggle to the death for the glory of western civilization, how could you turn around and explain that a compromise peace was in the offing? One cannot make deals with the devil. The propagandists who had offered their populations rationales for the way they were being squeezed for blood and money were hoist on their own petards. It became almost impossible for European governments to affect the sort of peace without victory called for by Wilson even if they came to think that such an approach was practical.

And so the awful war went on. If some wars are more rational than others, then World War I must be among the most irrational. We might be able to accept some of the unprecedented casualties had progress been made in terms of territory captured. The Allied landing in Normandy in 1944 and the subsequent march to Germany made sense because the armies were getting someplace. In World War I, millions died and nothing happened; neither side budged in that terrible war of attrition. Wilson saw this, as did many Americans, and so he vigorously, perhaps naively, and certainly unneutrally pursued the chimera of a just peace through American mediation.

In 1915 and 1916, Colonel House was sent on private missions to talk to the British, French, and Germans about prospects for peace. House, who admired the British, did not like the Germans. Knowing this, his friends in London greeted him more as a quasi-ally than an impartial mediator, although he claimed to be one. Theoretically, this personal favoritism for one side, if not discovered or resented by the Germans, could have worked to House's benefit since the British trusted him.

As early as 1915, some European leaders began to seek ways out of the bloody dead-end of trench warfare. It was difficult to talk peace in London where rumors of dovishness threatened to shatter the Anglo-French alliance. The story went that Germany would fight to the last German and England to the last Frenchman.

In Germany, rumors of a compromise peace threatened to spark a civil war between the right and a left that had not been very happy about voting for war credits in 1914. After visiting London and Berlin in the spring of 1915, House had to report back to Wilson that prospects for peace that year looked dim.

Our 1916 overture was more dramatic. Again, Colonel House played the major role as he journeyed to London in early January armed with a most unusual proposal. He hoped to obtain the belligerents' agreement to come to a peace conference and also to accept the basic outlines of a settlement that he promised would be in the Allies' interest. If the British would accept Wilson's plans for peace and if the Germans refused them, then the United States would "probably" enter the war on the British side. House planned to try to obtain Berlin's approval of Wilson's plans as well, but he did not make a corresponding offer about American intervention on *their* side; nor did he promise that his peace terms would be in the German interest. The so-called House-Grey Memorandum does not look very neutral given the asymmetrical nature of our promises.

The plan foundered on the word "probably" that hedged the American promise to come in on the British side. The year 1916 was an election year and the British thought it unlikely that Wilson would be able to bring his country into war, even had he wanted to, unless the Germans began attacking all American vessels. Furthermore, January 1916 was not a propitious time to talk of peace in the Allied camp for they were not doing very well in France. Supposedly, one must not sue for peace from a position of weakness.

Wilson's last major mediation proposal was more neutral. Indeed, as we have noted, the President appeared to be his most neutral during the last six months of 1916, between the issuance of the *Sussex* Pledge and Germany's decision for unlimited submarine warfare in January of 1917. This was the period of the British blacklist and other new affronts on the high seas. On top of this, failure of the House-Grey Memorandum convinced Wilson that the British were stringing him along: talking about peace but determined to continue the war. Here he was correct for we know that the British, who were sensitive to American opinion, tried to make themselves look like peacemongers when all along they hoped the President would peddle his idealism elsewhere.

After his victory in the election of 1916, Wilson found himself in a stronger position. With domestic politics squared, he turned again to peacemaking and issued a unilateral mediation proposal in December. In this instance, he called upon the belligerents to publicly explain their goals and programs for peace. His demarche frightened the British who suspected that he had turned from working with them to working with the Germans. It happened that the Germans were then considering a reopening of submarine warfare. Before they took that dramatic step, the civilians were allowed one last diplomatic attempt to bring about a peace favorable to their interests. Thus, Wilson's call for peace and the German proposals to open negotiations were made public during the same week in December. Despite Wilson's denials, the British felt that this was no coincidence—

Wilson was probably in league with the Germans. If so, London was in an awkward position.

Their concern was eased by the friendly advice of Secretary of State Lansing. More of an Anglophile than Wilson, by the end of 1916 he was convinced that we belonged in the war on the British side. Unbeknownst to Wilson, Lansing assured the British that there was no connection between the German and American proposals. To make things even worse, he advised them about the sort of response that would most please the President. Such behavior came close to treason or at least disloyalty. It compared to the actions of Alexander Hamilton who, in 1794, revealed to the British the cards we were holding as we prepared to negotiate the Jay Treaty.

In the end, both the British and the Germans offered unacceptable responses to Wilson's final peace plea. Because the British response was less unacceptable in tone than the German, Wilson concluded this phase of his peacemaking with renewed faith in the better intentions of the British.

THE KAISER GOES FOR BROKE

On January 31, 1917, the German Ambassador presented his government's proclamation of unlimited submarine warfare to Lansing. This unprecedented policy was fraught with danger for neutrals and Germany alike. Never before had Germany threatened to sink all vessels in the war zone, passenger and merchant, belligerent and neutral. Four days later, as the tearful ambassador bid the Secretary of State farewell, Wilson went before Congress to explain why he had to sever relations with Germany. The Kaiser's envoy agreed that we had no other choice but to honor our threats made during the *Sussex* crisis— his government had thrown down a challenge that had to be accepted. It was now only a matter of time before the submarine incidents mounted and Wilson asked for war. Why did the Germans do virtually the only thing that could bring us into the war against them?

Their decision to unleash the submarines was understandable if unwise. Not anticipating the first Russian Revolution, the German General Staff reported to the Kaiser that if they did not win the war in six months, they might never win it. According to projections of the comparative strength of the rivals, the Entente powers would have the upper hand were the war to continue into 1918. Consequently, Britain had to be brought to her knees quickly through all means possible, including the establishment of a submarine blockade of her territory. They argued that if all wraps were lifted from the submarine, Britain would be starved into surrender on terms favorable to the Central Powers. The German gamble was not outlandish. In January, operating under restrictions, the submarines destroyed 368,000 tons of shipping, in February 540,000, and the amount of tonnage sunk increased dramatically into the spring. More important, for the first time, neutrals began to steer clear of the war zone because of the submarine. Unfortunately for the Germans, since they did not have enough submarines to go around, a sizable number of merchants made it through the blockade with precious cargoes of food and war materials.

German advocates of unlimited submarine warfare were not concerned about neutral anger. People who did not worry about scraps of paper in 1914 would hardly worry about a diminution of their popularity in neutral capitals. As for those neutrals such as the United States that might satisfy their anger with a declaration of war, by the time their strength was added to that of the Allies, the war would be over. Again, German analysts were not far from the mark, since although our men and material proved helpful to the Allies by the end of 1917, we played a subsidiary role until the spring of 1918, fully a year after the initiation of unlimited submarine warfare. Had the submarine been able to deliver a swift, crushing blow, American entry into the war would have counted for nought.

German strategists did, however, undervalue the importance of American entry to the British. Knowing the Yanks were soon coming, they were able to commit reserves to the battle that they had been saving for 1918. Furthermore, with the United

States as an ally, the British no longer needed to worry about their dwindling monetary reserves and loan subscriptions. Such nuances were too subtle for German military men who thought primarily in terms of United States military might and preparations in early 1917.

The German General Staff had nothing but contempt for American military capabilities. They had just observed our pathetic attempt to find Pancho Villa in northern Mexico in the middle of 1916. Compared to their own and other continental forces, our army was too inexperienced and sloppy to pose a threat to them.

Finally, they argued that we had behaved so unneutrally in the past by supplying many of the weapons used by the British and French on the Western Front that even without the submarine issue, we had been nonbelligerent partners of the Entente. If anything, our entry into the war would weaken the British in the short run because we would have to keep some supplies and munitions for ourselves and also because German submarines could roam the world to sink our vessels at will.

Germany's civilian leaders could no longer match the generals' prestige or power. They had their chance in December and failed. Their more moderate arguments fell on deaf ears as the submarines were sent out to win the war for the Kaiser.

Wilson's policies had contributed to the German decision. Undoubtedly, his tolerance of English maritime activities and his intolerance of German made him appear to be anything but neutral in the eyes of Berlin. If Germany's submarines and spies had made Wilson think less of German trustworthiness, Wilson's skewed neutrality had exasperated the Germans. His nondefense policy also played a role in their decision. The man who once talked about being too proud to fight was a latecomer to the idea of preparedness. Had we been better prepared in the winter of 1916-1917, had we possessed an army ready to leap into troop transports, the Germans might have thought twice about their submarine policy. Their decision was predicated in part on the knowledge that we would not be a significant military factor in the Allied camp for quite a while.

At bottom, however, such a line of analysis is not fair to the President. Although we can understand their plight, the blame for the German decision must ultimately rest with Berlin. With their declaration of unlimited submarine warfare, they were converted into ruthless "Prussians" who had challenged not only the United States but also international decency.

WILSON LAUNCHES A CRUSADE

The severance of diplomatic relations with Germany did not mean that war was the inevitable next step. It was possible, for example, that the Germans would refrain from sinking American ships or that their submarine policy was just a bluff meant to frighten neutrals away from the war zone. In fact, several weeks passed before the first incident occurred that involved American deaths. In March, German intentions became clear. Up to the declaration of unlimited submarine warfare, 10 American vessels had been sunk by mistake. In March, 9 were sunk on purpose. Every few days, newspapers reported the latest sinking, the names of the dead, and survivors' tales of horror. With each such story, the nation became more upset. It was too late to consider truckling to the submarine by keeping Americans out of the war zone, although such an action would have headed off war. Through their flouting of the *Sussex* Pledge, the Germans had thrown down the gauntlet to the proud President and his countrymen. At the same time, the handful of sinkings themselves were not quite enough to convince all Americans that the moment for intervention had come. Wilson was among those who hoped against hope that we could find a dignified way to avoid war and defend national honor.

He first attempted to head off full-scale war through armed neutrality. The House of Representatives gave its approval to a bill that would have allowed American merchant ships to arm in order to defend themselves against U-boats. A "little group of willfull men" in the Senate, however, killed the measure. Nevertheless, the President found an allegedly legal way to effect the arming of vessels by executive order, and thus increased marginally the security of our merchant fleet. Submarines would no longer be able to attack from the surface where they were at their most mobile. All the same, the arming of the merchant ships offered no direct protection from submarines that struck from beneath the surface.

Two other events pushed Wilson and most of his countrymen over the brink. One was within his ability to control, the other was not. The first event, and the more important in the short run, was the infamous Zimmermann Telegram. Arthur Zimmermann, the German Foreign Secretary, asked his minister in Mexico to propose an alliance with our southern neighbor. For bait, he held out the prospect of the reconquest of the Mexican Cession as well as Japanese support. That the Mexicans would never countenance such a scheme, despite our intervention in their revolution, was not important here. The fact that the Germans were trying to incite them was another breech of international etiquette and a challenge to the Monroe Doctrine.

How we came to learn of the telegram is an amazing story. In a small irony, the Zimmermann proposal was sent from the American Embassy in Berlin. Since late 1916, we had permitted the Germans use of our equipment to transmit messages here in hopes that better access to transatlantic communication systems would facilitate peace conversations. The British, who were listening to most of Germany's worldwide communications and had cracked many of their codes by 1917, picked up the Zimmermann dispatch from *our* sender. Playing the role of the honest boy scout, they handed over the incriminating note to our ambassador in London for transmission back to Wilson.

If, by the end of February, Wilson was still serious about staying out of war, his treatment of the Zimmermann telegram did not serve that purpose. He could have responded with a strongly worded, *private* note to the Germans and awaited their explanations. Instead, he released the telegram to the American press which pounced on the story. Wilson's decision to make the telegram public, which inflamed American passions, inched us closer to formal belligerency.

Zimmermann made things even worse. The normal thing to do in such cases is to denounce the document as a forgery, a product of propagandists in the British intelligence service. One should not admit that she or he has lost a classified document or a spy. Had Zimmermann denied the authenticity of the telegram, a sizable minority of Americans would probably have believed him. Because of their unwillingness to reveal information about their intelligence operations, the British had no way to demonstrate the telegram's authenticity. The clumsy Zimmermann readily admitted that he had written the despatch and, in so doing, rubbed salt into the already festering wound of German-American relations.

The second major event of the period, and the one beyond Wilson's ability to control, was the Russian Revolution: the first, and from our point of view, good (non-Bolshevik) revolution of February-March 1917. All through the war, we had been skeptical about Allied claims of representing the forces of freedom. Although France and England were democratic countries fighting against German and Austrian autocrats, they were saddled with the Russians whose government was among the most illiberal in the world. In the spring of 1917, when the Russians toppled the Czar and established a democracy of sorts, the Entente's claims to moral superiority over their enemies were dramatically enhanced. Although the British and French were imperialists whose greedy plans for dividing up the possessions of Germany and Turkey violated Wilsonian conceptions of a just peace, such nasty business did not become common knowledge until the peace conference. For the nonce, the war could at last be sold as a struggle between the forces of light and the forces of darkness.

It is difficult to pin down the exact point when Wilson made up his mind that we had to go to war. During March, each new submarine outrage brought more Americans into the interventionist camp, a camp swelling with those angered by the Zimmermann effrontery and excited by the lifting of the yoke of tyranny in Russia. Though not all were clamoring for war, with some leadership from the President, the vast majority of the population was prepared to fight for democracy.

Wilson spent the second and third weeks of March in virtual seclusion, taking counsel with no one save his god. When he emerged from contemplative hibernation to face his Cabinet on March 20, he had decided for war. We can well-understand his thinking. Armed neutrality was not working and the Germans offered no indication of their willingness to relax the submarine policy. American prestige was under the gun everyday. Earlier, Wilson had argued that we had to defend our neutrality against the submarine in order to maintain the respect we would need to influence the construction of a just peace. Now, he convinced himself that we could best arrange a just peace, if we attended the peace conference on the side of the victors. Perhaps this new approach was merely a rationalization for a decision that had to be made on the basis of what Wilson perceived to be our national interests. It is true that our presence at the victor's table at Versailles did guarantee a less harsh treaty than that planned by revenge-minded leaders in France and England.

Aside from this general issue, it is probable that the unlimited submarine warfare policy and the Zimmermann dispatch, taken with prior broken promises and sabotage, had finally convinced him that the rulers in Berlin were indeed ruthless people who could be blamed for starting the war. Wilson had come full circle. When the war began, his immediate reaction had been to blame it on the Germans. After considerable reflection, he turned to the system and a multicausal approach. Now he was back blaming the Germans. Furthermore, he maintained that once they were eliminated from the international system, all nations could move toward capitalist democracy and peace. Whether he believed this simplistic approach to international relations or tried to convince himself that the Entente was fighting for freedom as a justification for his own resort to arms is difficult to say. It certainly made that decision more palatable to him and his countrymen.

Above all, Wilson felt that the physical attack upon the United States represented by the submarine outrages was an attack against our honor. That he gave much thought to economic considerations such as the need to protect our loans is unlikely. That he thought in terms of the balance of power and the implications of a German victory for our long-term security is also unlikely. For Wilson, it was the submarine and all that the submarine had come to represent. We had staked out our position on that issue as early as February of 1915. As a proud nation, we could not afford to cave in to an immoral weapon wielded by an immoral people.

From the time of the Cabinet meeting of March 20 to April 2, there was little doubt we had chosen war. Wilson delayed going to Congress so that we could alert our armed services and merchant marine and make other preparations for the day of reckoning with Germany. Once having decided for war, he never wavered from the conviction that he had made the correct choice. At least, he spent a good deal of time between the Cabinet session and his meeting with Congress on the golf links.

Washington was in a festive mood on April 2. As might have been expected, a minority contingent of protesters were not yet convinced that Wilson had exhausted all peaceful options. One protester became involved in an altercation with supernationalist Senator Henry Cabot Lodge who proceeded to punch and knock down his younger antagonist.

Eloquent and moving, Wilson's speech may have been more self-righteous and idealistic than it should have been. The submarine outrages were his prime reason for going to war but, he contended, they represented not just attacks against America but against the world at large. They were symbolic of the evils of the Prussian autocracy, a system of government that did not respect the liberties of individuals or nations.

Like many statesmen going to war, he emphasized that he had no quarrel with the good German people, only with their evil leaders. The Prussian leaders, and not the people, had sent out submarines, spies, and saboteurs, as well as the Zimmermann telegram. Ranged against the forces of darkness in Berlin were the forces of light now joined by the democratic Russians. Taking the high ground beyond the submarine issue, Wilson promised Americans a world made safe for democracy with the victory of the Allies. A new world would emerge from the ashes of the old—a world in which the Progressive dream of a liberally oriented system would be fulfilled.

Wilson did not mention the balance of power and control of the Atlantic or the relationship between our domestic economy and submarine warfare. Even specific German assaults against our sovereignty were submerged in their greater assault against mankind. His speech thrilled most listeners. It has the same effect on readers today. Yet, as we have seen, it did not tell the entire story and was especially deficient in its simplistic division of the world into saints and sinners. In the months to come, when people discovered that our allies were not terribly saintly and when the peace did not usher in an era of amity among peoples, they felt duped. Disillusioned with the manner in which Wilson's high-minded principles had been apparently ignored by the President himself at Versailles, they retreated into insularity and self-righteousness.

Wilson's reasons for going to war do not appear compelling, especially when we recall the way our behavior had provoked the Germans. Perhaps Wilson the politician knew what he was doing. Had he couched his message in terms of national security and the submarine alone, he might not have convinced a large minority of Americans who would have preferred to stay out of the war zone than fight. After all, one logical, if unlikely response to the submarine was to retreat to our shores.

Wilson's idealistic call for a crusade was difficult to reject. In appealing to the best in the American tradition and in elevating the conflict from another grubby imperialist war to a war to save democracy, Wilson was able not only to bring along those not quite resigned to going to war but also to bring them along enthusiastically. In 1812, Madison seemed to accept the war with resignation. In 1917, although more pacific than his Virginia predecessor, Wilson almost looked forward to his crusade against evil.

Whether he himself believed all that he said is difficult to ascertain. Undoubtedly, he felt that the Germans had broken faith with him. He never liked them or their culture, especially as compared to the British, and now their actions on the seas and in our country proved beyond a reasonable doubt that they · were fiends. But then to make the French, English, and Russians God's servants on earth is another proposition.

Most Congressmen approved of the speech. Debate in the Senate and House was brief but spirited. In the Senate, 6 Senators opposed the war measure on a variety of grounds ranging from the need to ask the American people directly for their approval of that fearful thing to the general attack on Wilson's perceptions of the two camps. In the House, 50 Representatives voted no to war, among them the first woman Representative, pacifist Jeannette Rankin. On April 6, we were formally at war with Germany. In the patriotic aftermath, dissenters in Congress were excoriated, many of them, including Congresswoman Rankin, lost their seats, while their antiwar supporters suffered persecution for failing to rally around the flag.

WORLD WAR I AND NATIONAL SECURITY

As we moved into the twentieth century, the question of the determinants of national security became more complicated. Revolutions in transportation, especially in the air, made it possible by the 1940s for an enemy to conceive of bombing or invading the United States.

During World War II, Walter Lippmann wrote an influential treatise in which he argued that Wilson went to war in 1917 for the wrong reasons. According to the philosopher-journalist, the United States had to enter the Great War because German control of the Atlantic was a threat to the balance of power and thus to our national security. This approach made sense to many in 1943 with the Nazis on the beaches of Europe's Atlantic coast and their airplanes developing transatlantic capabilities. Did it make sense in 1917?

First of all, we must deal with that sticky issue of intentions. Although the Kaiser and his friends did dream of world hegemony, in 1914 they did not have realistic hopes for taking over continents with anything more than German products and businessmen. Since they never came close to conquering France, let alone England and the rest of Europe, they spent little time planning ventures in our bailiwick.

Even more important than intentions are capabilities. Was it possible for the Germans to attack the United States physically or through the territory of a potential ally such as Mexico? Here the answer must be a firm no. In the foreseeable future, neither they nor anyone else possessed the means to invade the United States. Even had they been able to use Mexico for a staging ground and even had the Japanese been brought into an anti-- American alliance, such an incursion here would have been impossible without control of the Atlantic, and the defeat of the British Navy was not in the cards in 1917. Even if we grant them control of the Atlantic or at least the supplanting of the British as gatekeeper to the New World, they still could not have launched an invasion of our country. The logistics of the situation made it inconceivable that they could bring over enough men and materiel to mount an offensive against our territories.

It is true that Lippmann and realists who wrote after him worried less about an imminent attack on the United States than on the long-term effects of a German victory upon our security. They recognized the significance of a friendly England guarding the Atlantic throughout the nineteenth century. A German victory would have upset the balance on the continent and thus threatened our safety. Many theorists would accept that statement but what does it mean? Had the Central Powers and not the Entente become dominant on the continent (likely with a German victory) and on the Atlantic (less likely but plausible), how would our lives have been affected? Certainly we cannot apply the domino theory here. There is a lot of water between Brest and New York. Lippmann and his colleagues must have been talking about the economic impact of Germany assuming top-dog position in Europe.

With an alteration in the balance of power and the presumed emergence of Germany as a superpower, our worldwide economic interests would allegedly have suffered serious harm, especially in Latin America and Asia. According to this argument, the Germans would have erected an exclusive empire that would have stifled our economic growth. Leaving aside the debate over whether external expansion was necessary to internal growth, would our economy have suffered very much more than it had suffered previously in a system dominated by the free trade imperialism of England? Our friends in London had never been very generous about granting us access to their markets and they were fierce competitors in places they did not control outright. We had learned to live with British businessmen, why not with German? After all, in the period prior to the war, despite competition in the tropics, Germany was our second best customer, albeit nowhere near as important as England.

All the same, accepting the fragile assumption that a victorious Germany would have limited our markets enough to weaken our economy, we must ask, how much weaker? Suppose we talk about a decline in national income attributable to German world dominance of around 10%. Although that figure is inflated, we might have had to live more autarchically because of a German refusal to let us into the vast colonial areas that fell into their hands. Here we come to the kernel of the question — could we have accepted this sort of loss in exchange for peace? How many lives would be worth trying to make up that 10%? Naturally, that economic loss could lead to depression, followed by domestic violence, and even insurrection which, in the end, might have led to a loss of more lives than in World War I. Perhaps, and this may be where the defenders of our entry into war ultimately rest their case.

What about American prestige, our standing in the world, and our own self-image? Could we have allowed the Germans to sink our vessels and still maintain our integrity? To retreat from the defense of neutral rights and the laws of civilization allegedly would have made us less of a nation and would have brought everlasting disgrace. To have sullied our honor in such a way also would have made it difficult for Wilson to assist in the structuring of the sort of lasting peace he envisioned—a peace that would make the world safe for democracy or at least for the United States.

This is a complicated question indeed and one that may have been the most important of all to Wilson and our crisis managers who confronted the submarine. Evidently, nationalist Congressmen did not think that a cautious approach to the submarine would undermine our prestige. At least, the Neutrality Acts of the 1930s were enacted in order to keep Americans and their vessels out of war zones, even though with such legislation we surrendered our historic neutral right to ply the open seas. But that is getting ahead of the story and cannot in all fairness be used in our analysis of the prestige factor in World War I.

Let us imagine that Wilson had bowed to the submarine in 1915 or even in 1917 and pulled us out of the Atlantic. Had he explained to the American people *before* any submarine incidents had occurred that discretion was the better part of valor and that we ran the risk of war if we insisted on our rights, they might have accepted discretion. As for the world response, the British would have been very angry. Our image as a strong and independent power would have suffered in London. But would not other statesmen have interpreted our maneuver as shrewd and practical? We could stay out of the awful war awaiting the great powers' self-destruction and be the only one around at the end to pick up the pieces. Our image as a formidable and cynical world power might have been enhanced by such a superficially cowardly act as steering clear of the submarines.

Of course, by 1917, Wilson had put himself and the entire nation on record as the leading upholder of the law and defender of innocent neutrals against the immoral submarine. By the time Germany issued her declaration of unlimited submarine warfare, it was deemed impossible for us to turn tail and run. Nevertheless, one wonders if we had to go to war to maintain international prestige.

BIBLIOGRAPHY

The literature on the United States and World War I is voluminous. A useful, if somewhat outdated historiographical article is Daniel M. Smith's "National Interest and American Intervention, 1917: An Historical Reappraisal," *Journal of American History,* 52 (June 1965), 5-25. Smith built upon Richard W. Leopold's "The Problem of American Intervention, 1917: An Historical Retrospect," *World Politics,* 2 (April 1950), 405-425.

A judicious, short survey is Ross Gregory's *The Origins of American Intervention in the First World War* (New York: Norton, 1971). More detailed and especially good for the view from Europe is Ernest R. May's *The World War and American Isolation, 1914-1917* (Cambridge, MA: Harvard University Press, 1959). Both May and Gregory consider revisionist accounts but, in the end, generally support Wilson's decision. Another brief survey is Daniel M. Smith's *The Great Departure: The United States and the First World War, 1914-1920* (New York: Wiley, 1965). A classic defense of American policy written during the 1930s is Charles Seymour's *American Diplomacy During the Great War* (Baltimore: Johns Hopkins University Press, 1934). During the same decade, two other authors took issue with Seymour and his allies. Walter Millis, in the bestselling *Road to War: America 1914-1917* (Boston: Houghton-Mifflin, 1935), added fuel to the isolationists' fire. More scholarly was Charles Callan Tansill's *America Goes to War* (Boston: Little, Brown, 1938). Recently, Walter Karp in *The Politics of War: The Story of Two Wars Which Altered Forever the Political Life of the American Republic (1890-1920)* (New York: Harper & Row, 1979) was just as harsh on Wilson as he was on McKinley.

Scholars are still fascinated with Woodrow Wilson. The most impressive recent work is Patrick Devlin's *Too Proud to Fight: Woodrow Wilson's Neutrality* (New York: Oxford University Press, 1975). In his detailed, finely crafted monograph, Devlin offers reasonable explanations for the

President's actions as he blends political and psycho-history. Of course, Arthur Link is the Wilson biographer par excellence. Editor of the Wilson Papers, Link has written several books that all students of the period must examine. His series of essays, *Wilson the Diplomatist* (Baltimore: Johns Hopkins University Press, 1957), is an intelligent, not uncritical defense of Wilson's policies. In his multivolume biography, most useful is *Wilson: The Struggle for Neutrality 1914-1915* (Princeton, NJ: Princeton University Press, 1960). In *Woodrow Wilson and the Balance of Power* (Bloomington: Indiana University Press, 1955), Edward H. Buehrig argues that the alleged idealist was a realist who understood how to play the game of international politics.

For a study of British and other prowar propaganda, Horace C. Peterson and Gilbert C. Fite's *Propaganda for War: The Campaign Against American Neutrality, 1914-1917* (Norman: Oklahoma University Press, 1939) is still useful. Unfortunately, interested in keeping us out of World War II, the authors overemphasize their case. The last word on the *Lusitania* may be Thomas A. Bailey and Paul B. Ryan's *The Lusitania Disaster* (New York: Macmillan, 1975).

Chapter 5

WORLD WAR II

Yesterday, December 7, 1941 – a date which will live in infamy – the United States of America was suddenly and deliberately attacked by naval and air forces of the Empire of Japan.

—Franklin D. Roosevelt, December 8, 1941 –

Our involvement in World War II from 1939 to 1941 resembled our involvement in World War I from 1914 to 1917 in many ways. During both periods: we moved gradually from nonintervention to intervention; we were led by powerful, reforming Presidents; the war trade restored vigor to an ailing economy; and we ultimately came to the rescue of reputed forces of freedom beseiged by tyrants. Despite superficial similarities, the two cases are different. For one thing, our behavior during the early years of the second war was in good measure, determined by perceptions and memories of our behavior during the first. For another, problems that confronted us from 1939 to 1941, including the prospect of a two-front war, were more complicated than those that centered around the submarine and maritime rights 25 years earlier. For a third, while the first war could best be understood in terms of classic balance-of-power politics, ideological factors played a major role in the second war. Finally, by 1939, the continuing communication and transportation revolutions had brought us much closer, both spatially and temporally, to the rest of the world.

Franklin Roosevelt's activities seem familiar. Throughout this study, we have witnessed the steady growth of the powers of the Presidency. From a feeble performance by Madison who thought he was bullied by Congress, to Polk's brilliant manipulatory ploys, to McKinley's use of the *Maine* as well as his handling of Spanish concessions, and on to Wilson's mastery over opinion and events in early 1917, the crucial decisions came to be dominated by the President. His access both to the intelligence community and public—in addition to his role as commander in chief of the armed forces, executor of foreign policy, and symbol of the flag—makes any study of American entry into war in the twentieth century a study in Presidential decision making.

During World War II, the powers of the Presidency were stretched to new limits, marked by sweeping public and private executive agreements and especially, in the election of 1940, the blatant deception of the American people. Many hail Roosevelt for the imaginative and courageous way he led us through the trials of the early war years, walking a tightrope between intervention and nonintervention until we were ready to assume our responsibilities. With revelations of secret bombings in Cambodia and covert guerrilla raids in North Vietnam still ringing in their ears, others see in Roosevelt's devious practices ominous portents of things to come.

The pattern was clear. Diplomatic and military programs that would have been understood by Thucydides and Machiavelli were transformed into moral issues for a public unable to deal with the world as it was. Symptomatic of this approach was the title of General Eisenhower's famous memoir of his World War II command experiences, *Crusade in Europe.* A seamy American-Japanese dispute involving imperialist interests in Asia became transformed into a war to save the world from the anti-Christ—the league of Nazis, fascists, and Japanese militarists.

Undoubtedly, the enemy in World War II, especially the Nazis, was more bestial than any we had ever encountered. But that bestiality did not have much to do with the reasons for entering the war. The story of our entry has been obscured by Pearl Harbor, concentration camps, and countless Hollywood and television films about heroic exploits in Europe and the Pacific. For an explanation of how and why we became involved in World War II we must turn first to Franklin Roosevelt who, more than any other person or event, was responsible for our interventionist policies during the period of neutrality.

FRANKLIN DELANO ROOSEVELT

Franklin Delano Roosevelt exercised an enormous influence over his countrymen. President during our longest depression as well as the cataclysmic international crises of the 1930s, Roosevelt guided us through our most perilous period since the Civil War. Along the way, he enhanced the powers of the Presidency by quantum leaps. The strongest President in our history, he was beloved by most of the population and hated by a minority that opposed his centralization of powers, alleged socialist bent, and unbridled internationalism.

Like all great men, he is difficult to categorize, and even more so when we consider him as a diplomat. Was he a realist or an idealist? Did he understand the world or was he naive? Was he soft on Russia or an incipient cold warrior? Did he lead, or follow public opinion?

Clues to his *Weltanschauung* are found in his biographical data. Roosevelt was born into the Democratic branch of his old line cosmopolitan family. His early years were conventional for his class—travel, exposure to European culture, the best schools, Groton and Harvard, and a fashionable wedding attended by his cousin (also his bride's cousin), President Theodore Roosevelt. The young Franklin was intelligent enough but not bookish, well-liked but not yet a leader of men. After serving as Assistant Secretary of the Navy in the Wilson administration, from where, he boasted, he wrote the constitution of Haiti, Roosevelt was put up for Vice President by the Democratic Party in 1920. Handsome, inoffensive (except to antiimperialists), vigorous, he was a good choice, especially for a small segment of the electorate that assumed that Teddy was running again. Anything helped and the Democrats needed plenty of help in the "normalcy" election of 1920. The party's defeat was expected. As so often happens, the good team man, the losing Vice Presidential candidate, emerged as a likely contender for the top spot in the years to come.

During the summer of 1921, Roosevelt contracted polio. His recovery from that dread disease revealed something about his inner strengths. Biographers maintain that his sickness and painful rehabilitation contributed to the creation of a tougher, more mature adult than the carefree playboy of his healthy youth. Returning to New York politics, Roosevelt was elected governor in 1928, reelected in 1930, and was a natural choice to face Herbert Hoover in the Depression election of 1932. Blamed for the unprecedented economic and social dislocation, Hoover could not have been elected dog catcher in many locales.

Roosevelt had little experience in foreign affairs. During the 1920s, he had written articles about the League of Nations and the Kellogg-Briand Pact, but he had not held a post that dealt with diplomatic issues since he left the Navy Department in 1920. In 1933, he was a moderate internationalist who probably would have supported American involvement in the League of Nations had it been politically expedient. Elected during the Sino-Japanese War in Manchuria and the period that saw the rise of Hitler and the convening of important international monetary and disarmament conferences, Roosevelt nonetheless devoted his first years in office to domestic recovery and reform. Although he took an interest in the world and contemplated solutions to problems that made major war seem likely again, such matters took a back seat to domestic affairs until 1938.

When he finally did concentrate on the international sphere, he did so with a gusto and exuberance reminiscent of his hyperactive cousin. Above all, he was supremely confident of his abilities to influence world politics. For example, he once contemplated calling a summit conference on board an American vessel for all kings, presidents, and prime ministers. There, around a very long table with Papa Franklin at the head, the problems of the world would be settled. Later, in another celebrated example of his confidence in his negotiating skill, he told his friends that he could handle Uncle Joe—Stalin was "get-able." Exposure to the Roosevelt charm and personality would soften even the toughest of Bolsheviks.

Like most of his friends and family, Roosevelt was an Anglophile who linked our fate to that of the Mother Country, despite clashes with his friend Churchill over British imperialism. He had no sympathy for fascists or communists although the latter were the lesser of two evils. His liberal preferences did not always interfere with his practice of *Realpolitik.* Roosevelt is credited with saying about one Latin dictator, "He may be an S.O.B., but he is our S.O.B."

He was capable of wheeling and dealing like the best (or is it the worst?) of old school European diplomats. His much-criticized attempt to work with Vichy France from 1940 to 1942 demonstrated a realist streak. At the same time, his constant appeals to morality, his fear of appearing too scheming, and his genuine sentimentality toward the little people of the world suggested ambivalence in his approach to international relations. Although his moral paeans were carefully prepared for a naive and self-righteous audience that believed it constituted a unique nation, he too felt that we were guided by higher spiritual purposes. Like Wilson before him, he believed that we had a special role to play in the world—it was his task to convince his people, some 20 years after the fact, of the continuing relevance of the Wilsonian message.

Not surprisingly, the capable and unorthodox Roosevelt did not have much to do with his own State Department which he considered too conservative. Like Wilson, he relied upon personal emissaries and direct reports from ambassadors who were his friends. Presidential assistant Harry Hopkins traveled the world for him, while William C. Bullitt in the Paris embassy, Joseph P. Kennedy at the Court of St. James, and Undersecretary of State Sumner Welles kept him informed about the shape of the world in the late 1930s.

His official helpmate in foreign policy was Secretary of State Cordell Hull. Hull, who retired in 1944, holds the longevity record for that post. An influential Congressman and Senator from Tennessee for almost 25 years, Hull was inexperienced in foreign affairs. He too was a Wilsonian and, even more than his boss, devoted to idealism in foreign affairs—the worst of Wilson's legacy to American statesmen. Although Hull's congressional ties were useful to the President, he was more executor than originator of administration policy. In several areas, he did enjoy latitude. During the period of American neutrality when Roosevelt was preoccupied with European matters, Hull tended to Asia. Insisting upon a peace based upon sweeping principles, he helped undermine efforts to conclude an amoral compromise agreement. With good friends on Capitol Hill and respect from the public, Hull did, on occasion, win his point with an undecided President.

Whatever their policy preferences, Roosevelt and his advisors felt their options limited by the public and their representatives in Congress. Although they may have underestimated their own abilities to educate and lead, they ran scared of polls that revealed that Americans did not want to mix in world affairs. During the late 1930s, isolationism reached its peak in the United States and posed a problem for any leader bent on intervening in the European crises.

THE ISOLATIONIST IMPULSE

Even more so than the decade that preceded it, the 1930s was our classic isolationist decade. To be sure, Americans supported what they thought was the political isolationism of the covertly expansionist Republican governments of the 1920s, but since the world was relatively placid then, foreign policy was not a salient issue. As the dangers of war increased during the 1930s, Americans sought to erect formal barriers against internationalist impulses left over from the Wilson period.

Their isolationism, sanctified by George Washington and the subsequent history of the republic, was reenforced by the way they viewed World War I, the one great aberration in that history. The most important revisionist books appeared in the 1930s, not in the 1920s. The *Merchants of Death,* published in 1934, exposed armaments manufacturers who made millions on the broken bones of European youth. The best selling *Road to War,* published the next year, emphasized the economic forces as well as British propaganda that compelled Wilson to lead us into a war that was none of our business.

Responding to the international crises and the isolationist mood, Congress passed legislation in 1935, 1936, and 1937 that would have kept us out of *World War I.* The neutrality laws of the mid-1930s forbade American arms shipments to belligerents and prohibited our vessels and citizens from traveling in war zones. Although Roosevelt failed to obtain a provision allowing him to distinguish between aggressor and aggressee, he approved of the legislation. These neutrality acts were directed to the German submarine of World War I. Adherence to the letter of our laws would have kept us out of the European conflict that began in 1939 (and probably would have guaranteed England's defeat), and adherence to the spirit of our laws would have kept us out of the Asian war that began in 1937.

Although they erected defenses against involvement in war, Americans were not indifferent to the dangers posed to others by German and Italian fascism. At first, Hitler appeared as a Chaplinesque figure, more to be derided than taken seriously. After his success in the Rhineland in 1936 and the promulgation of anti-Semitic laws, Hitler became both despised and feared.

As war approached, the nation began to split into two unequal camps. The majority camp that opposed precipitate intervention was prepared to aid the democracies. A minority camp, whose organization and intensity of feeling made up for its lack of numbers, contended that any deviation from the policies prescribed by the Neutrality Acts would eventually bring us into the war. The major interventionist committee took the clever name the Committee to Defend America by Aiding the

Allies. Its most important opponents were found in the America First organization. The latter had the more plausible argument, or so it seems today. They contended that if we wanted to stay out of war, we had to mind our business and refrain from provoking one belligerent by helping the other. They were right. Our blatant unneutrality would have eventually led to war with Germany, had not the Japanese attacked Pearl Harbor. Those who were willing to help the Allies countered by saying that if Britain went down, we would be next. Since the British were not defeated, we are unable to test the validity of their position.

Interestingly, the debate concerned Europe and not Asia. Until late 1941, most everyone expected that our European policies were the ones that could bring us into war again. Our aid to China and condemnations of Japan were of little immediate concern for several reasons. First, the aid was legal since our neutrality laws did not apply to an undeclared war. Second, there was little debate about the United States' special relationship to China. And last, and most important, no one expected the Japanese to do anything that would force us into war.

Isolationism today is a naughty word. Its pejorative connotation relates, in part, to a perceived head-in-the-sand attitude out of place in a world in which supersonic airplanes and missiles can bring us to the brink of catastrophe within minutes. Nearly everyone now believes in the vague concept of collective security; not only did we belong in World War II but also we should have recognized that fact earlier than we did.

Furthermore, isolationism was sullied by those who opposed involvement in war for ulterior motives. Some isolationists were: blatant anti-Semites first who supported Hitler's crusade against the Jewish menace; anti-Bolsheviks first who hoped that Hitler would also destroy that menace (which, for some, was the same as the Jewish menace); pro-Bolsheviks first who supported Stalin's policy of neutrality toward Hitler until June of 1941; anti-British first who hoped to see the empire dismantled and England overrun; anti-Rooseveltians first who instinctively fought anything the dictator in the White House supported; and even profascists who hoped to bring the wave of the future to America. More savory were those who were isolationists because they feared for the future of domestic liberalism. They remembered how the Progressive Era had ended in 1917 and foresaw the same thing happening to the New Deal in wartime. Finally, some with a realistic or geopolitical perspective saw no relationship between the war in Europe and Asia and our own security. The rational strains in isolationism were forgotten after 1941 when it became synonymous with anti-Semitism, profascism, and even treason.

The triumph of the interventionists over the isolationists did not come easy. The outcome of the battle was still unclear in the late fall of 1941. Yet by then, we had come quite a way from the mid-1930s when just about everyone agreed that Wilson's mistakes would never be repeated.

"NEUTRALITY" ESTABLISHED

Where to begin the epic story of the origins of World War II? Some would look to the Treaty of Versailles that ended World War I, a treaty "purple with revenge" whose sweeping financial and spiritual claims on Germany made the survival of the democratic Weimar Republic problematic. Others might choose that day in Geneva in 1920 when the League of Nations first convened and a shadow fell across the empty chair of the United States. Still others would look to China in the spring of 1915 when Japan's Twenty-One Demands were assailed ,by Washington and the handwriting on the wall became clear—the Open Door could not coexist with Japanese programs for Asia.

Though we might go back even further, there is general agreement that the first substantial marker on the road to Pearl Harbor was the Manchurian Incident of 1931-1933. From that point on, few doubted that Japanese and Americans would one day clash in the Pacific. The seizure of the important Chinese province of Manchuria by a Japanese army operating independent of civilian authorities in Tokyo provoked a strong rhetorical response heard time and again through the next decade. We condemned Japanese aggression, urged them to withdraw, and refused to accept any alteration in the Asian status quo brought about by force. All of our notes, threats, and appeals to international law and League of Nations resolutions did not deter the Japanese either in Manchuria in 1931 or in the rest of China in 1937. Some day, it was expected, they would go too far and we would finally have to put some muscle behind the Open Door notes of John Hay that had guided our policy for almost two generations.

Our reactions to the European markers on the road to World War II were more restrained. To be sure, we disapproved of Mussolini's attack upon the Ethiopians in 1935 and Germany's seizure of Austria in 1938 and Czechoslovakia in 1939. France and England, however, protected our interests in Europe, or so we thought.

When war finally did come to the continent in the first days of September in 1939, we were ready for it, although not for Hitler's blitzkrieg in Poland. Supported by the vast majority of the American population, Roosevelt prepared to assist the Allies as much as possible consistent with the conviction that we did not belong in the war. His speech to the nation on September 3 was realistic. After proclaiming our neutrality, he broke with Wilson's precedent when he did not "ask that every American remain neutral in thought as well. Even a neutral has a right to take account of the facts. Even a neutral cannot be asked to close his mind or conscience."

Almost everyone in America echoed those sentiments. Over 80% of those polled thought the Allied coalition would defeat Hitler and well over 90% hoped they would. Our commitment to the British and French was signaled by the easy victory of neutrality law revision in Congress. After November 4, 1939, merchants were permitted to sell arms and other war materials to belligerents, as long as they picked them up here on a cash-and-carry basis. Since the British, as usual, controlled the seas, our neutrality revision helped only one side in the conflict.

It is instructive to contrast our policies with those of 1914.

Throughout our period as a neutral during World War II, we were not bothered by torpedo attacks. Even though the Germans possessed a first-rate U-boat fleet that harassed Allied shipping, Hitler was reluctant to provoke the United States. The neutrality act barring American vessels from the war zone made his job easier. On the other hand, when the British surface fleet instituted its blockade of German-controlled territories, the same sort of sweeping and extralegal blockade that drew our wrath in 1807 and 1914, Roosevelt offered a mild protest for the record, and then proceeded to cooperate with the Admiralty.

After a certain point, perhaps the spring of 1940, most Americans were convinced that war was inevitable. Each new escalation from the Japanese or Germans brought a corresponding escalation from us. Even though we maintained dialogues with the Axis, especially the Japanese, throughout the months preceding our entry, there was no turning back from our acknowledged drift toward belligerency. And unlike other wars, this scenario had nothing to do with defensive responses to challenges to our neutrality. Our reactions to Axis activities were only remotely connected to affronts to our flag or rights. We made no attempts to be even-handed; there was no talk of total embargoes or Gore-McLemore resolutions to keep us out of the way of Germany or Japan.

At the same time, each advance toward belligerency was made cautiously and only with the knowledge that the other side would not issue a declaration of war. As things turned out, our military was not ready in December of 1941. They would have liked another six months or a year to prepare themselves. In this case, the civilians in Washington were more anxious for war than the army and navy. Still, even the hawkish civilians knew that a declaration of war would have to be preceded by an attack upon our territory. Even though we were ready for war and expected it sooner or later, we told pollsters that we would not declare war without sufficient provocation. Perhaps this reluctance to go to war was illusory and reflected the normal response anyone would give to the question, "Do you want to go to war *now*?" Be that as it may, few opposed our neutral policies or lack of them—our role as a passive belligerent in the British camp stands in sharp contrast to our strained, yet generally successful attempts to maintain legal neutrality from 1914 to 1917.

THE LIGHTS GO OUT ALL OVER EUROPE

With western Poland occupied by the Germans and eastern Poland "liberated from capitalist exploitation" by the Russians, the principals settled down for the Phony War during the amazingly peaceful winter of 1939-1940. All eyes were fixed on France where the next blow would surely fall. Surprisingly, it did not fall in the west nor did it involve any of the major belligerents. On the last day of November, Russia invaded Finland. (The American *Daily Worker* saw it differently in a story headlined "Red Army Hurls Back Invaders.") Although the origins of the bloody Winter War are beyond our purview, American reactions were illustrative of the nature of isolationist thought.

As news of the Soviet invasion reached these shores—a modern David-Goliath story—our hearts went out to the Finns even more than they had to the Poles, British, and French. After paying their World War I debts and producing a record-shattering Olympic athlete, the democratic Finns were now fighting the Bolsheviks. Herbert Hoover, who was slow to embrace the Allies earlier, took up his traditional role when he became head of the Finnish Relief Fund. The editor of the isolationist *Chicago Tribune* joined internationalists such as Secretary of the Interior Harold Ickes in support of the Finnish cause. Many isolationists were among the first to leap aboard the Save Finland bandwagon, although they called for private, not official aid. Such a turnabout suggests a linkage between anticommunists and isolationists. Some anticommunists had been unhappy about aid to the Allies because whatever Hitler may have been, he was the enemy of the anti-Christ in the Kremlin. Now that someone else had taken up the battle against communism, we had to help with money and material.

The Winter War, with its tragic denouement for the Finns, was quietly forgotten when the Western Front heated up in the spring of 1940. First the Germans took over Denmark and Norway in April and then, in May, attacked the Low Countries and the allegedly impregnable French Maginot Line. During this phase of the war, Roosevelt put us firmly on record as partners in the Allied camp, a camp made more attractive when that uninspiring appeaser, Neville Chamberlain, was replaced by the indomitable Winston Churchill.

In several stirring speeches and letters, the President committed our moral, spiritual, and economic resources to the cause of the fast-failing French. When the French Prime Minister asked for clouds of American planes to save the day, however, Roosevelt came up empty-handed. During this same period, the President delivered his famous "hand that held the dagger has struck it into the back of its neighbor" address. Despite Roosevelt's pleas, Mussolini entered the war to pick up his piece of France.

The fall of France and the arrival of the Nazis on the Atlantic Coast quickened the pace of our preparedness movement. Many who had heretofore viewed the development of a large military establishment as costly, unnecessary, and provocative became frightened. Such relatively isolationist organizations as the National Association of Manufacturers and the National Chamber of Commerce soon began to support the official policy of all possible aid to Britain, our last line of defense on the continent. This new cooperation between business and reforming New Dealer was helped along by the President's eager acceptance of capitalist leadership in wartime agencies that sprung up every place in Washington where land could be found to erect a quonset hut. The businessmen might not have been so compliant had they known that Roosevelt was preparing new policies that almost dared the Germans to mix with us.

Churchill had asked Roosevelt for overage destroyers. Losing an increasing number of destroyers to Germany's ravenous submarine wolfpacks, the Admiralty desperately needed more vessels to assure delivery of our war materials. Despite a rare personal plea from King George, the President was fearful of taking up such a proposal in the summer of 1940. An election was near, an election in which he was going to try to shatter American tradition and win a third term.

Fortunately for Roosevelt (and Churchill), the Republicans offered the electorate an echo and not a choice. Wendell Willkie was a liberal internationalist who eventually approved the substance of the Destroyer Deal, as it came to be called. In September, the political coast was clear for Roosevelt to trade a bunch of useless, old, leaky white elephants, as they were described, for naval bases in Newfoundland and the West Indies. It seemed like a sharp Yankee bargain, especially when one compared some allegedly worthless ships to Bermuda. Republicans did complain about Roosevelt's employment of an executive order to effect the unprecedented transaction. Even Willkie, who did not oppose the deal itself, spoke out against its questionable constitutionality. Most of Roosevelt's other opponents remained silent since the public overwhelmingly applauded the deal.

Americans had other things on their minds as the nation prepared for the climax of our quadrennial exercise in invective and bunkum. The electorate was unaware of a September policy paper from the military chiefs reporting: that sooner or later the Japanese would attack our possessions in the Pacific; that in the ensuing war we had to concentrate on Hitler first (no clues were given as to how we were going to get into a war with Germany); and that we needed to work even more quickly on the development of a defense capability second to none. The Joint Chiefs predicted that war would break out within a year or two. Naturally no one expected the President to reveal the military game plan during the campaign, but his public position bore no resemblance to his advisors' secret policy. Perhaps we should not blame him for his deception. He was encouraged by Willkie's campaign rhetoric.

At the start of the campaign, the two candidates tacitly agreed to keep foreign policy out of the debate for national security reasons. Willkie approved of Roosevelt's program of aid to Britain and cautious interventionism. However, with election day approaching and the polls offering no solace for Republicans, Willkie violated the gentleman's agreement and took the low road. He began to say that a vote for the Democratic standard-bearer was a vote for war. This new approach, which appeared to be effective, scared Roosevelt. Backed into what he perceived to be a corner, the President came out fighting with categorical promises that he would keep America out of war and that American boys would not be sent to fight in foreign wars. Repeatedly, during the waning days of the campaign, he assured his listeners that his policies would keep us out of war. Privately, of course, he thought that we might have to go to war against Germany and Japan. Had he leveled with the American people and told them that although he found war abhorrent, the world situation was such that we might find ourselves swept into the maelstrom, he could have lost the election. Although not very happy about it, Roosevelt lied, or at the very least distorted the truth in order to win the election. Contributing to the unrealistic expectations of the public, he unwittingly increased his postelection problems.

His defenders contend that the President deceived the people for their own good. Because voters could never understand the heady issues of national security and military technology, they had to be dealt with simplistically and emotionally. When Willkie demagogically threatened that a vote for Roosevelt was a vote for war, Roosevelt responded equally demagogically. He was like the doctor who wants his or her patient to swallow awful tasting medicine. The patient might reject the medicine if the doctor told him the truth, so he or she tells him a white lie, the patient drinks the concoction and recovers, in the eternal debt of his doctor. A white lie was told, the President was reelected, and the country was saved.

Some have tried to distinguish between similar historical cases. Roosevelt's deceit is considered permissible because the cause was noble while comparable deceit from Lyndon Johnson and Richard Nixon is not. Not an isolated incident, Roosevelt's lauded deceit does not speak well for our system. Something is wrong when the person who speaks the honest, pessimistic truth will lose to the person who tells the dishonest, comforting lie.

TO THE BRINK

Although to determine why people vote for certain candidates is always difficult, Roosevelt's foreign policy was apparently endorsed by the American people. Of course, he did not offer them a candid view of that policy. Nevertheless, Roosevelt's electoral success emboldened Churchill to ask for even more from the self-proclaimed Arsenal of Democracy. The British needed planes, ships, ammunition, and every other kind of material imaginable. There was one catch. The once-bottomless British Exchequer was empty. In polite phrases, couched in eloquent Churchillian prose, the Prime Minister asked for a handout from that same Uncle Shylock who had proven to be such a heartless creditor during the interwar period.

From our point of view, the British were serving as surrogate soldiers in the war against fascism. Their purchases also helped keep our economy going. After some deliberation, the President decided to do away with the "silly foolish old dollar sign." If his neighbor's house was on fire, he would lend him our hose and not ask for a rental fee. If the fire was put out, we might expect to have our hose returned but that was of secondary importance. In a brilliant public relations gambit, the Lend Lease Bill was assigned the number House Resolution 1776. Roosevelt told a receptive American audience that Britain's defense was vital to our own. Since they were making unparalleled sacrifices, standing alone against the Nazis who had conquered almost all of Western Europe, the least we could do would be to lend them the material necessary for their survival. The Lend Lease Bill eventually sailed through Congress by a two-to-one margin in the Senate and better than four to one in the House. The margins accurately reflected the national consensus on the policy to aid the British however possible. Lend Lease was unprecedented for a neutral. Throughout 1941, we *gave away* material one side used against the other. And still the Germans maintained their cautious posture, unwilling to challenge the United States again. During previous centuries, such a blatant violation of the spirit, if not the letter, of the law might have resulted in a declaration of war from the offended party.

While supporters and opponents of Lend Lease testified in crowded hearing rooms in Congress, other meetings of vital importance to Anglo-American relations took place in more private surroundings in the War and Navy Departments. From January through March of 1941, American and British staff officers met to coordinate joint strategy. The fact they met together to plan wartime operations made them "common-law" allies. In the ABC-1 agreements that emerged from the sessions, a Europe first policy was endorsed and the means for cooperation spelled out.

After Lend Lease and ABC-1, the rest of 1941 was anticlimactic, at least so far as Europe was concerned. A pattern had been established. Step by step, Roosevelt led his insular nation closer and closer to the brink of full-scale intervention. Never moving too quickly, carefully protecting his weak congressional flanks, testing the water before he plunged in, he performed in an effective manner. Critics feel he was laggard in bringing the nation into the war, that he was overly cautious in leading a population ready to follow him almost anywhere. His defenders point out that although he did not lose any important congressional votes during the period of neutrality, his margin on some major issues was excruciatingly thin. This debate over the speed with which the President led us toward war is irrelevant to still other critics who oppose the overall thrust of his policies. For them, Roosevelt acted unconstitutionally time and again, withheld information from the people and Congress, and generally executed dangerous programs that led us into a war in which we did not belong.

No matter how we evaluate his actions, the President did move us in some remarkable directions for a nation still operating under the Neutrality Proclamation of September 1939. For example, in April of 1941 he received permission from the

Danish Minister in Washington, whose own country had been occupied by the Germans, to occupy Greenland. During that month, when Hitler extended his war zone further out into the Atlantic, Roosevelt met the challenge with an extension of our Safety Belt around the hemisphere half way across the ocean. Around the same time, we prepared to occupy Denmark's other major possession, Iceland, after the British asked us to lift that burden from their shoulders. All three policies involved a by-then-characteristic unilateral Presidential action. Although the Germans were unhappy, and said so, they did not challenge these incursions for the moment.

Each month brought new provocative policies. In June, because of increased German submarine activity, Roosevelt issued his Declaration of Unlimited National Emergency. The emergency in this case related to the necessity of getting our materials across the Atlantic to the British. The declaration was not enough. We needed a convoy system. However, even though the German sinking of the *Robin Moor* in late May offered an excuse, the President felt that the people would not accept convoy duties that could lead to a shooting war on the high seas. More important, his military advisors were not yet ready to confront the Axis.

The complexion of the war changed dramatically in late June of 1941 when the Nazis invaded Russia. As the pressure on the British eased, it appeared that our policies had paid off. In the days that followed, Roosevelt followed Churchill's lead and began to prepare his public for a new relationship with the Soviets. In a matter of months, we began sending Lend Lease aid to the bombers of Helsinki, as Roosevelt silenced detractors who hoped Hitler would finish off Stalin for us.

Further, in a secret meeting off the coast of Newfoundland in early August, he met with Churchill to discuss the shape of the postwar world as well as plans for military and economic liaison in the months to come. No one at the Atlantic Charter Conference doubted that we would be fighting allies. The question was when and where. More surprising, few voices were raised at home to question Roosevelt about the propriety of conspiring secretly with a belligerent while we were still neutral. Such acquiescence could not be expected on every issue.

Indeed, the wisdom of Roosevelt's cautious policy was painfully illustrated in the congressional debate over the extension of the military draft. The fact that a watered-down bill finally made it through the House by only one vote demonstrated the fragility of the President's congressional support. Although extraneous issues were involved in the debate over Selective Service, if the President had to fight for his life to get that one through, one can imagine his difficulties had he requested war in absence of a direct attack on our territory.

Nevertheless, even before his victory on draft extension, Roosevelt gambled that the country was ready for still another offensive gesture when he inflated the *Greer* incident of early September to justify a new submarine policy. The U.S.S. *Greer* had been shadowing a German submarine for the British for several hours. In frustration, the U-boat commander fired two torpedos in her direction. Although the details were known to Roosevelt, he chose to characterize the affair as wanton German aggression. In his *Greer* report to the nation, he referred to the submarines as the "rattlesnakes of the Atlantic" and announced a "shoot-on-sight" order. Our vessels patrolling the Atlantic could shoot first and ask questions later whenever they sighted a German submarine. He also ordered our navy to convoy British merchant ships from the United States to Iceland. International law gave us no right to shoot on sight or to convoy. The least we might have expected would have been naval retaliation from the Germans in self-defense. They still refused to take up our challenge.

Much of what was left of our neutrality legislation was wiped from the books in November. After spirited debate, Congress abrogated the prohibition against American shipping in the war zone. This was asking for it; there was every reason to expect that we would soon have a replay of World War I.

What else could we do short of declaring war? We were paying for and shipping material to the Allies, convoying their vessels across the Atlantic, shooting at submarines that dared challenge us, and planning war and peace with England.

Though we had gone about as far as we could go, war with Germany was still not on the horizon. With Britain unconquered, and with Russia holding her own, the Nazis could ill afford to provoke a third major fighting enemy. Yet American naval practices were becoming intolerable. Fortunately for the Germans, they were able to settle the matter in the most favorable of circumstances. Just as they were contemplating lashing back at us unilaterally, the Japanese delivered their crushing blow at Pearl Harbor. For that story, we must return to the Pacific where another drama was reaching the climax that had been building for several generations.

THE CLASH OVER CHINA

Of all our interventions in international and civil wars, none seems more defensible than our intervention in Asia on December 8, 1941. After ruthlessly attacking China on two occasions during the 1930s, the Japanese bombed Pearl Harbor without warning. Four decades have passed since that shocking event, the first major foreign attack on American territory since 1815. Today, the story of that attack is much more complicated and certainly a much less one-sided story than might be expected.

From the Japanese point of view, our Open Door policy was brazen effrontery. How could the United States make claims on the disposition of a country more than 6,000 miles away from her shores? When anyone entered the Caribbean, we invoked the Monroe Doctrine. The Japanese respected our rights there— why could not we respect their rights in East Asia?

Although the Japanese pacified Asia in a brutal manner, what was the difference, they asked, aside from body count, between American interventions in Haiti, Santo Domingo, Cuba, Mexico, and other Latin states and their interventions in China? Arguments about the democracy we spread and the stability we maintained were not accepted by the Japanese who enviously watched as United Fruit and Pan American Airlines counted their profits. Claiming that their Greater East Asia Co-Prosperity Sphere was just like the Monroe Doctrine, they also

planned to maintain peace and bring prosperity to their benighted cousins. They hoped to develop the area's raw materials,
process them into modern products, and sell them back to
poorer Asians whose living standards would consequently rise.
The Japanese would bring their fellow Asians the know-how
and political sophistication that had made them, alone in their
region, one of the great powers in the world.

Such a generous approach to Japanese expansion may seem
repugnant to those who remember the Rape of Nanking or the
prison camp near the River Kwai in Thailand. Looking at the
situation from their perspective, however, something we must
do in every diplomatic encounter no matter how evil our
adversary appears, we had as much right to tell them what to do
in China as they had to tell us what to do in Mexico. After all,
Japan and Mexico shared the Pacific basin as we shared it with
China. Yet as early as 1912, the Lodge Corollary to the Monroe
Doctrine warned our fellow Pacific power to steer clear of this
continent, even in the peaceful pursuit of trade.

The Japanese of the late 1930s felt that their future
depended upon their dominance of East Asia. In order to
maintain their economy as well as their relished membership in
the Great Power Club, they thought they had to control China
and the surrounding territories. It is depressing today to see
how mistaken they were in their estimates of what it would
take to keep them on top of the pile in Asia. In 1980, without
an army, navy, and formal colonies, but with American friendship, they have become the dominant economic power in the
Orient and the fourth most important economic power in the
world.

An American-Japanese showdown for control of the Pacific
had been predicted almost from the time that Admiral Matthew
Perry sailed into Tokyo Bay in the middle of the nineteenth
century. Certainly by 1895, after "tiny" Japan crushed China in
the first Sino-Japanese war of our times, the probability of such
a showdown increased. After Japan's upset victory over Russia
in 1905, stories of a war between the two young Pacific powers
appeared with growing frequency in both countries' media.

Both claimed the Pacific during the same period. In 1898, we secured the Philippines, which we hoped would become a valuable way station for the bountiful China trade to come. Two years later, Secretary of State John Hay announced our guardianship over China in the celebrated Open Door notes. Our own frenetic Asian activity was sandwiched between the two Japanese wars that marked her emergence not just as a regional leader but also as a world power with which all nations had to reckon. At stake was the limitless China market. Although other lands along the periphery of China possessed valuable treasures, the best of them—India, Indonesia, Indochina, Malaya—had already been claimed.

The war that broke out in 1941 was probably inevitable. Both Japan and the United States defined their national security in terms of control of China and the Open Door, respectively (some would argue both concepts are synonymous). Although war was headed off time and again through compromises from one or both parties, as long as both clung to diametrically opposed visions of the future in Asia, Japan and the United States were destined to meet on the field of battle. The story of the American-Japanese contest in the Orient is a sad one for diplomatic historians to contemplate. It suggests that some wars, which everyone wants to avoid, are unavoidable and, above all, that in most diplomatic encounters both sides can act rationally and, from their respective points of view, reasonably and still end up fighting one another.

From the turn of the century until 1941, each side in the Pacific contest steadily encroached upon the other's perceived interests. With every forward movement by the Japanese, we saw the Open Door closing another inch or two. With each protest from us, they saw their national development inhibited. Many in Japan, including a good portion of the civilian leadership, were wary about provoking us. They were naturally fearful that an American-Japanese war would be disastrous. We enjoyed economic and military supremacy, even taking into account the logistic advantages Japan had fighting in her own backyard. On the other hand, leading figures in the Japanese armed services, especially the army, were not so pessimistic, and in the Japanese system they were unrestrained by civilian authority.

The Japanese domestic situation posed a serious tactical problem for us. Each time their expansionists challenged our interests, we had to consider the effect our response would have upon their moderates. Unfortunately, whatever posture we adopted could weaken them. We could "hang tough" and alienate our potential friends. A firm response would lead to "I told you so" from the military adventurers—America *was* Japan's enemy. On the other hand, a gentle approach was similarly fraught with danger. A meek response to a military advance would allow Japanese generals to tell their civilian colleagues, "See, the United States is a paper tiger, we can safely proceed in our expansionist program."

This problem is not unique. How to appeal to doves in your opponents' camp always concerns policy makers. A hard line could convert them to hawks, a soft line might bolster the confidence of the real hawks. The policy maker must also be concerned about undercutting the doves by making them appear to be too friendly with the enemy. The dilemma is often insoluble.

A case in point which won us neither friends nor a policy change favorable to our interests was the Manchurian War of 1931-1933. The Japanese conquest of Manchuria was important for American decision makers in the 1950s who saw our tough words, but physical inaction then, as the first appeasement of the decade leading inevitably to world war. The lesson was clear; one cannot appease aggressors. Back in 1931, in the midst of our terrible depression and facing some legitimate Japanese claims in Manchuria, we could only condemn the aggression morally and place ourselves on record as refusing to recognize the new status of the former Chinese province.

The situation was different in 1937 when the Japanese attacked China proper and launched their assault that ended only when the bombs dropped on Hiroshima and Nagasaki in August of 1945. This time, Washington not only condemned

Japan but also began sending economic and technical assistance to Chiang Kai-shek whose military organization left much to be desired. Since the so-called China Incident never became an officially declared war, the American government was able to violate the spirit of its neutrality laws and assist the Chinese. They might not have been able to continue their struggle through to 1942 without our political and economic support, especially after 1940 when aid from Russia began to dwindle. All of which raises an intriguing what-might-have-been. As we will see, the chief issue between Japan and the United States was the future of China. The Japanese wanted to establish hegemony over China so that they could freely develop her resources and markets and even settle surplus population. Though they never expected to conquer the entire country militarily, they did hope to place themselves in a position from which they could effectively dominate her political and economic life. Had they been successful, they might have given us some share of the China market, that is, had we been amenable to a deal.

The key to such a deal would have been American withdrawal of support for Chiang Kai-shek. One can imagine the consequences of such a policy reversal. Chiang sues for peace but Mao's communists continue the struggle. Although most of China is pacified, Japan becomes mired in a protracted guerrilla war that might still be going on today. Whatever the outcome of such a war, we had to "win." If the Japanese eventually wiped out the Maoists, an unlikely proposition, communism in China would have been a dead issue, at least for our generation. Had they not been able to extinguish the movement, the Japanese would have become so enmeshed in an interminable little war that they would not have been able to make trouble for us elsewhere. Alas, such a delicious Machiavellian fantasy was not in the cards.

First of all, American policy makers and population alike were captives of almost two generations of rhetoric about the Open Door and our mission in the Orient. The defense of China was an unquestioned axiom of American policy taken in along with mother's milk and the Monroe Doctrine. We were certain that our future was inexorably linked to the future of China— her surrender to the Japanese could not be contemplated. Never were the basic premises of the Open Door challenged during official debates over policy in Asia in the 1930s. Everyone accepted the grand strategic overview, they disagreed only over tactics. Even though the China trade, upon which the Open Door notes were based, had never panned out, and even though Chiang Kai-shek was a corrupt and inefficient dictator, we would not surrender the historic legacy of John Hay and a generation of American expansionists from the Gilded Age. One looks in vain through the official papers of the 1930s for some prominent leader to say, "Wait a second, just why is China so essential to our security?" The question was never asked. Consequently, a realistic, if amoral deal with the Japanese was not possible.

A DEADLY GAME

Through 1939, we were implicit allies of the Chinese in their struggle against the Japanese invaders. Yet while the American government aided Chiang Kai-shek, American businessmen continued to sell minerals and oil to the Japanese that were converted for use against our Chinese friends. Our embarrassment was lessened in July of 1939 when, in response to growing public pressure, Secretary of State Hull announced that the American-Japanese commercial treaty would be abrogated in six months. After that date, Washington could begin limiting the export of strategic materials to Japan. We hoped our threat of economic embargoes would buoy the Chinese, restrain Tokyo, and make our policy more moral and logical. But we had to tread cautiously because we did not want to provoke the Japanese unduly. The specter of a two-front war haunted our policy makers, especially the military. We did not have enough men and materiel to go around to wage war against *both* Japan and Germany. Maybe we would be ready sometime in 1942, but no earlier.

Although our military leaders did not know it at the time, their preference for going slow and applying limited economic pressure on Japan almost worked. At least at the beginning of 1940, the Japanese considered retiring from China short of their goals. They had been fighting a long, costly, and indecisive struggle for almost three years. Faced with an interminable war, some of their leaders were prepared to bow out of China as gracefully as possible if they did not win by the end of the year. Germany's unexpected easy victories in the spring of 1940, however, squelched Japanese talk of withdrawal. After the Nazis demolished the western imperialists, Japan would have been foolish to think of peace.

Indeed, Hitler's triumphs paid dividends almost at once. From a truncated Vichy France reeling from defeat, Japan demanded and received certain rights in northern Indochina resulting in the severance of one supply line to Chiang Kai-shek from the south. Awaiting the invasion of their homeland, the British also agreed to a temporary closing of the Burma Road to China in an attempt, they said, to facilitate the search for peace in Asia. Since Japan controlled almost all of coastal China, the closing of two major southern supply routes was a blow to Chiang Kai-shek.

At this point, relations between the United States and Japan took on the coloration of a lethal chess match, as each well-calculated move drew a well-calculated countermove. The game would be a long one. In the spring of 1940, check, let alone check mate, appeared far off. Our gambit was the dispatch of the Pacific fleet to Hawaii where, three days closer to Japan, it remained as a constant reminder of our determination to protect our interests in Asia. Conspiracy seekers later claimed that the President sent the fleet to Pearl Harbor to provide the Japanese with a tempting target in December of 1941.

This relatively unaggressive action was followed by our National Defense Act of June 1940 which, among other things, permitted the President to restrict the exportation of materials vital to our defense. Under provisions of the bill, we immediately embargoed 40 key materials but still allowed Americans to sell scrap iron and oil to Japan. We held the latter items over Japan's head as an inducement to good behavior.

Our use of threats and sanctions to halt aggression failed. From this case, observers have concluded that such a policy is not viable—economic sanctions will never work. Whatever the validity of that generalization, the world was in a different shape in 1940 than it had been in 1931 and 1936 when sanctions were considered by the international community. In 1940, our potential allies were either conquered or bogged down in war; moreover, we never did apply our most severe sanctions against Japan until it was too late. In 1931 or 1936, had the League of Nations embargoed oil to Japan and Italy, respectively, the policy of economic sanctions might have emerged from that decade with a better reputation.

In any event, our policy of escalating sanctions did not deter Japan from taking actions that offended us. After we announced our initial embargo list, she began building bases in northern Indochina; after we banned the shipment of iron and steel scrap in September, she announced her formal entry into the growing Axis family of nations.

The latter offense was serious. The Tripartite Pact, in which Japan, Germany, and Italy promised to aid one another if they were attacked by a country not then at war, helped consolidate American opinion against the Axis. When the three perceived aggressors joined in alliance against the United States, millions in this country who were Asia-firsters became convinced of the danger of the Germans, and millions who were Europe-firsters became convinced of the danger of the Japanese. The alliance gave the impression of a global conspiracy against democracy, when in fact it was never anything more than a marriage of convenience between racist Europeans and honorary Asian aryans. Nevertheless, the existence of the pact strengthened the hands of interventionists in the United States who linked the unholy triumverate in their propaganda.

Tokyo and Berlin were not immediately concerned about how their alliance looked to American citizens. They had been attracted to each other because they wanted to confront the

United States with the threat of a two-front war. In addition, the pact augured ill for the British in Asia who would be helpless once the Germans made it across the English Channel. Unhappily for the Japanese, the Germans never came close to invading Great Britain and, more important, the Russian-German Neutrality Pact of 1939 came undone in June of 1941 when Hitler sent his legions into Russia. From that point on, as the Japanese themselves were threatened with a two-front war, the Tripartite Pact lost much of its attractiveness. Things looked even bleaker after the fall of 1941 when the Russians surprised the world by surviving the Nazi blitzkrieg, the same Russians who had won a huge tank campaign against Japan along the Mongolian border in 1939.

Of all the issues discussed during the extensive conversations between Japan and the United States throughout 1941, Tokyo was most compromising on the pact. It was one of the bargaining chips Japan tried to use to buy us off or, at least, trade for a deal on China. The three main issues separating us were Japan's membership in the pact, her movements in Southeast Asia, and her plans for China. She was willing to alter her role in the Axis alliance, to go slow in Indochina, but not to pull out of China. For our part, we insisted on her withdrawal from China as the *sina qua non* for an agreement, were interested in maintaining the status quo in the rest of Asia, and least concerned about the pact. This was our private bargaining position. In public, our spokesmen referred continually to Japan's partnership in Nazi aggression and inhumanity. The Pearl Harbor infamy, then, was subconsciously expected by an American populace that came to see little difference between Germans and Japanese.

Through the remainder of 1940, we systematically embargoed more and more strategic materials until only one, oil, remained. We reasoned that a precipitate severance of the oil line would force Japan to attack the Dutch East Indies and bring us into the war. Given our commitment in the ABC-1 agreements to Europe first and our inability at that time to conduct a one-front, let alone a two-front, war, we tried to steer clear of a final showdown. All the same, as 1940 came to a close, Secretary of State Hull opined that the odds for peace were about 100 to 1.

Hull knew whereof he spoke because we were privy to secret Japanese policy papers. In August of 1940, we pulled off one of the great intelligence coups by breaking the Japanese coding process through the employment of a deciphering system called MAGIC. After that date, whatever we could pick up around the world, mainly messages transmitted from Tokyo to diplomats, we decoded and read almost as quickly as they were in Japan's chancellories and sometimes, as was the case with the final peacetime note, even quicker.

We used intelligence obtained through MAGIC with circumspection because we did not want the Japanese to discover our breakthrough. Our diplomats had to react in a believable fashion while reading papers they had already seen in private. They had to know when to act surprised, when to raise an eyebrow, or when to pound the table, as their eyes scanned a document in the presence of a Japanese emissary. Although for some of the less guileful this was no mean trick, Cordell Hull had prepared for his role in one of the best theaters in the world, the U.S. Senate.

TOKYO TALKS PEACE

Ensconced in northern Indochina, the Japanese began the new year with a peace offensive. How serious they were is a difficult question. Although not prepared to compromise on basics, they were willing to try us out, to bend a little, albeit without offering what we considered a meaningful compromise. Several prominent Japanese visited Washington in January and February of 1941 to talk of peace, and a new ambassador, Admiral Kichisaburo Nomura, arrived here during the same period. An acquaintance of President Roosevelt from happier days, Nomura was a liberal, pro-American dove who, unfortunately, was also a diplomatic tyro. The highlight of the peace offensive was the spectacular Walsh-Drought proposals.

Bishop James E. Walsh and Father James M. Drought, two American clergymen stationed in Asia, were asked by Foreign Minister Yosuke Matsuoka to convey a new proposal to American authorities. The oral report the priests brought to Washington was so optimistic that they were sent back to their Japanese friends with instructions to get the offer in writing. In April, they returned with a draft agreement representing quite a concession from the Japanese; a promise to withdraw from China if Chiang Kai-shek agreed both to recognize Japanese control of Manchuria and to accept a coalition government with pro-Japanese Chinese. The Japanese were never again to offer such a proposal. We did not accept it because we thought that Chiang would never form a coalition government and also because other messages from MAGIC cast doubt on the validity of the Walsh-Drought draft. Nevertheless, all of these events suggested that the Japanese were sincere during the winter and spring of 1941 in their attempts to avoid a final break with the United States.

The Walsh-Drought proposals, an independent strain in Japanese-American negotiations, were among the first things Hull and Admiral Nomura discussed. From late February through December of 1941, the two men met in Hull's Washington hotel suite over 40 times. As historian Herbert Feis has written, "There, in the air, which like all hotel air, seems to belong to no one, they exchanged avowals of their countries' policies. And there, among furniture, which like all hotel furniture, is neutral, they sought formulas which would make them friends." All of their discussions came to naught. Hull insisted on a Japanese withdrawal from China and acceptance of the Open Door, while Nomura promised eventual withdrawal but stopped far short of renouncing the Greater East Asia Co-Prosperity Sphere. Both men honestly tried to avert war. The many meetings seem to belie the notion that once reasonable men sit down together they can settle any difficulties. There was no communication problem here except perhaps when Nomura occasionally found himself out of step with Tokyo.

As negotiations continued in Washington, Japan faced a hard policy decision involving her western flank. Germany's invasion of Russia in June of 1941 affected the balance in Asia almost as much as it affected the balance in Europe. The previous April, the Japanese secured Russian neutrality on paper. Presumably they no longer had to worry about an attack from their old rival in case of war with the United States. On the other hand, if they made the first move and invaded Siberia, they could have applied the knockout blow to the Russians. Despite such a temptation, there was time enough to start up with the Bolshe-viks—the first order of business was the Greater East Asia Co-Prosperity Sphere whose development would be aided only tangentially by the defeat of Russia. After all, Japanese armies were still bogged down in China with no end to that war in sight. In hopes of tidying up affairs there quickly, they decided on July 2 (in a policy paper to which we were privy) the following: Instead of moving north they would move south into the lower half of Indochina in order to prepare for actions further south; they would not enter the Soviet war until the Russians were on their last legs (shades of the jackal policy adopted by comrade-in-arms Mussolini); and the Japanese Empire would be placed on a war footing.

After studying the implications of the new Japanese strategy, American decision makers countered the proposed forward moves with two of their own: one covert, the other overt. On July 23, 1941, Franklin Roosevelt finally approved a plan to allow civilian American pilots in American planes with Chinese markings to bomb mainland Japan. Pearl Harbor came too quickly for the plan to be effected. One wonders whether Roosevelt would have gone through with it. What would have happened had Americans been shot down and captured by the Japanese?

The Japanese, and the American population for that matter, never learned of the proposed clandestine air war until the archives were opened in recent years. Our overt response to the Japanese forward move was startling enough. On July 26,

Roosevelt froze Japanese funds in the United States and thus effectively cut off trade between the two countries, including the trade in oil. Realizing the seriousness of his action, the President originally planned to allow Japan to obtain some oil through special permits. Inexplicably, his bureaucracy never got the message. When the Japanese made inquiries about purchasing oil, they were rebuffed by relatively junior government officials. This brought matters to a crisis point much quicker than Roosevelt had intended. At this point, Tokyo had a one year's supply of the vital fuel. Without oil, Japan would either have to give up the ghost in China or invade the Dutch East Indies whose government had also frozen Japanese funds.

Our perspicacious ambassador in Tokyo, Joseph Grew, was convinced that the freeze order came too late. The Japanese could never retreat from the program they had laid out for themselves; they would have to find oil elsewhere to lubricate their war machines. As Herbert Feis has written, "From now on the oil gauge and the clock stood side by side. Each fall in the level brought the hour of decision closer." The Japanese could no longer afford to wile away their time shadow boxing in those desultory meetings in Cordell Hull's hotel suite. A final solution to the American problem had to be devised in the weeks or, at best, months to come.

Although they should have expected it given what they perceived in the past to be unreasonable American actions, the Japanese were offended by the freeze order. After all, what had they done? With a bit of bullying, they convinced the Vichy French to permit a peaceful occupation of southern Indochina. For this, Roosevelt burnt the last economic bridge behind him? Of course, the Americans only used the new Indochina move as a rationale for a harder line that had already been decided.

Our policy appeared even more incomprehensible given political events in Tokyo in early July. First, the Emperor had intervened in an unprecedented manner on July 2 to urge a peaceful policy on his ministers. More important, on July 16 the most anti-American member of the cabinet and an architect of the Tripartite Pact, Foreign Minister Matsuoka, was pushed out of power. What else could the Japanese have done, short of withdrawing from China, to make clear their pacific intentions?

Undaunted, they tried another tack. Never excited about the prospect of war with the powerful United States, Prime Minister Fumimaro Konoye held off his impatient army with a new grand gesture. He proposed a summit conference with Roosevelt, a face-to-face meeting at which both leaders would try to solve the major issues separating them. We knew that if we rejected Konoye's overture, the peace faction in Tokyo would suffer a blow from which it might not recover. Ambassador Grew advised that Konoye, who was sincere, should be given a chance. The Prime Minister even tentatively approved the four principles that Hull had presented as a basis for negotiations three months earlier. Konoye suggested he might agree to the maintenance of the territorial integrity of all nations, the principle of noninterference in other nations' affairs, equality of commercial opportunity throughout the world, and the maintenance of the status quo in the Pacific.

Roosevelt was at first enchanted with the idea of a summit conference. A proponent of personal diplomacy and confident in his own ability as a negotiator, the President began half seriously considering meeting spots—maybe Alaska or Hawaii. However, Asia was Cordell Hull's domain. He had been minding that store while Roosevelt dabbled in Europe. Hull argued long and hard and eventually successfully against the meeting, suspecting that it would not have been beyond his chief to make some unprincipled deal that would have slighted our interests in China. Furthermore, Hull and his many allies contended that Konoye was a captive of his military, that he would not or could not offer us anything reasonable, and that in the past he had behaved less than honorably.

There are those who compare our failure to grant Konoye's request for a summit to McKinley's closing out of diplomatic options in the spring of 1898. Had Roosevelt met Konoye, the Japanese might have offered a face-saving, peace-keeping compromise we could have matched. What was to be lost by meeting him? At worst, we might have gained a few more months before a Japanese attack; at best, a firm commitment from them to retire from Indochina and portions of China proper. In other words, we might have been able to wangle more than half a loaf from our adversary, who was doing the best he could to avoid war with us. But even three-quarters of a loaf would have violated the principles that Hull and others had long argued were a *sina qua non* for an agreement. Principle number one was the independence and territorial integrity of China—the Open Door.

On October 16, Prince Konoye fell from power. His replacement, General Hideki Tojo, was not a friend of the United States, and he was not as nervous about an ultimate severance of relations with us. Still, Tojo had received a bad press here. As spokesman for the army earlier, he had been a leading hawk in the Konoye Cabinet. As a civilian prime minister now, he promised to do the Emperor's bidding and the Emperor wanted to continue negotiations. Konoye's final deadline for a settlement with the United States had been October 10. With the support of the doves, Tojo extended the deadline to December and immediately prepared a new peace plan. This time, it was clear that the deadline would not be extended unless the impasse was broken.

At an Imperial Conference on November 5, Tojo and his colleagues gave compromise one last chance. Naturally, their definition of compromise and ours were not identical. All the same, they decided to forward a new proposal to the United States. If no accord was obtained by November 25, the army and navy would begin their preparations for movement against the West. The proposal, later called Plan A, included economic equality for all in China and around the world, the retention of Japanese military units in North China, Mongolia, and Hainan for a necessary period (25 years according to Nomura), withdrawal of the rest of the troops from China within 2 years after the conclusion of peace, the end of American aid to Chiang, the evacuation of Indochina after the peace, and some modifications in Japan's role in the Tripartite Pact.

Plan A was clearly unacceptable to us and represented Japan's maximum demands. Foreign Minister Shigenori Togo recognized this and insisted that the Cabinet send along something more attractive, the so-called Plan B. Plan B was a *modus vivendi* to tidy things over for a while. It included the maintenance of the status quo in the Pacific, a promise to withdraw from southern Indochina when the war in China was over, American assistance in reopening trade with the Dutch East Indies, shipment of American oil to Japan, and the final point, the kicker that made the otherwise reasonable proposition ultimately unacceptable. "The government of the United States undertakes to refrain from such measures and actions as will be prejudicial to the endeavors for the restoration of general peace between Japan and China." Despite the final point, Tokyo was serious about Plan B and hoped it would serve as the basis for discussion of a temporary agreement to delay war.

Not only did we have an advance preview of A and B but we also knew of the plans sent to Japanese army and navy units beginning: "The Japanese Empire is expecting war to break out with the United States, Great Britain, and the Netherlands. War will be declared on X day. This order will become effective on Y day." Nomura's copies of the various informations included the following covering comment:

> Both in name and spirit this offer of ours is indeed the last. . . . This time we are showing all our friendship; this time we are making our last possible bargain . . . the success or failure of the pending discussions will have an immense effect on the destiny of the Japanese Empire.

Tokyo was not fooling.

Unbeknownst to the Japanese, we, too, had been drawing up guidelines for the approaching crisis. On November 5, the date of the Imperial Conference, the Joint Chiefs presented a program that called for the retention of the ABC-1 priorities, hoped that war could be avoided unless Japan attacked vitally important territories (i.e., British or Dutch colonies, Thailand, New Caledonia and the Loyalty Islands, Portuguese Timor), the maintenance of all possible aid to Chiang Kai-shek, and an admonition to refrain from provoking the Japanese. The Joint Chiefs did not want war yet, especially a two-front war. They would sit tight, keep their fingers crossed, and wait for Japan to make a move. Interestingly, the Joint Chiefs advocated war even if American territory was not attacked. One wonders whether Roosevelt could have convinced Congress to declare war to defend the British Empire.

On November 7, the next to last Japanese offer, Plan A, was presented to Hull and Roosevelt by an anxious Admiral Nomura. As he expected, it was rejected out of hand. To assist in the important negotiations over Plan B, the Japanese dispatched a second envoy, Ambassador Saburo Kurusu, who never hit it off with the Americans, even though he had an American wife. On November 20, he and Nomura offered the *modus vivendi*, Plan B, to Hull. We knew this was the last chance to avoid a break in relations and thus took the proposal more seriously than the first.

Undoubtedly, the provision for the freezing of the status quo in the Pacific would have been difficult to enforce. We also would have found it impossible to refrain from taking any action prejudicial to peace in China. Nonetheless, we did work up a counterproposal calling for a reopening of trade between the two countries, Japanese withdrawal from the pact, no further Japanese movement south, and American assistance in bringing about a just peace in China. On the surface, such an American Plan B was not too distant from Japan's. In 1946, the imprisoned Tojo claimed that had Roosevelt forwarded his Plan B to Tokyo, it would have been accepted. Had war been averted, even only for a few months, it might not have ever come, for a few months plus inclement weather in the Pacific would have taken us into the spring of 1942, and by then, the Japanese might have concluded that Hitler could not win in Russia. This conjecture rests upon Tojo's analysis. We cannot evaluate it because our planned *modus vivendi* was never submitted to Tokyo.

The domestic forces opposing a *modus vivendi*, led by Hull, were strengthened by the Allied response to the proposition. The Dutch, with much to lose, approved of it, but the British were lukewarm. As Churchill commented in his note of qualified acceptance, "What about Chiang Kai-shek? Is he not having a very thin diet? Our anxiety is about China. If they collapse our joint dangers would enormously increase." The Chinese themselves mustered their considerable influence in Washington to help nip an American Plan B in the bud.

Armed with the unified support of the China lobby, Hull came down strongly against the *modus vivendi.* Left alone, Roosevelt and his nervous military advisors might have tried it out. Ultimately, Hull's moral and practical arguments won the day, despite the fact that we knew that our rejection of Japan's *modus vivendi* meant the end of negotiations and, perhaps, war.

To make matters worse, instead of answering their Plan B with one of our own, Hull responded with a Plan A, our maximum terms. Not understanding what Hull was up to, the Japanese interpreted his 10-point, take-it-or-leave-it proposition as confirmation of what they had expected all along; they could not make deals with the United States. Hull never meant his plan to be a serious negotiating paper. He merely wanted to set the record straight. His final statement of American policy called for a nonaggression pact in Asia, a neutralization of Indochina, Japanese evacuation of China (the Japanese thought he meant Manchuria as well and were furious), an end to extraterritoriality in China, support from all principals for Chiang Kai-shek, a return to the old trade relationships, an end to our freeze order, stabilization of Japanese and American currency, Japanese withdrawal from the pact, and the creation of a new Far Eastern Concert. After dispatching the message to Tokyo, Hull dramatically told Secretary of War Henry L. Stimson, "I have washed my hands of it and it is now in the hands of you and [Frank] Knox [Secretary of the Navy], the Army and the Navy." Alerts were sent out to our military installations as we awaited the Japanese forward movement we knew not where.

There was one final peace proposal: 24 hours before the attack on Pearl Harbor, Roosevelt sent a personal plea to the Japanese Emperor to refrain from taking any action that would bring so much misery and suffering to the peoples of the world. He offered no new plans, merely good will. By the time the Emperor received the message, his army and naval units were in position for attack on several fronts throughout the Pacific.

Many Japanese accepted the final breakdown of negotiations in November with an air of resignation. They did not want war with the United States but they also wanted China. Although army officers thought themselves invincible, their navy counterparts were more realistic. Some planners of the Pearl Harbor attack considered it a desperate gamble that would probably fail. Even if it did take us by surprise, they knew they could never fight a long war against the United States. Facing the growing strength of the expansionists around them, the Emperor and many of the civilian cabinet members finally saw war as the only option available to maintain both domestic peace and international power. Although they could understand how the United States might misconstrue Japan's foreign and military policy, they felt that we had let them down when we failed to seriously consider their attempts to seek a compromise. From our point of view, the Japanese Empire was an aggressor nation, and as we learned from Munich, one could not compromise with aggressors. And that—especially for Hull and eventually Roosevelt—was that.

On December 6, Nomura and Kurusu received the first 13 points of a 14-point statement they were to present to the American government the next day. The document outlined the Japanese case against the United States and led, almost anticlimactically, to a 14th point severing diplomatic relations. We expected as much because we knew that Hull's 10-point statement had crushed all hopes for a negotiated settlement. Over the preceding week, we had noted a variety of Japanese naval and military movements but somehow lost track of part of their fleet, those aircraft carriers and their escorts stealthily making their way across the Pacific toward Hawaii. When the 14th and final point of the Japanese message arrived in Washington on the morning of December 7 and was decoded and translated in both Japanese and American decoding rooms, we still did not know what Japan's military plans were. We did not have to wait long to find out.

Owing to delays in decoding and translation in the Japanese Embassy, Kurusu and Nomura were late for their appointment with the Secretary of State. They did not present their indictment until 2:20, a full hour after the first bombs had fallen on Pearl Harbor. As the chastened envoys left the office of a furious Cordell Hull, Japan and the United States were already locked in mortal combat, combat to settle the destiny of the Japanese Empire, once and for all.

A DAY THAT WILL LIVE IN INFAMY

"My God, this can't be true! This must mean the Philippines." So did Secretary of the Navy Knox greet the news of the Pearl Harbor attack on December 7, 1941. Despite his and others' well-documented shock, an unsavory odor still lingers over the Pearl Harbor story. In these days of wiretapping, forged bombing reports, and government conspiracies to defraud, we must reexamine all of the charges concerning the Day of Infamy to discover how it came to be that the Japanese were able to destroy 18 ships, 188 planes, and kill over 2,000 military personnel in our worst military disaster.

At first glance, a Pearl Harbor plot seems plausible. As early as the middle of 1940, Roosevelt came to feel that some day we would most likely become involved in the war. We also have seen how he had done just about everything to the Germans short of declaring war by the late fall of 1941. We were shooting at their U-boats, convoying their enemy's ships laden with our material across the Atlantic, meeting with that same enemy to plan our war participation, and conducting a host of other covert and overt unneutral activities that made us an ally, in all but name, in the antifascist coalition. All of these moves bringing us closer and closer to full-scale intervention were accepted by most Americans. Indeed, on the eve of war, they considered Hitler and Tojo our enemies, the survival of England and Russia vital to our defense, and, above all, our entry into war probable. But when asked over and over again about going to war then and there, they responded with a resounding no. What would have happened had Roosevelt requested a war declaration? Though he might have been able to round up a majority in Congress to support him, he would have been confronted with a huge minority there, and in the public at large, that would have violently opposed war without an attack on our territory.

Thus, with Roosevelt's conviction that Americans did not share his desire for active belligerency hovering in the background, the seeds of the Pearl Harbor plot were planted. If only he could get the Japanese or the Germans to attack us. Treacherous and deceitful, yes, but *he* knew what was best for us. Where have we heard that one before? To this general argument, we can add a series of suspicious events surrounding the attack itself and we end up with a circumstantial case against the President and the alleged conspirators around him.

The circumstantial evidence involves five potentially incriminating happenings. First, and perhaps most important, Japanese messages in code indicating that Pearl Harbor was their target crossed the desk of several American decoders. Why were they ignored? The answer is deceivingly simple. Had we been expecting an attack in Hawaii, which we were not, then someone would have come across the documents amidst thousands of other pieces of intelligence our operatives obtained during the months before the attack. The relevant cues were ignored because no one could imagine a war scenario including Hawaii. This is not so difficult to understand. A man is walking in a busy city, surrounded by honking automobiles, jackhammers, and shouting pedestrians. Somewhere his brain picks up a vague rumbling noise. The rumbling turns out to be the sound emitted by an air conditioner tearing loose from its moorings some 100 feet above his head. He had never been hit by a falling air conditioner before and he had never heard about anyone being hit by such an exotic flying missile. Thus, he ignores the warning that competed unsuccessfully with other, more important noises for his attention. If Pearl Harbor is safe, then there is no reason to look for cues concerning its attack.

It is true that Joseph Grew, among others, predicted an attack on Pearl Harbor. On the other hand, our best military minds felt that such an attack was both impossible and illogical. It was impossible because the Japanese could never make it across the Pacific without being seen. As things turned out, they took an unorthodox route to Hawaii and were able to elude detection in that vast ocean. The attack was illogical because had they invaded a British or Dutch possession, the President might not have been able to convince the country to go to war. In their zeal to knock out our fleet, they made it easy for Roosevelt.

Second among the suspicious events, the approaching Japanese aircraft were picked up on our newfangled radar machines at Pearl. Again, since an attack was not expected, the radar technician thought the extraneous blips related to our own aircraft.

Third, Chairman of the Joint Chiefs General George C. Marshall went horseback riding on the morning of December 7 after he knew that the Japanese were going to attack—somewhere. All we can say to this charge is that Marshall was a creature of habit who took his exercise every day rain or shine, war or peace, and that his ride had little to do with our preparedness efforts.

Fourth, and most peculiarly, the message reflecting our foreknowledge of a Japanese movement on December 7 was sent to Hawaii by commercial RCA telegraph and thus arrived too late to allow the commanders to put their installations in a state of readiness. (The famous telegram that arrived some hours after the bombs had fallen was delivered by a *Japanese*-American messenger boy.) Why did not someone in Washington just pick up a phone and tell the Pacific command to be prepared for anything?

In the first place, we had to be very careful about the transmission of such a message. Had the Japanese picked up our alert, they might have figured out that we had broken their codes. But why RCA? We did have alternate means of getting the alert to Hawaii. As it turned out, the Army, whose responsibility it was to send the message, had been having problems

with its Paoific communication system. They refused to use the
Navy's parallel system because they did not want to admit that
theirs was not working. Thus, the important message was sent
via RCA telegraph without special priority. Of course, Pearl
Harbor was already on alert on December 7. It was, however, a
case of the boy who cried wolf. The base had been placed on
alert several times in 1941 and, more important, since Pearl was
not considered to be a Japanese target, the commanders greeted
the order casually.

Last in the series of questionable events took place at a
cabinet meeting on November 25. According to Stimson,
Roosevelt said that "we are likely to be attacked perhaps [as
soon as] next Monday. . . . The question was how we should
maneuver them into the position of firing the first shot without
allowing too much danger to ourselves." Suspicious yes, but
here Stimson was only reporting Roosevelt's concern about
what action to take when the Japanese invaded non-American
territory. Since he expected the Japanese would be clever
enough to avoid the Philippines in their new movements, how
could he come to the aid of the British or Dutch in a way that
would appear that we were on the defensive?

Each of these items by itself is not very important. When
taken together with Roosevelt's frustration, we can understand
how the Pearl Harbor myth developed. Suffice to say that not
one shred of evidence has been uncovered to show that the
President or any of his aides had foreknowledge of the attack.
Roosevelt's political opponents in Congress searched the records
and interrogated relevant witnesses in a vain attempt to crucify
him. Undoubtedly, he and his advisors should have been more
alert to the danger in Hawaii. The censure of the Pearl Harbor
commanders, as well as General Marshall, for being negligent, is
still a long way from participation in a plot to bring us into war
through the purposeful destruction of American lives and
materiel.

If there were a plot, scores of people would had to have been
involved and by now one of them should have talked or one
of their incriminating documents should have turned up.
Further, one hour before the bombs fell on Hawaii, Roosevelt

met with the Chinese Ambassador and told him that we expected an assault on someone else's property momentarily and that he hoped that he could bring his nation into the conflict in the absence of a direct attack. Other members of his entourage said similar things during the days before Pearl Harbor. Although they were politicians, even politicians would not have been able to execute the sort of grand obfuscation necessary to deceive those not in on the plot, as well as future investigators.

Ignoring for the moment the lack of incriminating documentary evidence, Roosevelt's alleged foreknowledge of the attack makes no sense when we consider the terrific beating we took at Pearl. There was no need to lose so many men and, to be callous, ships. Only one destroyed vessel or one bomb on Honolulu would have propelled us into the war Roosevelt wanted. The Japanese hoped that the destruction of the Pacific fleet would buy time for them to build an impregnable bastion throughout Southeast Asia. They almost succeeded. Their attack crippled us for half a year. The Battle of Midway, which took place in early June 1942, and which spelled the beginning of the end for Japanese naval power, was by no means a romp for us. Thus, the risk Roosevelt allegedly took was a foolish one that could have cost us everything in the Pacific.

On logical as well as evidential grounds, the case for the plot is weak or nonexistent. Still, many who remember Pearl Harbor also remember the rumors and allegations. Perhaps the pervasiveness of the myth relates to our unwillingness to believe that we could have suffered such a defeat through the natural order of events. The legend about American invincibility, however, may have finally been destroyed in the jungles of Vietnam. Pearl Harbor may be easier to understand today.

WAR WITH GERMANY, AT LAST

At the epochal December 7 Cabinet meeting, Secretary Stimson suggested that the Germans be included in our declaration of war. After all, he argued, not only were they responsible in part for their ally's reprehensible actions but also we would soon be at war with them anyway. Of course, since they had still not attacked us, a good number of Americans would have opposed entry into the European war through the backdoor of Asia. Roosevelt's Day of Infamy speech was therefore directed against Japan exclusively.

The congressional response to Roosevelt's request for war was predictable. Only one Representative dissented. In an amazing historical quirk, Jeannette Rankin, who had voted against war in 1917, had been returned to the House in 1940, after an absence of 22 years. With tears pouring down her face, she voted no and remained true to her pacifist's faith. As in 1918, she was denied her seat in the subsequent congressional election. Clearly, had Germany been slipped into Roosevelt's request for a declaration of war, other Congressmen would have joined the lonely Congresswoman Rankin in dissent.

That omission of Germany posed a serious problem. According to our joint military plan, we were supposed to devote the major effort to Europe while we fought a holding action in Asia. Without a declaration of war against Germany, we would have had to commit more and more troops to the Asian theater since Japan would have been our only *official* enemy. Hitler might have waited six months or a year before declaring war against us. By that time, we would have been oriented militarily toward an Asia-first strategy and so deeply involved there that we would have been unable to operate effectively in Europe.

Why did Hitler make it so easy for Roosevelt? This has been one of the unsolved riddles of World War II. We know that he was pleased with Japan's attack. His subsequent declaration of war meant a two-front war for us and a diffusion of our formidable strength. Had he waited too long, we might have made short work of the Japanese and then been able to concentrate everything we had against him, or so he might have reasoned. When Hitler did declare war on December 11, he did not mention the pact as a *casus belli,* but based his case on the fact that "from initial violations of neutrality [we] had finally proceeded to open acts of war against Germany." His charge was not far from the mark. Given his failure to invoke the pact, we cannot argue that he went to war because there was honor among thieves.

Psychological variables also play a role. The Germans had recently suffered their first setback of the war when the drive east came to a halt in the snows of Russia. Perhaps, Hitler may have reasoned, a declaration of war against the United States would serve as a morale booster. Similarly, he allegedly claimed that a great power did not wait for war to be declared against it; it acted first. He also may have reasoned that his declaration of war against the United States might produce a Japanese declaration of war against the Soviet Union.

Most probably, the explanation for Hitler's declaration involves all of the above factors, especially the fact that we were just about in the war anyway. In early December, without foreknowledge of Pearl Harbor, the Germany Admiralty was preparing to retaliate against the United States on the high seas. Since we were shooting at them and convoying vital goods to the British, they concluded that they might as well risk full-scale war, which had to come some day, by unleashing their submarines. Hitler did not have time to formally approve a change in his naval strategy before December 7, and after December 11 such a half measure was irrelevant. The probable alteration in German naval policy, in the works on the eve of Pearl Harbor, demonstrates that even without the Japanese attack, we might have been at war with Germany before the year was out. It would not have been easy for Roosevelt to go to war over German submarines again, but a handful of sinkings by Hitler, who was hated much more than the Kaiser had been, might have convinced most of Congress and the public that the time had come to get into the fray. In any event, German and Japanese American policies were running in parallel directions in the late fall of 1941. Hitler's unprovoked declaration eased our anxieties. Had he called off his submarines and kept his mouth shut, who knows what would have happened to ABC-1, the war in Asia, and especially the future of Europe? As Bismarck once remarked, the Lord looks after fools, drunkards, and the United States of America.

NATIONAL SECURITY AND WORLD WAR II

Of all of our examinations of American wars and national security, World War II poses the most difficult problem. Those who have grown up believing that Hitler was the scourge of the earth and that his Japanese allies were little better cannot question our entry into the war. Everyone knows that we had to fight to save civilization from the barbarians. Distinguished scholars such as Charles Beard were dismissed as deluded, senile, or even fascist for their attacks on the wisdom of our interventionist policies from 1939 to 1941. Images of German concentration camps and the brutality in Japanese prisoner of war camps make it almost impossible to deal with World War II on a rational basis. Yet we have dismissed such questions from our previous analyses and must try to do so again, even in the case of war against Hitler.

First of all, the direct military threat posed by Japan and Germany in 1941 was not a serious one. Obviously, Pearl Harbor more than justified a war declaration but such an attack would not have occurred in 1941 had we been more willing to acquiesce in Japanese plans for China. In the short run, there was no way for Japan to invade or occupy any part of our territories east of the Philippines. Moreover, she was not interested in American conquest, at least in the 1940s. As for Pearl Harbor itself, Japan merely destroyed our fleet and withdrew. She did, of course, invade the Philippines, a much easier logistic task, but the taking of our archipelago was not essential to the success of her Greater East Asia Co-Prosperity Sphere. The Philippines, our Achilles heel according to the Republican Roosevelt in 1907, were occupied because they were our base in her territory. Had we not been at loggerheads over China, Japan would not have taken the islands. Even in the heady days of early 1942, most Japanese strategists realized that they could never compete militarily against the United States over the long haul. One can thus envision a cold-blooded deal in which we gave them their head in China in exchange for a guarantee of our properties in Asia.

But what would have happened after the Japanese had sub-
dued China? Would they then have looked toward California?
We know that even in the 1930s, Japanese jingoes talked of
controlling all of the Pacific including our West Coast. Such
bravado was not taken seriously by those responsible for the
destiny of the Japanese Empire. In any event, we had plenty of
time to wait to see what they had in store for us since they
would have had to conduct a protracted guerrilla war against
the Chinese communists. That they had the capability of occasionally bombarding our shores or even launching balloons carrying small bombs across the Pacific goes without saying. But why
would they want to start up with us if they did not possess the
wherewithal to cross the Pacific and land an effective invasion
force? Given their logistic problems, even taking into account
technological developments over the next generation, we can
argue that both in the short and medium run, Japan was not a
military threat.

The Germans posed a more plausible challenge. By 1941,
they had reached the Atlantic. Hitler's dreams of world conquest, as documented by his second *Mein Kampf,* knew no
bounds. He could operate with more impressive resources and in
a smaller ocean than his Asiatic ally. At the time in question,
however, even had he not been bogged down in Russia, he did
not possess the technical capability to invade a defenseless Latin
American country. It took *us* three years to prepare the
amphibious invasion of France, an invasion that involved less
than 50 miles of water. An invasion of the United States in the
early 1940s was out of the question, despite Hitler's fantasies.

It is true that they were ahead of us in atomic bomb research
in 1941. We did not know much about this at the time or what
atomic power would mean for the balance of terror in the
world. Had they finished work on their first bombs in 1944,
which was possible had Hitler not diverted resources away from
that project, they might have terror-bombed us with the sort of
devices we used on Hiroshima and Nagasaki. Moreover, as we
were later to discover with their V rockets, they developed the

most advanced delivery systems of the day, systems that presaged intercontinental ballistic missiles. With rockets and atomic bombs in Hitler's hands, would we have been safe? All of this, of course, was science fiction in 1941 to American strategists. Many things could have happened to Hitler before he obtained the means to rain terror on us from the skies. Furthermore, on the eve of our entry into war, he had more serious things to worry about than an aerial attack and invasion in the Western Hemisphere.

Undoubtedly had the Axis powers emerged victorious from their wars in Europe and Asia, they would have eventually threatened our territories and developed adequate capabilities to do so, an attack 10 or 20 years in the future. Should we fight a preventive war now because 10 years from today a country harboring malevolent feelings toward us will be in a position to conquer us?

Although the Germans and Japanese clearly posed the most serious threat to our military security up to that time, we had enough breathing space to wait until the dust had settled from World War II. In 1941, they presented no immediate or intermediate military problem.

The United States had less to fear from the Axis on economic grounds. In 1940, Ambassador to England Joseph P. Kennedy suggested an informal division of the globe into five spheres— German, British, Russian, Japanese, and American. Each major power was to be supreme in its own sphere where it would develop an autarchic economy. Since there were enough economic spoils to go around for everyone with major power status, there would be no need for conflict.

At the time Kennedy offered his scheme to an unimpressed Washington, Germany controlled most of Central and Western Europe and might have been able to seize a few of the choice colonies of the British and French. Clearly, Hitler enjoyed a more favorable economic position than did the Kaiser a generation earlier. Once (and if) he settled his European affairs, we might have been squeezed out of markets and denied vital raw materials.

During the 1930s, however, foreign trade constituted only 3% of our gross national product. Given the Depression, this was not to be sneezed at, yet it is not an impressive figure. Moreover, some of that trade was with countries such as Canada and Cuba that would never be controlled by Berlin. As for raw materials, we might have had some problems with rubber and tin, but when confronted with shortages during the war, we were able to develop serviceable synthetic substitutes. All of the foregoing assumes a Germany bent on warring upon us economically, something not necessarily in the cards, especially if a Kennedy-type plan could have been worked out. But if worse came to worse, our economy could have suffered. As in the case of World War I, we must ask, how much of a drop in gross national product or living standards merited a war?

The economic threat was even less credible in Asia. At bottom, we were contending with Japan for what had proved to be a phantom Chinese market. Prior to the war, trade between Japan and the United States flourished while the dreams of John Hay and his crowd had never materialized. We had every reason to suspect that a friendly Japan would maintain the mutually advantageous trade with us indefinitely. We could do without the Asian market she might have ended up controlling.

It is true that the war production and war trade did seem to solve our economic problems in 1939. The New Deal had failed—the recession of 1937 put us back almost to where we had been in 1933, although the psychological climate had changed for the better. Without a war, our artificially stimulated economy might have faltered again. Did we need a war to combat economic instability and maybe even political unrest? Even if we did, the contradictions of American capitalism did not justify going to war in 1941.

What then about our honor? Did not the continued military success of both the Germans and Japanese represent an indirect assault on our honor? John Hay had announced our support of an independent China in 1900. In succeeding decades that pledge was repeated by Woodrow Wilson, Herbert Hoover, and Franklin Roosevelt. Although such promises were honored more in the breach than in the observance, some Americans considered an attack upon China to be almost an attack on their own country. The complete loss of China to Japan would have been unacceptable to those Americans who had been involved for so long in her educational, religious, and business enterprises. How many Americans are we talking about here? Most likely, those prepared to die for China were few and far between. Everyone would have clucked their tongues about the fate of their little yellow brothers and might have thrown a few coins into the collection box. Few were prepared to do much more to save China. Had Roosevelt himself asked for war with Japan over China, in the absence of an attack on our territories, he would have been laughed out of the Congress. As for other nations, they had never taken our Open Door proclamation seriously, so any unwillingness to put our money where our mouth was would have been shrugged off. Our fellow great powers knew that prudence called for some sense of proportion in international relations and anyone could see that China was not essential to our security.

Even more than Japan, Germany's repressive system and conquest of democratic Europe, if unchecked, threatened to undermine our image of ourselves as the defender of freedom throughout the world (although not in our own South). Yet republicanism had taken a beating many times before without jeopardizing our international status or even self-esteem. Up until 1941, our role as democracy's champion involved merely holding the torch for everyone else to see and refraining from joining in Old World contests between tyrants and free men. One wonders if we could have remained aloof once we learned of Hitler's death camps, although Stalin's death camps of 1937 and 1938 never came close to sparking sentiment for a war against the Soviet Union.

Neither the Germans nor Japanese were violating our legal rights to any significant degree in 1941 nor did they offer any indications that they planned to do so in the immediate future. We had no real *casus belli* based upon honor or rights until Pearl

Harbor. And, as we have seen, the Pearl Harbor attack could have been avoided had we been willing to make an amoral settlement with Tokyo.

BIBLIOGRAPHY

The literature on the origins of World War II continues to proliferate with some of the most important works written in the past few years. The most exhaustive and up-to-date historiographical introduction is Justus Doenecke's "Beyond Polemics: An Historiographical Reappraisal of American Entry into World War II," *The History Teacher*, 12 (February 1979), 217-251. Doenecke builds upon an earlier article by Wayne S. Cole, "American Entry into World War II: A Historiographical Appraisal," *Mississippi Valley Historical Review*, 43 (March 1957), 595-617.

Much of the debate about the war involves the character and policies of Franklin D. Roosevelt. Indispensable is Robert Dallek's *Franklin D. Roosevelt and American Foreign Policy, 1932-1945* (New York: Oxford University Press, 1979). Dallek captures the complexity of Roosevelt's policies which defy categorization. His monograph now supplants James McGregor Burns's *Roosevelt: The Soldier of Freedom* (New York: Harcourt Brace Jovanovich, 1970). Both authors, who pull no critical punches, end up with a generally favorable estimation. Useful also is William E. Kinsella's *Leadership in Isolation: F.D.R. and the Origins of the Second World War* (Cambridge, MA: Schenkman, 1978). Analyzing the materials that crossed Roosevelt's desk, Kinsella characterizes him as a defensive interventionist. Much earlier, Charles A. Beard attacked Roosevelt's alleged deceitful and unconstitutional leadership in *President Roosevelt and the Coming of the War, 1941* (New Haven, CT: Yale University Press, 1948). More recently, Richard W. Steele offered new evidence of Roosevelt's violation of the civil liberties of his opponents in "Franklin D. Roosevelt and His Foreign Policy Critics," *Political Science Quarterly*, 94 (Spring 1979), 15-35.

A useful introductory survey that approves of our entrance into the war is Robert A. Divine's *The Reluctant Belligerent: American Entry into the Second World War* (New York: John Wiley, 1965). Arnold Offner makes use of his own research in the 1930s, as well as more recent material, in *The Origins of the Second World War* (New York: Praeger, 1975). Pro-

Roosevelt and prointervention is the standard two-volume study by William L. Langer and S. Everett Gleason, *The Challenge to Isolation, 1937-1940* (New York: Harper & Row, 1952) and *The Undeclared War: 1940-41* (New York: Harper & Row, 1953). The first volume's title is misleading as the authors devote little attention to the years from 1937 to 1939. A reasoned critique of American entry based upon national security criteria was written by political scientist Bruce Russett. In *No Clear and Present Danger: A Skeptical View of the United States Entry into World War II* (New York: Harper & Row, 1972), Russett concentrates on the strategic situation in 1941 and possible scenarios had the United States stayed out of the war.

For German-American relations, James V. Compton's *The Swastika and the Eagle: Hitler, the United States, and the Origins of World War Two* (Boston: Houghton-Mifflin, 1967) is the best of several books on the subject. In general, the United States relation to Europe is less controversial than the Japanese connection. Thomas A. Bailey and Paul B. Ryan do offer new evidence of Rooseveltian unneutrality in their readable *Hitler vs. Roosevelt: The Undeclared Naval War* (New York: Macmillan, 1979).

That rarity, a good symposium collection, is Dorothy Borg and Shumpei Okomoto's (eds.) *Pearl Harbor as History: Japanese American Relations, 1931-1941* (New York: Columbia University Press, 1973), which covers almost all dimensions of the relationship as seen by academics on both sides of the Pacific. Generally critical of the Japanese is Robert J.C. Butow in *Tojo and the Coming of the War* (Stanford, CA: Stanford University Press, 1961) and *The John Doe Associates: Backdoor Diplomacy for Peace, 1941* (Stanford, CA: Stanford University Press, 1974). Butow has mined the relevant Japanese documents. More sympathetic and much more readable is the first-rate popular history by John Toland, *The Rising Sun: The Decline and Fall of the Japanese Empire, 1936-1945* (New York: Random House, 1970). A sound analysis of Japanese policy is found in Louis Morton's "Japan's Decision for War," in Kent Roberts Greenfield (ed.), *Command Decisions* (Washington, DC: Government Printing Office, 1960), 99-124.

The most influential early study of the Pacific conflict is Herbert Feis's masterful *The Road to Pearl Harbor: The Coming of the War between the United States and Japan* (Princeton, NJ: Princeton University Press, 1950). A brilliant analysis of the Japanese attack, as well as one of the best introductions to the intelligence business, is Roberta Wohlstetter's *Pearl Harbor, Warning and Decision* (Stanford, CA: Stanford University Press.

1962). An extreme version of the alleged plot is found in Charles Callan Tansill's *Back Door to War* (Chicago: Henry Regnery, 1952). The amazing story of the covert plan to bomb mainland Japan before Pearl Harbor is well told in Michael Schaller's "American Air Strategy in China, 1939-1941: The Origins of Clandestine Air Warfare," *American Quarterly*, 28 (Spring 1976), 3-19.

Chapter 6

THE KOREAN WAR

*The Security Council of the United Nations called upon
the invading troops to cease hostilities and to withdraw
to the 38th parallel. This they have not done.... The
Security Council called upon all members ... to render
every assistance to the United Nations in the execution
of this resolution. In these circumstances I have ordered
United States air and sea forces to give the Korean
Government troops cover and support.*
—Harry S Truman, June 27, 1950—

Unlike the five previous wars, the Korean War was called a
"police action." Police action came to be a euphemism for a
bloody international war in which we suffered more than
54,000 battle deaths, our allies more than 500,000, and our
opponents more than 1,400,000. In other ways too, the Korean
War seems different. First, whereas we enjoyed a decent breathing space between our earlier international wars, the Korean War
followed almost immediately on the heels of World War II.
Second, as of this writing, the war has not been officially
terminated. Although an armistice was signed in 1953, the
consummation of a peace treaty still appears to be a long way
off. Last, and amazing as it may seem, the Korean War involved

an extensive military action in a country designated by the Secretary of State as beyond our immediate security interests.

Since 1950, we have participated in other undeclared limited wars. Most notably in Southeast Asia from 1961 to 1973, Presidents sent troops into combat without obtaining a formal declaration of war. And we are not alone. Of the more than 100 wars fought throughout the world since 1945, very few have produced an old-fashioned declaration of war.

The Korean War differs from most of the other contemporary conflicts in that it began in a traditional manner with one country apparently invading another. It was not a classic civil war spawned by a guerrilla insurrection or struggle for national liberation. This factor is of paramount importance. Coming just five years after the close of World War II, the events on the Korean peninsula superficially resembled the events of the late 1930s, only this time, Stalin and his alleged puppets played the role of Hitler and the Japanese.

Like the Mexican War, World War II, and the Vietnamese War, the Korean War underscored the virtual omnipotence of the President as commander in chief. As in 1846, and more recently Tonkin Bay in 1964, Congressmen, as well as the public, had to accept the President's report of an international crisis and then support his dispatch of units to the combat theater before our ramparts were breached.

The Korean War was the prototype of today's limited war. Although the North Koreans appeared to be aiming for total victory in July of 1950, we were initially interested in pushing them back across the border and restoring the *status quo ante bellum.* Such a war, fought for limited goals and with our atomic arm tied behind our back, was difficult to understand and accept, especially as the battle death figures mounted. Yet, there was then, as there is now, no alternative to limited war, if war must be fought.

Finally, and perhaps most important, the Korean War was the major visible symbol of our coming of age as a global power, a global power willing, and in some cases anxious, to play the game of international politics anywhere at any time. From 1812 through World War II, the American people had to be tricked and coaxed into involvement outside their hemisphere. In 1950, we were ready to confront communists everywhere as we took up England's nineteenth century role as world peacekeeper. Korea, The Land of the Morning Calm, seemed an unlikely place to display our alleged new maturity.

LAND OF MORNING CALM

A remote nation, Korea had been an object but never a participant in international diplomacy. The United States had been the first to open Korea to the West when in 1882, after several naval forays against the so-called Hermit Kingdom, we secured a treaty guaranteeing commercial rights. A backwater of the Chinese Empire legally tied to Peking but virtually independent, she became a major issue in the Japanese-Russian fin-de-siecle struggle for control of Manchuria and adjacent territories. The Russo-Japanese War of 1904-1905 was fought, in part, over Korea, and in the peace treaty signed at Portsmouth, New Hampshire, in 1905, that defenseless country was acknowledged to be a Japanese spoil of war. In 1910, Japanese suzerainty over Korea was legitimized by a formal treaty of annexation. From that point until the termination of World War II, Korea was a colony of Japan.

Although Koreans in exile, such as Syngman Rhee in the West and Kim Il Sung in Russia and China, called for the overthrow of the Japanese, the Korean independence movement was a feeble one. During the turbulent 1920s and 1930s, the world had more important things to worry about than her plight. Over the course of World War II, the Allies discussed Korea's future at Cairo, Teheran, and Yalta. The Big Three ultimately decided to liberate Korea at war's end and to establish an international trusteeship to provide time for her to develop institutions suitable for the maintenance of independence in the modern international system. Independence itself might come in 5 to 20 years. Because she was small potatoes compared to Eastern Europe, Germany, and larger colonial entities, long-range Korean policy was left in an inchoate state.

In the short run and to facilitate the surrender of the Japanese, *temporary* provisions were made for the Russians to occupy Korea north of the 38th parallel and the Americans, the area to the south. In the months following the Japanese capitulation, the arbitrary 38th parallel boundary became a permanent demarcation line between emerging Cold War antagonists. In both the north and south, Russians and Americans developed their own systems run by their own friends in a pattern similar to that which was becoming familiar in the divided sectors of Germany. After several failures in 1946 and 1947 to convince the Soviets of the justice of our proposals for unification, normalization, and free elections, we turned to the United Nations which assisted in the running of relatively free parliamentary elections in the south in the spring of 1948. In August, the Republic of Korea was proclaimed with conservative nationalist Syngman Rhee as President. In the following month, the Russians announced the formation of the Democratic People's Republic of Korea with Kim Il Sung as Premier. They also informed us they would withdraw all of their military forces by December of that year. After hurriedly trying to build and equip a viable army in the south, we pulled our military forces out of Korea in the summer of 1949.

Rhee's position in the south was more tenuous than Kim's in the north. Many South Koreans opposed Rhee's conservative programs, his tendencies toward dictatorship, and the way they thought he contributed to the hardening of the 38th parallel division. Others, fearful of the communist Chinese, felt that rapprochement with the north, and consequently Russia, might bring a measure of security to the entire peninsula. Still others who worked against Rhee were agents of the northern regime sent south to subvert and agitate. Although neither Kim nor Rhee was a democrat, Rhee did tolerate a greater degree of freedom of the press and speech, perhaps because he did not have sufficient power to control his people or offend American sensitivities. To the outside world, the south appeared to be in political and economic turmoil, the north orderly and united. Additionally, the south, primarily an agricultural region, had been cut off from the mineral and electrical power resources of the north.

Americans on the scene realized that Rhee was not universally popular. Despite his self-promoted role as the George Washington of his country, his policies had alienated a good portion of the middle class and intellectuals whose support he needed to maintain stability. In fact, in the parliamentary elections of May 30, 1950, his party lost a significant number of seats to independents who threatened to challenge his power. Still, on the eve of the war, Americans thought that with aid, technical assistance, and advice, the South Koreans, and maybe even Rhee, would make it through the difficult period of nation building.

THE MAN FROM INDEPENDENCE

By 1950, Harry S Truman was not only President in his own right but had become a strong and forceful national leader. Like Chester A. Arthur and John Tyler, two other accidental Presidents, he grew with the office. In a celebrated poll of historians conducted during the 1960s, Truman was ranked as a "Near Great" President. His reputation was not always so good and, interestingly, may not withstand the scrutiny of the latest generation of historical tastemakers.

During the late 1950s, historians and political scientists began to hail him for the masterful way he guided us through the perilous early days of the Cold War with such unprecedented instruments as the Marshall Plan and NATO. At first, the general public scoffed, for they only remembered his scandals, Palm Beach shirts, and crude manners. Then, as such things happen, the expert evaluations, or at least the evaluations of Cold War liberals who defined the consensus in the scholarly world, began to trickle down through college texts to high schools and into popular literature and magazines. Today, a good portion of the population, excluding some partisan Republicans, admires the feisty Missourian. To complete the cycle, revisionist historians now argue that Truman may have been responsible for creating the conditions that led to a need for NATO and for even planting the seeds of McCarthyism. However, this evaluation is still only heard in the rarified atmosphere of historical conventions and scholarly journals—for the time being, the general public remains surprisingly enthusiastic about Truman.

Harry Truman was a professional politician for most of his life. After service as an artillery captain in World War I and a fling as an unsuccessful haberdasher, Truman read law and became involved in Missouri politics, first as a judge of the commissioner type in Jackson County and then as a U.S. Senator in 1934. He was a product, albeit an honest one, of the corrupt Pendergast machine. Such a background was not uncommon for Democratic politicians. As Senator, he made few waves until 1941, when his Special Committee to Investigate the National Defense Program made his name almost a household word and served to bring him forward from the back benches.

Truman was a member in good standing of the card-playing, bourbon-drinking southern Democratic fraternity that ran the Senate. Like many of his colleagues, he loved belonging to what has been called the most exclusive club in the world. Indeed, in the early 1940s, he looked forward to spending the rest of his political career within its pleasant confines. Even had he had higher ambitions, he lacked the charisma and major-state base from which to launch a Presidential campaign. In 1944, however, Roosevelt again dropped a Vice-President, this time the unpredictable and uncontrollable, Henry A. Wallace.

With apparently little thought given to the awesome responsibilities facing the man "a heartbeat away" from the Presidency, the Democratic leadership chose Truman as the ideal Vice-President, a man who would operate in the John Nance Garner mode of being seen only in the Senate and little heard. The rather casual selection process seems astonishing today given the very real possibility that Roosevelt would not survive his fourth term. Although the President appeared healthy enough, the Depression and war had taken their toll of a man who already was an invalid. But Truman was safe, well-liked, relatively liberal (somewhere between Wallace and Garner), and was expected to behave.

While a perfect choice for Vice-President, Truman was ill-prepared to become President and certainly ignorant about international politics in 1945. Indeed, when he took office after Roosevelt's death in April, he had to be informed of the existence of the Atomic Bomb project.

Truman prided himself on being a tough customer in foreign relations. Blunt and often undiplomatic, he pounded the desk in situations in which Roosevelt would have cajoled and coaxed. Controversy still clouds the question of the degree to which American policy toward Russia changed with Roosevelt's death. Suffice to say that Truman, who said in 1941:

> If we see that Germany is winning, we ought to help Russia and if Russia is winning we ought to help Germany and that way let them kill as many as possible. Though I don't want to see Hitler victorious under any circumstance. Neither of them think anything of their pledged word.

was less a believer in Soviet-American rapprochement than Roosevelt. His experiences with Stalin at Potsdam in July of 1945 confirmed his instinctive hard line. During the five years following that inconclusive conference, Truman reacted aggressively as he perceived the Russians breaking promises, stealing secrets, and subverting nations. To combat Soviet expansion, the President and his advisors adopted the Containment Policy calling for the application of pressure at every point on the globe where Russian troops or communist agitators threatened our friends.

No intellectual or even a college graduate, Truman did read books, especially history books. Contemporary history taught him two things: One could not appease aggressors and the President had a powerful role to play in the conduct of his nation's foreign policy. His conception of the Presidency was symbolized by the famous plaque that rested on the desk in the Oval Office—"The Buck Stops Here."

In 1950, this active President, who had learned international politics on the job, was aided by Dean Acheson in the State Department. Urbane and sophisticated, Acheson had been in and out of government over the previous 20 years and was an articulate defender of the Containment Policy. A trusted advisor and executor of Truman's program, Acheson knew his place and respected his chief's untutored judgment. Though they worked together as a grand team, no one doubted who was boss. Surprisingly, the proud Acheson rarely overstepped his bounds.

Both Acheson and Truman were disheartened about the political situation in 1950. Acheson himself had become an object of scorn among Republicans who resented his arrogance and seemingly studied British demeanor. An intensely partisan politician, Truman had to be concerned about a Gallup poll of April 1950 that showed his popularity at one of its lowest points since 1945. At the same time, anticommunism, tough foreign policy talk, and the sensations of a young Wisconsin Senator seemed to be capturing the public's fancy. A congressional election was coming up in the fall and the opposition was certain to use the communist issue against the increasingly beleaguered Democrats. Like McKinley's Republicans in 1898, Truman's party was on the defensive, in part because of perceived foreign policy failures. Although the Democrats enjoyed a healthy majority in Congress (263-171 in the House and 54-42 in the Senate), they would lose some seats in the fall if previous patterns held true. Truman hoped to hold those losses to a minimum. Any defense of the party's policies was going to be difficult given the despair of the American people about the Cold War we seemed to be in danger of losing.

DEFEAT SNATCHED FROM THE JAWS OF VICTORY

For Americans, 1950 may have been the bleakest year of the Cold War. In rapid succession during the preceding two years, democratic Czechoslovakia was forced behind the Iron Curtain, the Russians exploded an Atomic Bomb, and China fell to those who seemed to be Stalin's minions. In addition, through investigations of the House Un-American Activities Committee, Americans were told that Russian spies who had infiltrated the Roosevelt administration had sold out the nation to international communism. Then, in February of 1950, Joseph McCarthy launched his career as the nation's premier witch hunter. Five years earlier we had stood at the threshold of a new era of peace and freedom; now we were faced with a menace even greater than Hitler.

The environment in which Truman operated in the summer of 1950 was, in part, of his own making. In 1947, feeling that he had to awaken the American people to the menace of communism as well as their new worldwide responsibilities, he "scared the hell" out of them and helped create a monster that eventually consumed some of its parents. Well before McCarthyism had infected the entire nation, Truman pushed through his Marshall Plan, NATO, and Point Four which, he felt, saved the West from imminent peril. Most Americans accepted Truman's Containment Policy. They argued only whether he had been tough enough. After 1948, fewer and fewer respectable leaders called for a soft line toward the Russians.

By the eve of the Korean War, we had become almost used to the role of world policeman against the communist conspiracy, a conspiracy that had to be fought at home and abroad with the FBI, money, arms, and, probably some day, soldiers. In May of 1950, almost 60% of the American people thought that we would have to fight Russia within five years. The concept of Fortress America of the 1930s was abandoned. Not surprisingly, our new international activism was related to that period in two ways. First, we had apparently learned that aggressors could not be appeased; if they are not stopped in Manchuria or Czechoslovakia, they will eventually reach your shores. Second, the contrast between the way we responded to communism in the 1950s and fascism in the 1930s revealed much about the new internationalism. Fascism represented military aggression in a traditional form. Communism, however, did not just arrive with the tanks of the Red Armies but through the more insidious weapons of subversion and propaganda. The Soviet doctrine, it was thought, threatened the very fabric of the American way of life at home and abroad. Some of the most ardent old isolationists, who really were anticommunists first and isolationists second, supported the new internationalism. In the 1930s, one fought Stalin through isolationism, in the 1950s through internationalism.

In June of 1950, then, we were primed for action against the Reds. Air raid drills, frightening Hollywood movies, vituperative speeches, and a host of Cold War clashes created a mood that countenanced military intervention in another hemisphere.

WHO PULLED THE TRIGGER AND WHY

Still, war in Korea came as a complete surprise to Americans. Some movement was expected from the Kremlin, perhaps in Germany but not in Korea. Like Hitler's attacks in the 1930s (and thus the parallels began at once), the North Korean attack took place on a weekend when our leaders were on holiday. Harry Truman was in Independence with his family while our chief United Nations delegate was off in the New Hampshire woods. Manning the fort in Washington, Dean Acheson learned of the incursion across the 38th parallel in the early evening of Saturday, June 24 (Korean time is 13 hours ahead of Washington time). Our first reports came from the United Press and not from the embassy in Seoul. In fact, 90 minutes passed before our ambassador cabled a confirmation of the wire service story. Notified immediately, Truman prepared to leap aboard the Presidential plane and dash back to Washington, but Acheson advised him to spend the night in Missouri so as to not alarm the already jumpy American populace.

The place the Russians chose for an attack against the Free World suggested a second parallel with the 1930s. Like Pearl Harbor 10 years earlier, Korea was an unlikely spot for the enemy to test our mettle. During the months following the defeat of Japan, the Joint Chiefs of Staff had concluded that the Korean peninsula was of no strategic value to the United

States in case of war with Russia. In 1947, Secretary of Defense James Forrestal, confronted by demobilization and budgetary stringency, began the process of withdrawal from Korea. We just did not have enough troops to protect all of the places around the world where Americans and Russians shared common boundaries. Moreover, because our strategic planning envisaged a total war begun in the conventional way by the Red Army in Europe, a Korean incident was not anticipated. Limited war was still a fuzzy concept as some Strangeloves in Washington were willing to employ our atomic arsenal to halt Red "aggression," once and for all.

In January of 1950, Acheson formalized our military withdrawal from Korea when he explained, in a celebrated public address, that our defense perimeter ran from the Aleutians to Okinawa to the Philippines. Other Asian countries, including Korea, would have to defend themselves as best they could with their own forces and those of the United Nations. Although Acheson did not explicitly preclude an American commitment to Korea, he did imply that we would react differently to an attack against Japan than to an attack against Korea. The Secretary of State was later pilloried for setting up the South Koreans, for giving a green light to the predatory North Koreans and their Russian masters. At the least, one must criticize him for laying too many cards on the table. If the North Koreans did invade the south with the intention of total conquest, they might have thought twice had they suspected that Korea was within our defense perimeter.

What would have happened had Acheson included her under our protective umbrella? Would that have deterred the North Koreans, who suspected that we would not, and certainly could not, maintain adequate defense forces on the peninsula? More important, considering our track record in the Orient, replete with extravagant pledges to defend the Open Door, any promise to support Korea might have looked hollow. Nevertheless, it is probably a good idea to keep one's putative opponents guessing about one's responses, and here the experienced Acheson violated a classic principle of diplomacy.

The Secretary was not alone in offering invitations to the North Koreans. During the month in which he defined our Asian defense strategy, Congress, the same Congress that was to excoriate him for his gaffe, killed a $60 million supplemental aid bill for South Korea. Thus, if the Communists did not get the message from Acheson, they certainly picked it up from the hawkish anticommunist Congress. And so Joseph Stalin *apparently* sent his legions hurtling southward down the Korean peninsula.

Just about everyone assumed that the order to invade South Korea came from the Kremlin. North Korean puppets were employed to probe the West's defenses along a forgotten and obscure flank. Since communism was thought to be mono- lithic—then-Assistant Secretary of State Dean Rusk claimed that Mao was not even Chinese—such an interpretation made good sense. Even today, few doubt the original designation of Stalin as the villain who both loaded the gun and pulled the trigger. However, some unanswered questions raise doubts about that once clear-cut story of Russian aggression in Korea in the summer of 1950.

First of all, and most interesting, if the Soviets did launch the attack, why were their United Nations envoys unprepared for the event? As things turned out, we intervened in Korea under a UN banner, a banner that added legitimacy to our efforts. Had the Russians attended the relevant sessions of the Security Council, they could have vetoed any attempt to resist aggres- sion. At the time, they were boycotting all UN organs in which the Chinese Nationalists were represented. Though Secretary General Trygve Lie was prepared to go to the General Assembly if the Soviets returned to block Security Council actions, he might have had a difficult time transforming that body, some- what unconstitutionally, into an agency for the protection of collective security. Incidentally, owing to the Security Council's rotating chairmanship system, the Soviet delegate was soon due to take his place at the head of the table. Thus, two questions must be answered. First, why was the Soviet delegate absent when the Korean discussion began and, second, why did not the

Russians delay the attack until their man was in position to hamstring deliberations, even without resorting to his veto?

Furthermore, although the Security Council session of Sunday, June 25 resulted in a resolution of condemnation against North Korea and a general appeal for her to withdraw from the south, not until Tuesday were the collective security provisions of the UN Charter invoked. The Russians were inexplicably absent from that session as well. In other words, Russian UN policy is mysterious even to this day, especially if we argue that Stalin orchestrated the events in Korea.

Conceivably, the Russians made a gigantic miscalculation. Perhaps they failed to communicate with their UN mission because they did not expect the Security Council to react so firmly. After all, the council was directed by a United States that had written off Korea. Then, when the United Nations became a major actor in the crisis, events moved too quickly for the bureaucrats in Moscow to decide upon the proper course of action and to communicate it to their emissaries in New York. Or perhaps the security-conscious Russians were unwilling to give their UN operatives advance knowledge of the Korean venture because they were afraid that American agents had bugged their offices.

The Russians did label the United Nations action illegal because their absence from the council was, according to them, tantamount to a veto. The council considered the Russian nonvote an abstention and so the work of the United Nations continued unhindered until August 1. Only then, a full five weeks after the crisis began, did the Soviets drop their boycott and take their place at the table. By that time, the damage had been done. Their delegates could do nothing to extricate the United Nations from Korea.

The several explanations for Soviet policy are not completely convincing, especially when we examine their press response to the crisis. Had Stalin planned the Korean invasion, his journalists should have been ready with a cover story about a South Korean attack on the north or something to that effect. Yet they did not report the Korean incident until two days after the fact, and then, in succeeding weeks, changed the party line several times. Is it possible that Russian editorial cadres were unprepared for the Korean attack and did not know how to handle the story? If *they* were surprised, what about their bosses?

When we turn to the logic of the situation, the circumstantial case against Russian foreknowledge of the attack is strengthened. Up to this point, they had not invaded any other nations either with their own army or a surrogate. In Eastern Europe, internal conspiracies and coups d'état had been the primary means of satellization. Moreover, in the weeks before the invasion, a relatively anti-Rhee legislature had been elected. This event, plus American lack of interest in Korea, suggested that the anticommunist government in the south might soon be toppled and replaced with a liberal, maybe anti-American or neutralist, regime. Thus, why invade South Korea before the dust had settled from the latest political crisis in Seoul?

To take another logical tack, if the Russian move was meant to be a symbolic ploy unrelated to Korea, a test of our resolve and nothing more, then why did they not call off their North Korean friends once it became apparent that both the United States and the United Nations were willing to respond decisively? It is true that at the outset we were almost pushed into the sea. Later, Soviet purposes were served by allowing the United States to bleed herself dry in a stalemated conflict. But if this latter line is accepted, why did not Stalin launch some political or military offensive in Europe while we were trapped in the snows of Korea in the winter of 1950-1951?

The conquest of South Korea can be related to Russia's military security. The destruction of the West's power there would have made the Soviet Empire a little more defensible by giving Stalin one less border to worry about. In addition, developments in Japan augured ill for Russian interests as the United States prepared to bring the defeated Japanese into a symbiotic relationship with the West. Perhaps the Kremlin decision makers reasoned that a quick march down the Korean peninsula would strengthen the arguments of Japan's leftist neutralist bloc that wanted to stay out of the Cold War. On the other hand, a successful invasion of South Korea could have just as easily driven the Japanese closer to the United States, and so this approach is somewhat tenuous.

Finally, if we are to accept the notion of Soviet culpability and treat the Korean affair as a calculated gamble, then they lost and lost heavily. Indeed, they lost so much that one wonders why they risked such a defeat. For example, our initial military setbacks demonstrated to skeptics in Congress that our armed forces were spread too thin and that we needed a massive rearmament program to guarantee security in the years to come. This is exactly what had been argued in NSC 68, the very important policy paper that the Truman administration had drawn up in the months prior to the outbreak of the war. Alliances, technical assistance, and other offensive Cold War programs had easier going on Capitol Hill after the Russians fulfilled Truman's direst prophecies in Korea. In a related vein, those remaining few who had hoped to soften Russian hostility through policies of accommodation were now effectively silenced by the vast majority who supported a hard line with no holds barred.

Internationally, the Russians suffered a black eye because of their apparent invasion of South Korea. From 1945 to 1949, they were the self-proclaimed apostles of world peace (they had no atomic weapons), but to many, in 1950, they seemed two-faced. Indeed, some heretofore neutralist nations began to move behind the West's defenses in fear of what the aggressive Russians might try next. As for Asia, the Korean War squelched any chance for Chinese-American rapprochement. Early in 1950, tentative voices were heard in the State Department calling for a normalization of relations with the Chinese communists. That policy was shelved for 20 years as a direct product of Mao's alleged close relationship with both Stalin and Kim. Of course, maybe the Russians, worried about possible Chinese-American friendship, wanted to fill in the crevices in the Bamboo Curtain.

Considering all of this fallout, one must ask again, what were the Russians trying to achieve in Korea and was it worth the possible losses they must have perceived in the gaming rooms of the Kremlin? Or were they just stupid?

If not the Russians, who was responsible for the invasion of the south? Mao would have to be eliminated for two reasons. First, he was in no economic or political position to become involved in a war with the United States and, second, and more important, Kim Il Sung was a Moscow-oriented communist who was wary of the Chinese across the Yalu.

All of this brings us down in the communist hierarchy to Kim himself. In the summer of 1950, the Premier of North Korea enjoyed military superiority over his disorganized countrymen to the south. He would not be so secure in the future for things could hardly get worse for the Rhee government. Furthermore, some in the south who looked longingly to the order and stability of the Democratic People's Republic of Korea were not averse to the unification of the entire peninsula by force. According to this line, Kim invaded South Korea on his own without telling the Russians, whom he knew would have restrained him. Moscow, then, was as surprised as we were and maybe even angry. As one author has suggested, "Stalin may have loaded the gun, but it was Kim Il Sung who seized it and pulled the trigger." On the surface, this scenario seems plausible and helps to explain the Russians' UN and press policy—except for two things. First, the large number of Russian advisors and technicians attached to the North Korean Army, as well as Kim's reliance upon his benefactors for supply, made it likely that the Kremlin would have gotten wind of his allegedly secret plans. Second, since South Korean political affairs appeared to be moving in directions favored by the north, why did not Kim merely wait for the apple to drop neatly and peacefully into his lap?

Some revisionist historians look to a fourth possible culprit. For them, the real organizer of what they label the Korean Civil War was none other than Syngman Rhee, who feared that the United States was about to withdraw from Asia. According to this convoluted analysis, fearing for his political life, Rhee provoked the North Koreans into crossing the parallel. By tricking Kim into coming south, Rhee could rally anticommunist forces in Asia and the United States and shore up his rapidly disintegrating position. Thus, and some of this is documented, during the first half of 1950, he ordered a variety of commando and guerrilla incursions north, staged troop maneuvers along the border, and in other ways tried to telegraph *his* imminent invasion of the north. When Kim took the bait and sent his armies over the border, Rhee pulled his men back to Seoul, sucked the communists deeper and deeper into his country, and then called for help against the unprovoked invasion from the Pyongyang aggressors.

Interesting and imaginative but not likely, especially considering the subsequent military history of the war. For a while, it looked like Rhee would lose everything. His armies, as well as our reenforcements, were pushed southward into a tiny salient before MacArthur saved the day with his daring Inchon landing. If Rhee maneuvered the north into war, he should have taken into account the possibility that the affair could be over before the UN cavalry arrived, if at all. Then again, he might have underestimated the quality of the North Korean troops and overestimated his own, as well as the occupation-bloated American troops available in Japan. Washington was surprised by the quality of Kim's armies pouring over the 38th parallel.

Each of the explanations for the events of June 24, 1950 is full of logical and evidentiary mysteries that remain murky. Suffice to say that the most plausible scenario might be the one in which Kim launches a *relatively* unilateral attack or incursion after being provoked by Rhee's pesky military activities. In any event, it appears unlikely that the Russians wanted a full-scale war.

As we have seen, the origins of the Korean War are not as unambiguous as they once appeared to the American government and population during the waning days of June in 1950. There are too many unanswered questions that will have to await the opening of the archives in Moscow, Pyongyang, and Seoul before we can come to any closure on the story. Without knowing for certain who started the war and why, our subsequent analysis becomes tenuous. Such are the frustrations of the historian of recent international relations.

WAR AGAINST THE UNITED NATIONS

Few in Washington were riven with doubts about the meaning of the news emanating from Korea. This was it—the first direct military challenge to Free World security since the end of World War II. Korea was the first round just as Manchuria and Ethiopia had been the first rounds in the 1930s. All agreed with Republican foreign affairs expert John Foster Dulles who pointed out that unless we moved, subsequent rounds would take us from Korea to Japan, the Philippines, Hawaii, and on to our West Coast. Moreover, the North Korean attack tested our resolve. We were on display for our new European allies to see. Could we be trusted? Would we stand by them in similar circumstances? This was our Rhineland Crisis. It was also the United Nations' moment of truth. As the less than neutral Secretary General Trygve Lie commented, "My God, this is war against the United Nations." During the first days of the crisis, American policy makers worried openly about letting down the United Nations.

The generals and diplomats gathered in the early morning of June 25 to plan strategy. For several hours, they tended to treat the incursion as a large-scale incident, the sort of thing that had been going on along that hot border over the past year. But as more complete reports arrived, it became clear that it was more than an incident. They also realized that they could not afford the luxury of a congressional debate. This was Pearl Harbor all over again. They had to move with dispatch before Korea was lost and the balance of power upset.

The Americans organized their responses in two places—Washington and New York. In a 2 am phone conversation on June 25, Truman ordered Acheson to call for a Security Council meeting that day. The Secretary called Lie who in turn woke up the relevant officials to set the wheels in motion for an emergency session. Meeting that Sunday afternoon, while American strategists in Washington planned their own response, the council, minus Russia, hastily heard reports and discussed the issues. By 6 pm it produced a resolution that called for political support for the South Koreans and requested that the northerners return home or else. The vote was 9-0 with Yugoslavia, at war with the Cominform, abstaining. The next day, June 26, marked the fifth anniversary of the United Nations Charter.

By the time the council acted, Truman was back in Washington engaged in a round of talks with his advisors. According to the President's own account, he kept on thinking of the 1930s and what inaction then meant for our security. During his first few hours back in the capital, he ordered our fleet to protect Chiang Kai-shek, just in case the Korean attack was part of a larger communist Asian plot, and authorized air and naval units to supply South Korean troops with needed equipment and also to protect our dependents fleeing southward in the face of the northern advance. At this point, the President and his advisors hoped that the southern armies would be able to hold the line against their northern brothers. Then Stalin would note our resolve and call back his communist soldiers. On June 26, as the battle reports became grimmer, we realized that the American-trained South Korean troops were unreliable. Truman was thus compelled to order American naval and air forces into combat. He issued this directive to the Pacific Command without consulting Congress and *before* the United Nations authorized its members to offer all possible assistance to the victims of aggression. In a technical sense, we had gone to war without authorization from the United Nations. Only the next day, June 27, did we receive the legitimation from the world body. At the same time, the President summoned congressional leaders to the White House to explain what he had done. If the participants in the decision making are to be believed, at no time did domestic political considerations enter into the discussions.

Few in Washington objected either to the methods or substance of Truman's policies. The challenge the military incursion posed to our national security could not await the pleasure of Congressmen in the manner prescribed by our Founding Fathers during an earlier epoch. Tanks moved too quickly for that sort of deliberation. Moreover, against whom could Congress declare war? Russia? China? North Korea? And had we formally declared war, we might have found ourselves in a much bigger affair than we or our enemies had imagined. After all, what would it take to repel an invasion from a country not very far removed from the Stone Age? The Koreans were Asians and not even as clever as the Japanese. A contingent of American soldiers would cut through them like butter, the contest would be over, and the Korean "war" would become another incident in the war of nerves between Moscow and Washington.

RALLY ROUND THE FLAG

Almost to a person, Congress approved of Truman's unilateral dispatch of military forces to Korea. Even such fierce Republican partisans as William Knowland (soon to be known as the Senator from Taiwan) applauded the President's action. Others such as Senator Robert Taft (Mister Republican), who paused in their supportive speeches to complain that the Korean mess was a product of misguided American Asian policy, rallied around the flag. After June 30, when Truman sent ground troops to the peninsula, another Republican exclaimed almost gleefully, "We've got the rattlesnake by the tail and the sooner we pound its damn head, the better."

Although several Congressmen did question the legality of the President's action, most ignored the issue. We had scores of precedents beginning with expeditions against the Barbary pirates back in the early days of the nineteenth century. Of course, the Korean police action was expected to be a brief clean-up campaign. One wonders whether Congress would have been so acquiescent in the usurpation of its war power had it known that the action was going to last three years and cost us over 50,000 battle-related deaths.

The American people, who only a decade earlier had recoiled at any thought of saving France, now were fighting for Korea. In June of 1950, not more than 10% of them could have located Korea on the map. In August, according to the public opinion polls, they supported Truman's action by a margin of 73% to 15%. The President took pride in the fact that of the 12,000 letters and telegrams he received in the days after his decision was made public, almost 11,000 were favorable. Indeed, at the start, the Korean War had more popular support than any war in our series, except for World War II. Later, as the war dragged on through an interminable stalemate, its unpopularity was instrumental in bringing down the Democratic Party in 1952. But that was far off. In August of 1950, with World War II hero Douglas MacArthur in charge, the boys would be home for Christmas.

Our new allies in Europe clambered aboard the collective security bandwagon, although few sent substantial numbers of troops and supplies to Korea. It would have appeared unseemly of them to criticize our actions in 1950. They did not want to bite the hand that was literally feeding them with economic aid. Though later they became distressed about our decision to pursue the North Koreans across the 38th parallel, for the time being, like Congress and the public, they stood foresquare behind Harry Truman.

How do we account for this support from virtually every quarter of our population and the so-called Free World? Although some military men were surprised by the American civilians' response, they should not have been. For one thing, the combination of Cold War tensions and coups of the previous years, along with the analogy of appeasement in the 1930s, conditioned the public to accept the necessity of intervention in Asia. The widespread perception that we would be fighting Joseph Stalin in Korea made it easy for Americans to break historic precedent and go to war 6,000 miles from their shores.

Many observers were pleased we had finally accepted the mantle of international responsibility rejected in 1919. With Korea, America had come of age as a great power. Or had it? The answer to that question brings us once again to the relationship between the war and national security.

KOREA AND NATIONAL SECURITY

Militarily, the North Koreans, acting either for the Russians or themselves, posed no direct threat to the American mainland. Their conquest of South Korea, certain without our intervention, would not have made our coastline or possessions and allies in the Pacific any less secure. Indeed, our precipitate withdrawal of troops in 1949 and our unwillingness to establish a permanent base in Korea, as well as Acheson's frank admissions, suggested that Korea was not vital to our military security.

A successful invasion would have moved the forces of communism a little closer to Japan. Although the Russians glared down at the Japanese from Sakhalin Island in the north, another outpost across the sea might have been valuable. But valuable for what? As a staging base for an amphibious invasion of Japan? Most unlikely in 1980 let alone 1950. If we adopt the calculus that you must deny to your enemy anything he deems important even though it is not important to you, then our security was enhanced by Russia's continuing insecurity. That is, for her, the 38th parallel was not as desirable a boundary as were the waters around the tip of South Korea. Since she was uneasy about the land boundary, our retention of South Korea made Russia less strong. In terms of the global balance of power, however, communist seizure of South Korea would have mattered little.

Perhaps a victory in Korea would have emboldened the Russians at other pressure points such as Germany, Vietnam, Yugoslavia, Malaya, or the Philippines. Here, of course, we can see the 1930s what-might-have-beens applied to the 1950s. Had we only stopped Japan in Manchuria and Hitler in the Rhineland there would have been no world war. If we stop Russia in Korea, they will not try their funny business elsewhere—Korea as example and symbol. Such an analysis presupposes direct Russian participation in and foreknowledge of the North Korean attack, something that today appears not at all certain. Nevertheless, it is true that they never tried a "Korea" again, even though our policy makers were once convinced that they did so in Vietnam.

Of all the wars, the economic factor appeared to be least important in Korea. South Korea was an impoverished land whose economy survived by the grace of American handouts. Although today we hear of the miracle of South Korean economic development and some vital materials have been found in her seas, at the time, no one thought Korea had or would have any importance for our economy. Rather, our loss of the country would have meant a considerable savings in money and other forms of assistance to a regime that squandered whatever we gave it.

More indirectly, the industrial north's conquest of the agrarian south would have enhanced Kim Il Sung's economic strength, but that should have been of little interest to us. If anything, a strong Kim, separated from his Russian masters by China, might have developed into the Asian Tito some hoped to find in Ho Chi Minh.

Even more indirect was the effect of the war on our domestic economy. We had never quite righted ourselves after we shifted to a peacetime economy in 1946, and 1949 had been a recession year. On the other hand, the first half of 1950 had been promising—boom times had returned *before* the start of the war in Korea. Nevertheless, some corporate leaders may have thought that a medium-size war, with its orders for our military-industrial complex, would pull us out of the doldrums more rapidly. Such had been the case during World War II, why not again?

Another seductive conspiracy, but it is unconvincing. In the first place, there is no evidence that the decision makers or their alleged confederates on Wall Street thought of using the initial incident as a pretext to spur our economy. There simply was not enough time for such planning. In fact, news of the war resulted in a temporary, downward trend in the leading economic indicators. We do know that the war probably had a relatively positive short-run impact on our economy in the months to come, especially since it led to huge defense expenditures, but the Joint Chiefs were in the process of turning the corner on rearmament before Korea. Economic issues appear unimportant here as a justification for rushing to the aid of Syngman Rhee.

As in all of the other cases, the prestige factor might have been the most powerful argument for going to war. Although we had stood fast in Turkey, Iran, and Berlin, we had "lost" Eastern Europe and our willingness to provide troops for any ally had yet to be demonstrated. The eyes of the world, free as well as communist, were on us. Some Europeans, perhaps those not yet in power, were not entirely convinced about the efficacy of NATO. For them, the safest path to security and survival rested in rapprochement with Russia. Had we faltered in Korea, so goes the argument, why would any of our European allies have taken our word that we would be there when the Red Army appeared on their border?

Yet we had never given our word to the Koreans and, if anything, had set them adrift physically in 1949 and spiritually in 1950 with Acheson's speech. No doubt, our closest allies were heartened by our reaction to the crisis. We could be trusted. If we went to war over remote Korea, we would surely go to war to save European democracy.

In addition, the reputation of the United Nations and the entire concept of collective security was thought to be at stake in Korea. The world body had been involved in the elections in the south and now one of its charges was under the gun. Would the United Nations operate effectively to resist aggression or was it doomed to the impotency of the League of Nations? As things turned out, the UN did work in this case, but only because the Russians were boycotting the Security Council. In reality then, we knew, as did the rest of the world, that the United Nations could never work against one of the major powers. Collective security presupposed great power solidarity and from the early days at Lake Success, Russians and Americans had been anything but cooperative. Had the UN been unable to step in, the emperor's new clothes would have been discovered, but with what ultimate effect for our national security?

BIBLIOGRAPHY

Despite widespread interest in the early years of the Cold War, the Korean War has not received as much scholarly attention as our other wars. John Lewis Gaddis's "Korea in American Politics, Strategy, and Diplomacy, 1945-50," in Yonosuke Nagai and Akira Iriye (eds.), *The Origins of the Cold War in Asia* (New York: Columbia University Press, 1977), 277-298 is an excellent place to launch an investigation.

The best book on the subject remains Glenn Paige's *The Korean Decision, June 24-30, 1950* (New York: Macmillan, 1968). A political scientist, Paige was more interested in testing a model of decision making than in the war itself. For him, the Korean War was a convenient case study. Most interesting and courageous is his apologia, "On Values and Science: The Korean Decision Reconsidered," *American Political Science Review,* 71 (December 1977), 1603-1609. Now oriented toward pacifism, Paige is embarrassed by the prowar assumptions that lie behind his seemingly value-free empirical analysis. Earlier, Carl Berger published *The Korean Knot: A Military-Political History of Korea* (Philadelphia: University of Pennsylvania Press, 1957), a useful account of the war and its historical roots.

During the war, journalist curmudgeon I. F. Stone layed the groundwork for the revisionist approach when he contended that Syngman Rhee and right-wing Americans orchestrated the events of June 1950. Stone's *The Hidden History of the Korean War* (New York: Monthly Review Press, 1952), ignored at the time, was reissued during the Vietnam period. Another suggestive revisionist account is found in Joyce and Gabriel Kolko's *The Limits of Power: The World and United States Foreign Policy, 1945-54* (New York: Harper & Row, 1972), 565-599.

Although in *Korea: The Limited War* (New York: St. Martin's, 1964), David Rees devotes most of his attention to military history, his discussion of the early diplomacy is sound. Rees's volume is still the best single work on the entire history of the war from 1950 to the armistice in 1953.

We still do not know very much about what was going on in North Korea, Russia, and China during the months before the war. The most intelligent guesswork is done by Robert R. Simmons, *The Strained Alliance: Peking, P'yongyang, Moscow, and the Politics of the Korean Civil War* (New York: Macmillan, 1975). Simmons should be supplemented with the classic monograph by Allen S. Whiting, *China Crosses the Yalu: The Decision to Enter the Korean War* (New York: Macmillan, 1960). A reasonable interpretation is offered by Okonoyi Masao in "The Domestic Roots of the Korean War," in Y. Nagai and A. Iriye (eds.), *The Cold War in Asia* (New York: Columbia University Press, 1977), 299-320, who is fairly certain that the Russians agreed in principle to the North Korean attack.

An influential early analysis of American policy is found in Alexander L. George's "American Policy-Making and the North Korean Aggression," *World Politics*, 7 (January 1955), 209-232. That alleged aggression is described in a stereotypically homey fashion by Harry S Truman in the second volume of his *Memoirs, Years of Trial and Hope* (Garden City, NY: Doubleday, 1956). As might be expected, Dean Acheson's own account, *Present at the Creation* (New York: Norton, 1969), is a bit more sophisticated.

CONCLUSION

From 1812 through 1950, the United States fought in six international wars. That their nation resorted to arms to resolve international conflict so infrequently pleases most Americans. Six such wars are well below the norm for major powers over the last 200 years. Americans believe also that their nation entered those wars only after others struck at vital national security interests. This exploration suggests otherwise.

Did the United States have to enter the War of 1812, the war with Mexico in 1846, the war with Spain in 1898, World War I, World War II, and the Korean War? We are not interested here in examining rationales for intervention offered at the time. Indeed, considering their motives, the spirit of the times, and the intelligence available to them, the Presidents' actions are defensible. Like most national leaders, they were honestly convinced they had little choice when their moments of truth arrived. Rather than analyzing the situations as contemporaries viewed them, we are engaged in an exercise in historical hindsight. Such an exercise is warranted because of the uncritical way most Americans view their war entries. Returning to our discussions of the six cases, was national security threatened sufficiently to justify the decisions for war?

On the eve of five of the six wars, our military security was not directly threatened. Except for the bombing of Pearl Harbor, we did not face a military attack or invasion from any of our opponents at the time of our war entries.

Although still a potential threat in 1812, the Indians along the frontier had suffered reverses during the previous year. Furthermore, engaged in a titanic struggle with Napoleon, the British were reluctant to launch a major North American campaign that could eventuate in the invasion of vulnerable Canada. Even when his nation stood astride the world in 1814, Wellington counseled against continuing the war with the United States. The Iron Duke was neither an admirer of republics nor a pacifist. For him, the costs of a full-scale war with the Americans outweighed any potential benefits to be gained from a victory.

In our next international war, the Mexicans were not a serious military rival, unless their extremely long shot of European support materialized. Though they had attacked our young men in the disputed territory between the Nueces and the Rio Grande, we had provoked them by occupying a region to which we had no clear title. After the initial contact, they took no further action to menace either our soldiers or lands.

Like the Mexicans in 1846, the Spanish in 1898 had no real prospect of arousing European states to come to their aid. By themselves, the Spanish were absolutely incapable of threatening our territory. We exposed their weakness when we destroyed their decrepit fleets in the Caribbean and the Pacific.

In the twentieth century, the advent of air power and other innovations in transportation and communication, as well as the growing strength of new rivals in Europe and Asia, began to alter our strategic position. In 1917, the Kaiser's submarines allowed him to make war on our vessels. He also conspired with our putative enemies in Mexico. Naturally, we could have avoided U-boat attacks by keeping our ships and citizens out of the war zone, as the Neutrality Acts of the 1930s proscribed, or by using convoys to protect armed merchant ships. Moreover, in the throes of a massive revolution, the Mexicans posed even less of a danger in 1917 than they did in 1846. Although in his wildest moments Wilhelm contemplated world empire, such a program was logistically impossible until the 1940s, if then.

The military challenge the Axis posed during World War II is more difficult to evaluate. American territory was attacked on December 7, 1941. Yet, the Japanese struck Pearl Harbor primarily because of the impasse over China whose conquest would not have jeopardized our security. Satisfied with the destruction of the bulk of our Pacific fleet, they had no immediate plans to occupy Hawaii, although they did seize the Philippines. Tokyo hoped to take over all of our Pacific territories some day, even the American West, but this was not feasible in 1941.

The Germans are a different story. Once his European enemies were crushed, Hitler planned to isolate and conquer the United States. His scientists (many of whom later became our scientists) would have won the missile race and developed the atomic bomb before we did. Without the impetus of war, there might not have been a Manhattan Project. We are, however, assessing the situation in 1941. Invasion of, or even war with, the United States was the last thing on Hitler's mind after the Wehrmacht bogged down in the Soviet Union in the winter of 1941-1942. He might have unleashed his submarines in 1942 and thus have provided Roosevelt with a *casus belli,* tainted though it was by the experiences of World War I. Only if we accept the worst-case scenario, however, could the United States have expected a frontal assault from Germany and her allies before the late 1940s. Does prudence call for joining the battle in 1941 before the Germans reached the point in 1947 or 1948 where they *might* have become an immediate military threat?

Entry into the Korean War is much easier to critique on the military dimension. The North Korean invasion of South Korea was not an attack against an American base or formal ally. In fact, government officials had earlier announced Korea's marginal relationship to our security. Although the North Koreans, or Russians, in possession of all of the Korean peninsula might have been in a somewhat stronger strategic position against Japan, this outcome has little to do with our definition of military security.

For some, myself included, this is where the evaluation should end. In five of the wars, and perhaps the sixth up to December 7, 1941, the United States was not threatened with military attack. If national security can be defined in such narrow terms, then American entry into her international wars was not justified. For many, such a definition of national security is naive. Among other things, economic factors are considered an important part of that definition. An attack upon a nation's commerce may lead to a general decline in the standard of living that might threaten physical well-being and domestic political stability. In addition, a nation with an unhealthy economy might become too feeble to meet successfully the inevitable military challenge. Considering the wide acceptance of such an analysis, we must reexamine the relationship between economic security and American entry into war. We must remember, of course, the difficulty of establishing the threshold at which an economic offensive justifies launching a retaliatory war.

The War of 1812 was preceded by a long series of British and French attacks upon our commerce. Unbeknownst to Madison, as Congress deliberated his message of June 1, the British had begun to modify their Orders in Council. Even had they not made this gesture, their protective maritime legislation was tolerated by most American merchants and shipowners who treated the occasional seizure as a business cost. In 1812, the economic issue relates more to questions of sovereignty than to the bookkeeper's ledger.

When Mexico refused to sell to the United States her western properties in 1846, she temporarily foiled our expansionist program. Expansion to the Pacific was a major element in our drive to compete in international commerce. Nevertheless, our inability to buy California and the Mexican West did not pose an immediate problem. The American economy was capable of much greater development within the boundaries that existed in 1846. In addition, although this was not as certain then as it is today, European powers did not contemplate taking economic or political control of Texas and California. More narrowly, the failure of the Mexican government to pay the several millions that Americans claimed were owed to them did not affect the economic survival of the United States.

During the 1890s, American leaders confronting the latest in a series of depressions were convinced that expansion was the key to prosperity. Even if contemporary economists were correct in their analysis, the relationship between the perceived need to expand and the war in Cuba is tenuous. Certainly, to those who sought to make the Caribbean a peaceful American lake, the Cuban war was unsettling. The areas around the sealanes to a proposed isthmian canal had to be stable and secure. American tobacco and sugar interests were also suffering from the dislocation brought about by the savage struggle for Cuban independence. All of this does not amount to a major threat to our standard of living. For one thing, until March of 1898 the majority of business leaders opposed entry into war because they felt that a prolonged military engagement would be harmful to recovery. For another, the taking of the Philippines, that fits so neatly into an alleged plan to establish way stations to the China market, was an afterthought. Our territorial war booty, in any event, did not turn out to be especially profitable, with the Philippines costing more in treasure and lives than any dollars earned in the islands' development as a market and entrepôt.

In many ways, World War I was a replay of the War of 1812 with a new wrinkle, the submarine. The war trade with England and her allies apparently pulled us out of the recession of 1913. The submarine, and especially the way the Germans began to use it in 1917, threatened that lucrative trade. The Kaiser's supporters maintain that we forced him into declaring unlimited submarine warfare because we accepted British violations of neutral rights. Had we retaliated against the Royal Navy, the possible severance of trade with London would have thrown us back into recession. The submarine, then, was not only a threat to our honor but also to our economic security in the early spring of 1917. The degree of that threat and its potential consequences for our political stability are impossible to determine precisely.

We must consider the long-range economic outlook as well. For some, a German victory in 1917 or 1918 was inimical to our development. Had Germany replaced England throughout the world, she might have made it more difficult for us to secure access to raw materials and markets. This line of reasoning is not entirely convincing. First, the British, who had never practiced free trade in their empire, had been fierce competitors wherever we had encountered them. Furthermore, that they would have been beaten so badly to have been removed from their position in the developing world was unlikely.

A similar argument is made for American entry into World War II. Hitler had both the means to supplant our friends around the world and the malevolent intentions to attempt such a policy. His second *Mein Kampf* talked of the economic strangulation of the United States as a prelude to military conquest. As with the prospects for a conclusive German victory in 1917, the day when the Fuehrer would be able to launch this final assault was far off. At the time the United States entered the war, his submarines had not even begun to threaten our war trade, let alone access to the developing world. In fact, from 1939 through 1941, our immediate economic interests were less threatened by Hitler than they had been by the Kaiser from 1914 to 1917.

In the other theater, China was the most important issue in our conflict with Japan. We did not want China to become part of Japan's Greater East Asia Co-Prosperity Sphere. In prewar negotiations, Japan tentatively agreed to halt her advances in Southeast Asia in exchange for American acquiescence in her plans for China. How much of our strategic thinking in 1941 was affected by economic considerations is unclear. By that time, the Open Door Policy meant more than just guaranteeing our merchants and bankers equal access to China. In so far as that policy was still economically based, China was of marginal importance to our economy. The fabled China Market had never materialized. The Japanese-American trade link was our most important Asian economic connection.

The Korean case is uncomplicated. In 1950, the conquest of South Korea by the forces of international communism, or even just the North Koreans, posed no direct, intermediate, or long-range economic challenge. Conceivably, such a conquest might have weakened our overall position in Asia or even pointed a symbolic dagger at Japan, our soon-to-be vital economic partner. At the time, however, South Korea meant nothing to us in terms of markets or materials.

Looking at the economic factor in our six wars, the strongest case can be made for the German threat to our shipping in the winter of 1917. And there, we helped drive them to that extreme because of our unneutral policies. In the other cases, our war entry did presumably enhance economic development. The draw with England in 1814, the territorial gains of the Treaty of Guadalupe Hidalgo, the colonies and bases picked up in 1898, the destruction of the Nazi World Order and the Greater East Asia Co-Prosperity Sphere, and the protection of our Asian commerce from communist encroachment in 1950 all ultimately redounded to our economic benefit. Such gains do not constitute compelling post hoc justifications for war based upon immediate threats to our material well-being.

Threats to a nation's honor or prestige are often perceived to be more serious than economic threats. A government that permits the harrassment of its citizens, the illegal seizure of its vessels, or other violations of its sovereignty is said to lose the respect of the international community *and* its own citizenry. Such a loss of respect may lead to more serious physical violations or even internal instability. In all six wars, American decision makers perceived national honor to be threatened. To evaluate those perceptions today is a tricky business that will call for even more subjective judgments than those made in the analyses of the military and economic factors.

From the 1790s to 1812, European participants in the French Revolutionary and Napoleonic wars continually violated neutral rights. Our retaliatory legislation did not bring an end to their illegal practices. For many, the integrity of the young nation had been challenged, as well as its ability to function as an independent actor in the international community. The republic had to be defended against both the assaults of the British and those of little faith at home who thought that our noble experiment had run its course.

This approach overlooks the fact that we had been putting up with European insults for many years. We could have waited a bit longer—the damage to our prestige had been done. When the British modified their Orders in Council in the spring of 1812, we won our point. We had stood them down without recourse to arms.

Most contemporary observers agreed that the Mexican attack on American soldiers in 1846 and their refusal to accept our territorial demands challenged our honor and prestige. These same observers ignored our provocative movement into the area between the Nueces and the Rio Grande and the lack of any legal basis for our demands for California. If anything, Mexican prestige was challenged by our policies.

In 1898, American elites felt that they had to keep order in their hemisphere. The Monroe Doctrine and our role as protector of liberation movements in Latin America had allegedly been challenged. As with the Mexicans in 1846, the Spanish had international law on their side when they declined to accept our solution to their problem. They had already gone more than half way to meet McKinley's March ultimatum. As for the *Maine* issue, the President could have placed the explosion in perspective in order to cool down those who wanted to remember the *Maine* by killing Spaniards. Finally, Europeans did not need more evidence of our strength and maturity in 1898. By that time, especially after our success in Venezuela against the mighty British in 1895, they had reluctantly recognized both our claim to great power status and our supremacy in this hemisphere.

The German declaration of unlimited submarine warfare in January of 1917 was a clear challenge to the honor of the United States. The Kaiser had violated our interpretation of the *Sussex* Pledge. For the first time, his U-boats were prepared to sink every sort of vessel in the war zone. After two years of protesting against the illegal use of submarines, and after he had established himself as the guardian of international law and morality, Woodrow Wilson had been blatantly insulted. Furthermore, he believed that in order to guarantee his influence at a future peace conference, he had to defend American integrity. The Germans maintained that Wilson had driven them to desperate measures. Moreover, war could have been avoided in 1917 had we kept our citizens and vessels out of the war zone. For Wilson, the right and American prestige was more precious than peace.

The question of the protection of national integrity in World War II is comparable to the World War I case. By 1941, we had made it clear that we would not allow the Chinese or the British to be defeated. In a series of unprecedented agreements, we had become a cobelligerent. Nevertheless, on the eve of Pearl Harbor, our allies were in relatively good shape thanks to the Nazi invasion of the Soviet Union the previous June. No new challenges had been thrown down during the second half of 1941 that demanded action to perserve our position.

More generally, as self-proclaimed leader of the world's democratic forces, Americans were uncomfortable sitting by as our friends were menaced by aggression. We did feel good about the assistance given the Allies in violation of our principles of nonintervention. With massive Lend Lease aid, as well as the convoy system, the occupation of Greenland and Iceland, and other actions, we had protected our good name. Forcing the point with Japan in the fall of 1941 had little to do with the redemption of our international reputation. We had continually adopted hostile, unneutral policies that the Axis were compelled to ignore. As with similar arguments about World War I, as well as the original position of the Committee to Defend America by Aiding the Allies, a wise nation may best protect its security by providing material but not human treasure to belligerents defending its interests.

In the Korean War, our honor as an ally of South Korea was not at stake. We had all but written her off in the months prior to June of 1950. What may have been at stake was our credibility as an ally of Western Europe. Had we not gone to the aid of remote South Korea, the British and French, among others, might have thought twice about the value of the new NATO arrangement as a protection against Soviet attack. Such an argument is seductive except for the improbability that our Western European friends would have altered their policies from antagonism toward the Soviet Union to neutrality or even Finlandization. Even then, many doubted that the Red Army was poised to invade Western Europe. Of course, if the North Korean move was planned by the Russians as a test of American resolve, then our action there proved to them that they had better not try anything else. If we would fight in god-forsaken Korea, we would certainly fight in Germany or Italy. That argument hinges upon the interpretation of the invasion as a Russian probe, an interpretation no longer accepted by all observers.

Concluding this summary, no matter how we define national security, we cannot justify American entry into most of her international wars. World War I may be the most justifiable in terms of the events in the early spring of 1917. Our economy and sovereignty were under serious assault when the Kaiser issued his declaration of unlimited submarine warfare. As we have seen, however, Wilson's policies from August of 1914 to early 1917 had placed us in a position from which retreat would have been difficult. Clearly, we contributed to the dangerous situation in which we found ourselves when the Kaiser cast down his gauntlet. In all of the other wars, including World War II through late November of 1941, American military, economic, and political interests were not threatened sufficiently to justify a resort to arms.

Undoubtedly, were we to examine all important international wars over the past 200 years we would encounter a comparable pattern. Analyzed with hindsight, few wars can be justified in terms of national security interests. What is surprising, perhaps, is how well *American* wars conform to this pattern. Such a conclusion is no cause for hand wringing. By understanding, at last, that the American diplomatic record resembles the diplomatic record of most of history's major powers, we might be able to shape future policies that reflect the promise of our idealistic rhetoric.

APPENDIX: THE CORRELATES OF AMERICAN WARS

To identify the causes of any group of wars is problematic. The task is even more tenuous since I have described only one side of each belligerent dyad in detail. Given this limitation, I cannot consider here the ostensible causes of the six international wars in which the United States participated from 1812 to 1950. I can, however, retreat from causation to correlation and ask, under what conditions did the United States enter her wars? Were there uniformities in the prewar environments that offer clues about scenarios that predict American entry into war?

Unfortunately, because of the small number of wars, a rigorous empirical analysis cannot be undertaken. With only six cases, we must assess the meaning of our primitive correlations with caution. Even if we discover a particularly fascinating uniformity, the likelihood that it occurred by chance would still be relatively strong. In some future study, it might be useful to increase the number of cases to a scientifically respectable size by grouping our wars with other American diplomatic crises that did not result in armed conflict.

One final problem merits attention. Some historians contend that it is impossible—and maybe even dangerous—to compare a nineteenth century war with a twentieth century war. For them, changes in transportation, communication, weaponry, and political systems make the War of 1812 as unlike the Korean War as an apple and a pear. Social scientists respond that apples and pears are both fruits with common familial properties that can be measured and compared. So, too, can we compare events belonging to the tragic family of war.

Bearing in mind the tentative nature of this exercise as well as its unscientific design, let us turn to Table 1 which presents, in summary form, selected prewar descriptor variables. In the rows, I list a variety of factors that historians and political scientists associate with the causes of war. The six wars, identified by their beginning dates, head each column.

Beginning with the crudest and most general factor, the temporal factor, we find that the United States entered five of her six wars in either April, May, or June, roughly the months of spring. The one outlier, World War II, interestingly enough, is the only war intervention not initiated by the United States. In the five prewar crises in which the United States determined her own entry date, combat was begun during the spring months. The appearance of a pattern becomes even more striking when we note that both the Revolution and the Civil War began in April.

This finding conforms to a more universal pattern. Of the 50 international wars that resulted in more than 1,000 battle deaths from 1816 to 1965, 19 (38%) began in the spring.

TABLE 1   Factors Associated with American War Entries

	1812	1846	1898	1917	1941	1950
Month of Entry	June	May	April	April	Dec.	June
Years since termination of previous war	29	31	33*	19	23	5
President's age at start of term of war entry	57	49	54	60	59	64
President's months in office at war entry	39	14	13	49	104	62
President's combat experience	No	No	Yes	No	No	Yes
President's diplomatic experience	Yes	No	No	No	No	No
President's party	Dem	Dem	Rep	Dem	Dem	Dem
Months to congressional election at war entry	5**	6	7	19	11	5
Months to Presidential election at war entry	5**	30	31	43	35	29
Years since recession or depression at war entry	0	4	2	3	2	1/2

*includes Civil War
**difficult to estimate because no set election days in 1812.

We can explain this phenomenon in several ways. In the first place, generals prefer to fight in the spring and summer when the days are longest and when climatological factors are least likely to upset precise logistical planning. Even today, monsoons, mud, and cold still may determine the outcome of warfare. At the same time, military men or men with military minds played minimal roles in decision-making circles in our first four wars, at the least. Consequently, we might look elsewhere for explanations for our seeming propensity to war in the spring.

Omitting for now the relationship between astrological signs and aggression, it might well be that nations and their leaders need to flex their muscles after a long, perhaps depressing winter of inactivity. Psychologists suggest that individuals are most bellicose when they emerge from a depression. Whether we can transfer such a theory to a nation or its leadership is questionable but we cannot discount it until we develop better explanations for the disproportionate number of wars begun during the spring.

Another temporal factor relates to cyclical patterns. In the second row, I show the number of years between the beginning of each war and the termination of the war that preceded it. I have included the Revolutionary War which terminated in 1783 and the Civil War (1861-1865) in my calculations. Our first five wars are spaced apart rather neatly with the interregnum ranging from 33 years, from the end of the Civil War to the Spanish-American War, to 19 years, between the latter and World War I. Coming on the heels of World War II, the Korean War upsets the pattern.

Again, there is some correspondence between the American experience and that of the rest of the international system. From 1816 to 1965, major international wars appeared to come in cycles from 20 to 40 years in length. Such cyclical patterns are understandable. Most likely, leaders are unable to mobilize their populations for major military efforts twice within the same generation. Breathing space is required for people to forget the carnage and resulting disappointment produced by each massive military struggle.

Looking at those factors idiosyncratic to the American political system, we turn first to the President, the chief decision maker in all of our cases. The age of a decision maker might be important for a variety of psychological and physiological reasons. Young men might be more unsure of themselves or even more aggressive than older men. Older men might be more stubborn or lethargic than younger men.

In row three, I show the ages of our 6 Presidents at the time they took office in the term they went to war: 3 went to war during their first term, 2 during their second terms, while Roosevelt went to war in his third. In any event, the figures reveal no significant pattern. Of the remaining 33 Presidents, 6 were in their 40s when they entered office for the first time, 20 in their 50s, and 7 were in their 60s. Thus, the ages of our six "special" Presidents—1 in his 40s, 3 in their 50s, and 2 in their 60s—fit the general distribution.

Of course, chronological age is often meaningless; some people are old at 35 while others maintain both a youthful body and mind into their 60s. Questions of experience, however, are a different matter. In row four, I present the number of months each of our Presidents had been in office before he led the nation into war. Theoretically, one could interpret this issue in several ways. Early in a term, a President might be cautious while he learned the ropes or, conversely, impetuous because of his insecurity. In any event, the figures again reveal no patterns of importance with the only interesting finding being that not one of the Presidents entered war during the first 12 months of his first administration.

As for the backgrounds of the Presidents, in the next two rows, I record binomially whether they had military and diplomatic experience prior to their elections. Four of the six had no combat experience, McKinley fought in the Civil War, and Truman in World War I. The others had opportunities to participate in an international war—Madison in the Revolution, Polk in the War of 1812, Wilson in the Spanish-American War, and Roosevelt in World War I. The latter did serve as Assistant Secretary of the Navy in Wilson's War Cabinet and thus helped direct naval combat operations. Two out of six with combat experience is slightly below the Presidential average. Of the remaining 33 Presidents (counting Cleveland twice), slightly more than half fought in major wars.

Of the 6, only Madison held a diplomatic post prior to taking office. Like many of the early Presidents, Madison was well-schooled in international affairs. Roosevelt's position in the Navy Department was a quasi-diplomatic post. Moreover, from 1933 to 1941, he was almost constantly engaged in international politics. The same could be said for Harry Truman who was the nation's chief diplomat for five years before he faced the Korean challenge. As for the other 3, their lack of diplomatic expertise should not be surprising because only 7 of the other 33 Presidents had been diplomats prior to their entering the White House.

To conclude the Presidential section of this table, I note in the seventh row the party of each war President. Counting Madison as a member of an emerging Democratic Party, we see that five of the six Presidents belonged to that party. Things look a little better for Democrats when we start our tabulation from the 1850s when the Republican Party was founded. Then, and including the Civil War, we find that Republicans presided over two of the five post-1850 wars. Yet, 3 of the 9 Democratic Presidents since Buchanan were involved in international wars while only 2 (counting the Civil War) of 16 Republican Presidents were similarly involved. Thus, the old political slogan about the Democrats being the party of war is confirmed, to a limited degree, by these data.

There is a variety of other Presidential biographical data that we might consider. For example, although 3 (or 4 if Truman is included) of the war Presidents came from Scotch-Irish backgrounds only 3 of the remaining 33 boasted similar origins. Or to examine ethnicity from another direction, only 1 of our war Presidents was of purely English ancestry. Such an outcome is unexpected since more than half of the other Presidents had English backgrounds. Similarly, we might look at marital status, personality factors, ages of children, region, religious orientations, and a host of other factors which, while seemingly irrelevant by themselves, might offer suggestive ideas when grouped.

More interesting, perhaps, is the relationship between the timing of our entries into war and impending elections. The prospect of an imminent election, as we have seen in the cases of Madison and McKinley, can affect the war decision. When jingoist opposition leaders rally around the flag and when many citizens perceive their national security to be threatened, few Presidents show more courage than profile

As we see in the next row, congressional elections were on the horizon at the time we entered four of our six wars. However, since five of the six began in the spring and since congressional elections occur every other year, such a distribution may not be significant.

The figures for our quadrennial Presidential elections are shown in the next row. Naturally, they relate to those in the fourth row discussed earlier. With the exception of Madison, Presidential elections were at least two years distant when Presidents entered wars. Moreover, all war Presidents were potential candidates for another term. (Wilson and Truman both flirted with the idea of making another run for it.) Does this mean that wars are bad politics? A Machiavellian President might maneuver his country into a war on the eve of a Presidential election. At that point, the patriotic electorate would be reluctant to change leaders in midstream. Of course, although we called most of the shots in our six diplomatic crises, our mastery over each situation was not so complete that Presidents were free to choose the month or even the year in which to launch a war.

The state of the economy is one of the most important of all background variables. Marxists, among others, maintain that international conflict is intimately related to imperialism and the search for markets for capital and exports. Other economic determinists see war as an option exercised by a leader when domestic instabilities threaten to undermine his regime. War is generally thought to be good business for almost all segments of the economy. In recent memory, the United States was pulled out of depression by the war trade and war production during

World Wars I and II. Folklore also suggests that bad times are more likely to produce foreign conflict behavior than are good times. Naturally, since I have proven one half of the old saw—the Democrats are the party of war—and the other half points to the Republicans as the party of depression, we should not find strong correlations between war and depression.

In the tenth row, I show the number of years between the termination of the last depression or major recession and the onset of war. Although precise dating is difficult, historians agree on a rough time frame for each periodic economic dislocation. Here we see that one war, the War of 1812, was fought while a good portion of the economy, especially the farm areas of the west, was in a depressed condition. All of the others were entered into *after* a depression. Even in the case of the Korean War, a previously depressed economy was on its way out of the doldrums before June of 1950.

Dexter Perkins, one of the deans of American diplomatic history, suggests that such data are among the most useful for the construction of a general theory of American war. As noted in the section on seasonal distributions, psychologists claim that individuals are their most bellicose when they rise from a personal depression. Transferring this theory to economic cycles and nations, we see that the theory holds, more or less, in five of our cases. Further, when we add the Civil War, which followed on the heels of a serious recession (1857-1859) and the Vietnamese War, in which one major turning point occurred as we were recovering from the recession of 1959-1961, the case is strengthened. In any event, it is interesting to note how infrequently we went to war *during* a depression, despite the prevalence of those occurrences every decade or so.

What, then, has this exercise shown? Americans seem predisposed to initiate their military hostilities in the spring. Except for Korea, we usually waited a decent interval before we took up the cudgels again. None of the six Presidents entered a war at the beginning of his term and only one became involved during the last year of his term. The martial record of the Democratic Party is not very savory. And finally, economic cycles do correlate with American entry into international war.

Slim pickings, perhaps, but they offer suggestions for further study. Comparative analyses of other countries' experiences, as well as American behavior in crises that did not result in war, might produce more convincing findings. The discovery of patterns and variables associated with the onset of international war by contemporary peace scientists, peace researchers, and diplomatic historians may be as important as discoveries of alternate fuel or food sources. It is regrettable that such a small proportion of human energies and treasure is devoted to the study of war, the scourge that threatens us all.

ABOUT THE AUTHOR

MELVIN SMALL is Professor and Chair in the History Department of Wayne State University and co-investigator in the Correlates of War Project. Editor of *Public Opinion and Historians: Interdisciplinary Perspectives* (Detroit: Wayne State University Press, 1970) and coauthor (with J. David Singer) of *The Wages of War, 1816-1965: A Statistical Handbook* (New York: Wiley, 1972), Small has published articles on diplomatic history and world politics in, among other journals, *The Historian, Journal of Peace Research, Journal of Conflict Resolution, Historical Methods Newsletter, Film and History, The Americas, World Politics,* and *The American Political Science Review.*

WARNER MEMORIAL LIBRARY
EASTERN COLLEGE
ST. DAVIDS, PA. 19087